Israel's Wars, 1947–93

Warfare and History
General Editor
Jeremy Black
Professor of History, University of Exeter

European warfare, 1660–1815
Jeremy Black

The Great War, 1914–18
Spencer C. Tucker

Wars of imperial conquest in Africa, 1830–1914
Bruce Vandervort

German armies: war and German politics, 1648–1806
Peter H. Wilson

Ottoman warfare, 1500–1700
Rhoads Murphey

Seapower and naval warfare, 1650–1830
Richard Harding

Air power in the age of total war, 1900–60
John Buckley

Frontiersmen: warfare in Africa since 1950
Anthony Clayton

Western warfare in the age of the Crusades, 1000–1300
John France

The Korean War
Stanley Sandler

European and Native-American warfare, 1675–1815
Armstrong Starkey

Vietnam
Spencer C. Tucker

The War for Independence and the transformation of American society
Harry M. Ward

Warfare, state and society in the Byzantine world, 565–1204
John Haldon

Soviet military system
Roger Reese

Israel's Wars, 1947–93

Ahron Bregman

London and New York

First published 2000
by Routledge
11 New Fetter Lane, London EC4P 4EE

Simultaneously published in the USA and Canada
by Routledge
29 West 35th Street, New York, NY 10001

Routledge is an imprint of the Taylor & Francis Group

Typeset in Bembo by Taylor & Francis Books Ltd
Printed and bound in Great Britain by Biddles Ltd,
Guildford and King's Lynn

British Library Cataloguing in Publication Data
A catalogue record for this book is available from the British
Library

Library of Congress Cataloging in Publication Data
Bregman, Ahron.
Israel's wars, 1947–93 / Ahron Bregman.
p. cm.
Includes bibliographical references and index.
1. Arab–Israeli conflict. I. Title.
DS119.76.B74 2000
956.04–dc21   99-054115
ISBN 0–415–21467–X (hbk)
ISBN 0–415–21468–8 (pbk)

In memory of my great uncle
Ahron Friedman
killed in the 1948 War of Independence

Contents

List of Maps

Preface

This book is the result of a suggestion made by Jeremy Black, general editor of *Warfare and History*, who thought that an account of Israel's wars would be a useful addition to the series. Its publication was delayed by an invitation to act as a consultant and write the companion book for a six-part BBC Television documentary about the Arab–Israeli conflict (*The Fifty Years War: Israel and the Arabs*). This has proved a benefit since, in the course of my work on the series, I came across material which I could never otherwise have obtained.

Israel's Wars, 1947–93 is, first and foremost, an overview of Israel's wars with the Palestinians and Arabs. I start with the 1947–8 Jewish-Palestinian struggle for possession and mastery of the land of Palestine, and conclude with the Israeli–Palestinian confrontation which took place between 1987 and 1993, the so-called *Intifada*. In between I examine Israel's wars with its Arab neighbours, principally Egypt, Jordan, Syria and the PLO in Lebanon, in the years 1948, 1956, 1967, 1968–70, 1973 and 1982.

Israel's Wars is not, however, only about battles and fighting, but also about the people of Israel, a nation-in-arms, who are, it is often said, 'soldiers on eleven months' annual leave'. By looking at almost five decades of Israeli–Palestinian–Arab conflict we can see that the Israelis, in spite of tremendous difficulties, have for many years demonstrated an extraordinary willingness to carry the burden, pay high taxes, endure long military service, and fight both in wars and between them. But after, and as a result of, the Six Day War of June 1967, as I will demonstrate, Israelis became more critical of their leadership, dissent grew, and there was also a pronounced tendency to reject the idea that preparations for war need always be at the expense of social services and justify indifference towards domestic problems. Still, in spite of growing dissent and criticism, the Israelis remained, in the post-1967 war period, loyal to their leadership, always rallying behind it in times of war. The turning point, however, came during the 1982 war in Lebanon when, for the first time in Israel's history, national solidarity showed signs of breaking down, and while the battle was still in progress Israelis protested against the war, and some even declared their refusal to take part in it. This unprecedented challenge and decline in the motivation of Israelis to serve gathered pace after the Lebanon war and reached a peak during the *Intifada*, the Palestinian revolt in the occupied territories between 1987 and 1993.

I link this trend mainly to a reduction in the level of the external threat to Israel's existence, and suggest that during the first two or three decades of the state, a strong sense of external threat, fresh memories of the Holocaust and collective ideals and priorities had stiffened the will of Israelis to serve, fight and sacrifice. This determination was strengthened by the leadership's success in cultivating the image of Israel as a small defenceless state surrounded by evil Arabs bent on her destruction; and, ironically, by the Arabs themselves, who played into their hands by exaggerating their own military capability and talking of dismantling the Jewish state, wiping it out and driving the Jews into the sea. However, with the external danger subsiding, the gradual disappearance of the Holocaust generation and a general shift from collective ideals and priorities to individual ones, there was also a decline of will among Israelis to serve and bear the burden, as was made very clear in Lebanon in 1982 and during the *Intifada*.

This book is intended chiefly for the use of university students, and is designed to be rather more than a chronicle of events. There are frequent pauses to examine how things operate and for what reasons; and I often go beyond the task of narrative and description to comment and explain, so that the reader can elicit from the sequence of events some better understanding of how things turned out as they did.

The book also contains new – never before published – material. Perhaps most notable is the revelation that Anwar Sadat's right-hand man (who also worked for Sadat's predecessor President Nasser as confidante and member of his presidential staff) was an agent of Mossad, Israel's secret service. I expose, for the first time, the documents he passed to the Israelis which became the foundation of Israel's strategy before the Yom Kippur War ('The Conception') and claim that from being an agent working exclusively for Mossad, he later became a double agent and worked also for Sadat, who sent him, on the eve of the Yom Kippur War, to meet the head of Mossad in London and to mislead him regarding the time Egypt would open fire.

I have always believed that while one can learn history from documents, articles and books, it can be better understood if heard from those who have made it, for motives and personalities are important in the making of history. And though a person's recollection tends to be clouded by later events, oral history is still an important complement to the written word and to our better understanding of history. In the last decade or so, in addition to sieving through piles of written material, I have had the opportunity to meet many who have taken part in making the history about which I am writing here. Their names are too numerous to mention, but I wish in particular to thank the following, from whom I have benefited most: Amos Amir, Moshe Amirav, Meir Amit, Moshe Arens, Ehud Barak, Haim Bar Lev, Mordechai Bar On,

Benyamin Begin, Yossi Beilin, Yossi Ben-Aharon, Avigdor Ben Gal, Benyamin Ben-Eliezer, Yosef Burg, Warren Christopher, Ben Zion Cohen, Avraham Dar, Robert Dassa, Uzi Dayan, Abba Eban, Rafael Eitan, Miriam Eshkol, Yeshayahu Gavish, Mordechai Gazit, Eli Geva, Benjamin Givli, Mordechai Gur, Eitan Haber, Yehoshafat Harkabi, Isser Harel, Yair Hirschfeld, Mordechai Hod, Yitzhak Hofi, Yehiel Kadishai, Lou Keddar, David Kimche, Yitzhak Levi-Levitza, Uri Milstein, Amram Mitzna, Uzi Narkiss, Yitzhak Navon, Benjamin Netanyahu, Marcelle Ninio, Meir Pail, Dan Pattir, Matityahu Peled, Shimon Peres, Leah Rabin, Yitzhak Rabin, Itamar Rabinovich, Gideon Rafael, Ran Ronen (Peker), Elyakim Rubinstein, Yehoshua Saguey, Yossi Sarid, Uri Savir, Amnon Lipkin-Shahak, Shlomo Shamir, Yitzhak Shamir, Yaacov Sharett, Ariel Sharon, Yisrael Tal, Avraham Tamir, Yair Tzaban, Ezer Weizman, Aharon Yariv, Re'havham Ze'evi, and Eli Zeira. Last, but certainly not least, my love and thanks go to Dana, and to my children Daniel and Maya, whose constant interruption is a good reminder that there is more to life than the long and lonesome business of writing.

Ahron Bregman
London, 1999

Abbreviations

The following abbreviations are used in the notes:

ISA   Israel State Archive

BGA   Ben Gurion Archive

BLA   Brian Lapping Associates (interviews carried out by this production company and kept at the Liddell Hart Centre, King's College London)

HA   Hagana Archive

IDFA   Israel Defence Forces Archive

LILR   The Lavon Institute for Labour Research

LPA   Labour Party Archive

YTA   Yad Tabenkin Archive

CHAPTER ONE

The 1947–9 war

A conflict is born

'Some years', J. K. Galbraith once wrote, 'like some poets and politicians and some lovely women, are singled out for fame far beyond the common lot'.[1] For the Middle East in general, and for the people of Palestine in particular, 1948 was clearly such a year. It was the year in which the British Mandate for Palestine terminated, a Jewish state called Israel was established, thousands of Arab Palestinians became refugees, and regular armed forces of Transjordan, Egypt, Syria and other Arab countries entered Palestine-Israel and clashed with Israeli forces. Thus begun the first all-out Arab–Israeli war which – like the civil war which preceded it – revolved around land.[2]

The ancient land of Palestine – small in size, covering some 10,000 square miles – formed a narrow strip stretching along the Levant. In the south it was separated from Egypt by the dunes of the Sinai desert, in the east it was bordered by the Syrian Arabian desert, and in the north it was marked by the city of Dan. Although described in the Bible as 'a land of milk and honey', Palestine was in fact a barren, rocky, neglected and inhospitable land with malaria-infested swamps. Nevertheless its strategic importance was immense, for it provided a bridge from Asia to Africa – a junction for traffic crossing from the south (Egypt) to the north (the highlands of Hittite Anatolia), to the east (Mesopotamian Anatolia) and to the west (Cyprus). Because of its strategic importance Palestine had been, throughout its history, the battle-ground for military campaigns and invasions by the pharaohs, the kings of Assyria, Babylon and Persia, Alexander the Great, the emperors of Byzantium, the Arabs, the Crusaders, the Mamelukes and the Turks. Finally, British forces during the First World War had taken it from the Turks, who had ruled this land ever since Sultan Selim I occupied it in 1517.[3]

It was under the British rule, which lasted from 1917 to 1948, that the struggle between Jew and Arab for the mastery and possession of the land of Palestine reached 'an unprecedented peak.[4] A *modus vivendi* between the two peoples in Palestine had been always hard to achieve, because here was a clash of *rights* – the claim of two races to one land – and thus any solution could be

1

found only on the lines of least injustice. In their struggle to win the argument and the land, the Jews claimed that the rocky land of Palestine which they called *Eretz Yisrael* was their traditional and spiritual home, one promised by God to Abraham and 'to [his] posterity'.[5] But the Arabs of Palestine also regarded Palestine as their rightful home, for 'posterity', as they saw it, also included themselves, since they were the descendants of Ishmael, Abraham's son by his concubine Ketirah. But it was more than a conflict between two rights, for the Jews felt that *Eretz Yisrael* was their only safe haven after years of persecutions and endless pogroms in their native countries.[6] The Arabs of Palestine, on the other hand, resented the idea that they, the majority of whom were Muslims with no tradition of anti-Semitism, had to pay the price for evils committed against the Jews by others, often within European Christendom. They also argued that in contrast with the Jews, who had been moving in and out of Palestine and had always been the minority in this land, they – the Arabs – had never abandoned the land, and had for hundreds of years constituted the majority of its population. This was true, but as the years passed and Jews continued to arrive in Palestine, the demographic scales tilted steadily in their favour. There were Jews who had come to Palestine to die and be buried in the Holy Land, others who had immigrated to Palestine to escape persecution, and there were also Zionists who had immigrated to Palestine in order to build a new Hebrew society which they wished would be, as Dr Chaim Weizmann, a Zionist and chemist at Manchester University, put it, 'as Jewish as England is English or America is American'.[7]

Scrutinizing the speeches and writings of Zionist leaders of the late nineteenth century and the beginning of the twentieth, one comes to the inevitable conclusion that some of the Zionist leaders did truly believe that Palestine was derelict and empty – 'A land without a people waiting for a people without a land'.[8] This, it is worth noting, was not an unusual thought, for some early Zionists suffered from the common Eurocentric illusion that 'territories outside Europe were in a state of political vacuum'.[9] But there were also Zionists who did realize that an Arab community existed in Palestine – working the land, bringing up children, living and dying[10] – however, they took it for granted that the native Arabs would welcome the new arrivals, whose zeal and skill and, of course, money would help develop the barren land for the benefit of all of its inhabitants. Herzl, a Budapest-born Viennese journalist and the father of modern Jewish nationalism (Zionism), who in 1896 had published an eighty-six-page book called *The Jewish State*, knew, as emerges from his writings, that Palestine was not an empty land. But he thought that the Jews could buy the land from Arab landlords and spirit the 'penniless [Arab] population [living on this land] ... across the border by procuring employment for [the Arab population] ... while denying [them] any employment in our country'.[11] It is easy with hindsight to criticize this way of thinking, but we should bear in mind that such thinking was not unusual in the age of colonialism, when the rights of indigenous inhabitants were often ignored.

Persecuted, and often encouraged by their leaders to leave their native countries, Jews began pouring into Palestine. From 1882 to 1903, some 20,000–30,000 Jews arrived to join the small Jewish community, mostly religious, living especially in Tiberias, Jerusalem and Tzefat; and in the short period between 1904 and the beginning of the First World War another 35,000 Jews were added. It is estimated that in 1917 about 85,000 Jews lived in Palestine alongside 600,000 Arabs.[12] Jewish immigration to Palestine was relatively restricted under Ottoman rule because the authorities suspected that the Jews were being used as cat's-paw by the West, but with the defeat of the Turks during the First World War, Jewish immigration to Palestine increased. From the end of the war to 1923 another 35,000 Jews came mainly from Russia, and in the second half of the 1920s the flow of Jews increased, with 82,000 arriving between 1925 and 1930. Troubles in Europe, notably the rise of Nazism in Germany, meant that immigration to Palestine gathered momentum, with 200,000 arrivals between 1932 and 1938. Here it is worth remarking that many of these Jewish immigrants would have preferred to go elsewhere, especially to America, one of the most sought-after destinations for immigrants, but the gates to America were half-shut. Among other reasons, this was because 'The leaders of the Zionist movement exerted all the influence they could muster to make sure that the US did not open up immigration to these Jews for the simple reason that they wanted to herd these same Jews to Palestine'.[13]

The mounting influx of Jewish refugees had quite dramatically changed the demography of Palestine, and the balance had begun to shift remarkably in favour of the Jews. Jews, who comprised only 4 per cent of the total Palestinian population in 1882, formed 13 per cent in 1922, 28 per cent in 1935 and about 30 per cent in 1939. By 1947 there were 608,230 Jews in Palestine compared with about 1,364,330 Arabs.[14] Not all the Jews remained in Palestine, where harsh living conditions were hard to bear, and there were periods where more Jews actually left Palestine than entered. But of those who did remain there emerged the future Jewish-Israeli leadership: David Ben Gurion (Gruen), who had arrived from Poland in 1906 and later became the first Prime Minister of Israel; Levi Eshkol (Shkolnik) who had arrived from the Ukraine in 1909 and later became the third Prime Minister; and Golda Meir (Meyerson), who had arrived from America in 1921 and would succeed Eshkol to the premiership.

Demographic modification aside, a geographical transformation was also under way in Palestine; for Jews not only poured into the country but also bought large tracts of its land. For this purpose, The Jewish National Fund (*Keren Ha'Kayemet* in Hebrew) was established in 1901 with the task of buying land in Palestine, and in 1908 the economist and agronomist Arthur Ruppin set up at Jaffa the first Zionist office, which bought land from Arab landlords. So successful was the Jewish policy of purchasing land, that in 1935 the quasi-religious politician and leader of the Arab Palestinians, the Grand Mufti of Jerusalem, Haj Amin Al-Husseini, had to issue a *fatwa*, which is a decree or a religious order, defining Arabs who sold land to Jews as apostates to be denied burial in Moslem cemeteries. This was to no avail, even though the growing demand led to the value of property in Palestine soaring: Jews had mustered the money and bought large tracts of it. It is estimated that between 1920 and 1939 Jews acquired 845,198 acres in Palestine, most of which belonged to absentee landowners, and towards the end of the 1930s they possessed around 1,533,400 acres.[15] From a modest fifty-five Jewish settlements in 1920, the number had rocketed to 218 in 1939.[16]

It perhaps deserves mention that the Jews did not, as is sometimes alleged, 'rob' the Arabs or 'steal' their land, but rather they bought it from them for hefty sums of money. As for the Arab aristocracy of landowners who had sold the land to the Jews, they did so voluntarily and with open eyes, and they must have known that for the Arab peasants who had been living on their lands for generations this would be a devastating blow. Indeed it proved to be so, for when the new owners of the land voluntarily became hewers of wood and drawers of water and worked the land themselves (they called it: *Avoda Ivrit*, 'Jewish work') – as a means of recovering contact with nature and also disproving the slander of their detractors that they were fit only for commerce and not for labour – they inevitably deprived Palestinian labourers of employment.

What made matters far worse and increased the anxieties of the Arabs of Palestine, was the fact that the massive influx of Jews and their purchase of large tracts of land in Palestine was accompanied by a gradual commitment of the British government to the idea of establishing a 'National Home' for the Jews in Palestine. Most notable was the Balfour Declaration, approved by the British cabinet and enshrined in a letter dated 2 November 1917, which was sent by the British Foreign Secretary Arthur James Balfour to a prominent member of the Jewish community in England, Lord Rothschild. In this short but most significant letter the British minister expressed the support of His Majesty's Government for the idea of establishing a 'National Home' – a term undefined by international law and a complete novelty – for the Jewish people.[17] The subsequent commitment that this should not 'prejudice the civil and religious rights of existing non-Jewish communities in Palestine' did little to dispel the fear of the Arabs for their own future. Indeed, it angered them, for they, who were referred to in this 117-word letter as the 'existing non-Jewish communities in Palestine', formed at this time the overwhelming majority of the population – they made up around 87 per cent of the total population while the Jews were only 13 per cent – and the land of Palestine was *theirs* in the generally accepted sense of the word. What the Arabs feared, and with hindsight we know that they were right, was that as soon as a large Jewish population had built up in Palestine, the idea of a Jewish 'National Home' would turn into that of a Jewish state. The Arabs, though, found some comfort in the joint Anglo-French declaration which was issued simultaneously in Palestine, Syria and Iraq on 7 November 1918, stating that 'The goal envisaged by France and Great Britain ... is the complete and final liberation of the peoples who have for so long been oppressed by the Turks ... and the setting up of national governments'. This was taken by the Arabs as a pledge for Arab independence in Palestine.[18]

The British promise to the Jews of a 'National Home' in Palestine was turned into an international commitment when the League of Nations, on 24 July 1922, reiterated the British pledge in a document which assigned a mandate of Palestine to Britain.[19] On this Arthur Koestler commented in *Promise and Fulfilment*: 'The League requisitioned Palestine from its [Arab] owners to provide the Jews with a permanent abode, and appointed Britain to act as billeting officer'.[20] The promise to the Arabs expressed in the joint Anglo-French declaration of 7 November 1918 was all but forgotten. For the Jews the pledge of the international community was a significant political victory, for after all, the Balfour Declaration was without legal force because Britain had no sovereign rights over Palestine and had no authority to dispose of the land. The declaration was no more than a statement of its intentions.[21] But now with the Balfour Declaration incorporated into the Palestine mandate, the British promise had received explicit international recognition. One can only be puzzled by how little thought was devoted to the Arab Palestinians, who were the overwhelming majority in Palestine, and by how much was promised to the Jews, who were the minority, by both the British and later the international community in issuing, respectively, the 1917 Balfour Declaration and the 1922 British Mandate. The explanation seems to be that those who endorsed these critical documents and sealed the future of the two communities, had all been nurtured on biblical reminiscences of the eternal bond between the children of Israel and their promised land, and that they knew next to nothing of the Arab community of Palestine.

It is ironic that in their growing opposition to the Jews, the Arabs of Palestine were now led by prominent Palestinian clans and families who had sold their lands to the Jews through middlemen at high profits, and thus visited on the Palestinians the very problems which were now causing such tensions with the Jews. In fact, tensions between the two peoples had already risen dangerously in the early 1920s. On 3 April 1920, for example, which was the first day of Passover, Arabs attacked Jews in the old town of Jerusalem,[22] and on 1 May 1921, disturbances in Jaffa led to the killing of nearly 200 Jews and 120 Arabs. A few quiet years followed, but then on 23 August 1929, Jews and Arabs clashed in Jerusalem and the next day Arabs slaughtered fifty-nine men, women and children in Hebron. Arab dissatisfaction reached its peak between 1936 and 1939, a period known as 'The Arab Revolt', when they began a general strike which soon turned into clashes, mainly with the British who had allowed Jews to enter Palestine, purchase land and establish the infrastructure for a future state.

The British authorities, the caretakers of Palestine, crushed the revolt, but overall they failed to calm the situation in Palestine, because their tendency to veer first one way and then the other, and their policy of appeasement which 'in practice meant endorsing the claims of the stronger' invited even more violence from the parties involved.[23] Thus when the British had allowed Jewish immigrants to enter Palestine they angered the Arabs, and in their attempts to appease the latter they angered the Jews. British attempts to find a way out of the dilemma and offer solutions to which both Arab and Jew could agree came to little. In August 1936, for example, the British government entrusted Lord Peel (grandson of Sir Robert Peel, the nineteenth-century British Prime Minister) with the mission of recommending a solution to the problem in Palestine. After investigating the matter, Peel published his report on 7 July 1937. The report proposed that Palestine should be partitioned between Arabs and Jews. While the Jews accepted the proposal, the Arabs of Palestine rejected it; they were not prepared to give up Palestine either in part or in whole, which in retrospect seems to be a grave error of judgement, for their insistence on having all the land resulted, as we shall later see, in their losing it all.

In the summer of 1939, with increasing tension in Palestine, the British summoned an Arab–Jewish conference to try and sort out their differences; but the conference quickly broke down. The British government then imposed its own solution, expressed in a White Paper of May 1939 stating that a final batch of 75,000 Jews was to be admitted to Palestine between 1939 and 1944, and that, after this, further entry of Jews would be subject to Arab approval. Additionally, it empowered the High Commissioner of Palestine to prohibit the sale of land by Arabs to Jews in specified areas. The White Paper caused an uproar among the Jews, who turned on the British and accused them of retreating from previous pledges. Here without doubt the British government had miscalculated, for they were imposing restrictions on Jewish immigration to Palestine at a time when Jews in Europe were the first targets of the Nazis. As a result of the White Paper, the Jewish underground organizations, including Irgun but mainly the small but violent Lehi (the so called 'Stern Gang'), viciously attacked the British in Palestine and in less than two years rendered the mandate unworkable.

At the close of the Second World War and with the ending of their rule in India, Britain's primary motive for staying in the Middle East had gone, and there seemed little reason for the British to pursue a policy in Palestine – 'a hell disaster' as Winston Churchill once described it – that imposed financial burdens (there were 100,000 British troops there), was difficult to implement, and was increasingly unpopular both at home and abroad. A growing number of British politicians – and they had broad British public support – now urged the government 'to lay [the] Mandate at the feet of the United Nations Organization and thereafter evacuate the country [with which Britain had] no connection or tradition'.[24] And indeed, even before a final decision regarding Palestine was made, the British government on 31 January 1947 ordered the evacuation from Palestine of all British women, children and male civilians in non-essential jobs. About two weeks later, on 14 February 1947, the British Foreign Secretary announced that his government intended to refer the Mandate of Palestine back to the two-year-old United Nations, the successor of the League of Nations; he repeated the announcement to the House of Commons on 18 February, and it was debated on the 25th.

'The Palestine question' was put on the agenda of the UN, whose assembly met on 28 April and on 15 May to discuss the matter. It then decided to appoint a special committee, called UNSCOP, to investigate conditions in Palestine and decide what recommendations should be made to Britain as Mandatory Power.[25] The committee duly arrived in Jerusalem on 16 June, stayed for five weeks and met Jewish representatives; the Arab Higher Committee, the body representing the Arabs of Palestine, boycotted it, arguing that the departure of the British should be followed by one thing only, which was the establishment of an Arab state on the entire land of Palestine. The boycott was a grave error of judgement, for the absence of the Arab side made it easier for the Jews to put a forceful case before the UN committee for partitioning the land with the Arabs and having their own state on part of Palestine. It is sometimes alleged that, in fact, the real intention of the Jews was to have the whole of Palestine (including parts allotted to the Arabs), but that they wished to obtain it in stages – first get what they could from the UN and then expand it by force. This claim is supported, for example, by a letter of Ben Gurion to his wife, where he says: 'Establish a Jewish state at once, even if it is not in the whole land ... the rest will come in the course of time'.[26] That the Jewish hidden agenda was indeed to occupy all of Palestine was also believed by leading Palestinians. At a meeting in September 1947 with a British official in Lebanon, where he was in exile, the leader of the Arab Palestinians, Haj Amin Al-Husseini, said: 'No form of partition ... would finally satisfy the Zionists. Whatever they got would merely be a springboard from which to leap on more'.[27]

Back in Geneva, the UN committee produced a report of sixty-seven printed foolscap pages in which it recommended that the Mandate for Palestine should be terminated at the earliest practicable date.[28] But the committee was divided with regard to the nature of the regime which should be set up after the British departure. A minority of three suggested a federal state, and a majority of eight was in favour of passing a 'Judgement of Solomon' which would partition the land between Jews and Arabs but maintain the economic unity of Palestine.

On 29 November 1947 the matter was brought before the General Assembly of the UN, which voted 33 to 13, with 10 abstentions, in favour of Resolution 181 to partition Palestine. Britain abstained, all the Islamic Asian countries voted against, and both the USA and USSR – the latter regarding

Map 1 Palestine 1947: the UN Partition Plan

Britain as a greater menace than the USA in world politics – voted in favour. According to the UN partition resolution, the 10,000 square miles of Palestine was to be divided between Arabs – then numbering 1,364,330 including 127,000 Bedouin – who were to retain 4,300 square miles, and Jews – then numbering 608,230 – who were allotted 5,700 square miles. Jerusalem and Bethlehem were to come under United Nations control.

For the Jews this was a significant political victory, which could be compared in magnitude only to their success in obtaining the Balfour Declaration of 1917. For the Arabs of Palestine, however, the vote for partition was a devastating blow; they vowed to oppose it by force and called for a three-day protest in Palestine. In Haifa, where 70,000 Arabs were living along-side 70,000 Jews, an Arab gathering took place where a leading Palestinian, Sheikh Sabri Abdeen, announced: '"If the Jews are going to take our land then by God we will throw them into the sea" and he pointed to the Mediterranean which was only a few hundred metres away to the cheering, clapping and shooting-in-the-air of the crowd'.[29] In such a charged atmosphere, the more moderate Palestinian Arabs such as the Nashashibi family (many of this moderate clan had previously been assassinated by fellow Arabs during the 1936–9 Arab revolt), the Nablus group and the communists who were more willing to accept partition were silenced.[30]

With the benefit of hindsight, it is obvious that the failure of the Arabs to accept the 1947 UN partition proposal was a colossal historical mistake, as was their previous rejection of the Peel partition plan of 1937. If they had accepted either, they could have had an independent Palestinian state along-side Israel. But this, as we know, was not to be the case.

Civil war in Palestine

Although significant, the UN partition resolution did not envisage the imme-diate creation of either a Jewish or an Arab state on the land of Palestine. Yet, rather than easing tension, the resolution to partition the land and the subse-quent British decision, made on 4 December 1947, to depart on Friday 14 May 1948, had increased tensions between the peoples of Palestine and 'it was as if on a signal Arabs and Jews squeezed the trigger and exchanged fire'.[31] On 15 December 1947, Lieutenant General Sir Alan Cunningham, the British High Commissioner for Palestine, sent a top-secret memorandum to the British Colonial Secretary Arthur Creech-Jones, outlining the situation in Palestine in fearful detail. 'Situation now is deteriorating', he wrote, 'into a series of reprisals and counter-reprisals between Jews and Arabs, in which many innocent lives are being lost, the tempo of which may accelerate'.[32]

The initial phase following the UN resolution to partition Palestine was characterized mainly by Arab attacks on Jewish convoys and street fighting on the Jaffa–Tel Aviv border and in the Old City of Jerusalem.[33] This was not yet a full-blown civil war but rather skirmishes and a vicious circle where an action was followed by a reprisal with disturbances and clashes between Jews and Arabs spreading to all parts of Palestine.

With all its energy directed to the evacuation and removal of some 210,000 tons of stores and a huge retinue of colonial administrators, the British in Palestine, under the command of Sir Gordon Macmillan, chose to stand aside and to protect only their own evacuation routes. Britain now simply washed its hands of the problems of Palestine and refused to assume responsibility for implementing the UN partition plan. And with the 'policeman' standing aside, the condition of Palestine deteriorated into anarchy, with Jews and Arabs fighting out their differences in what gradually slid into an all-out civil war which was to last about five months.

The opposing forces at the outbreak of the civil war

On the eve of the civil war in Palestine, Jewish forces comprised Hagana, which was the largest underground organization of the *Yishuv*, the Jewish community, and two smaller dissident organizations: the *Irgun Zvai Leumi*, better known as 'Irgun' and *Lochamai Herut Yisrael*, known also as 'Lehi' (or 'The Stern Gang'). The Hagana comprised 45,000 men and women, about 2,100 of them in Palmach, making up the striking force of the organization. In Irgun and Lehi there were about 3,000 fighters and, although independent of Ben Gurion's Hagana, the two small organizations often coordinated their actions with Hagana, as they did in the notorious battle at Deir Yassin.[34] Expecting a strong Arab response to the UN resolution to partition the land of Palestine, the Jewish leadership under Ben Gurion began mobilizing the whole community, and just a day after the UN resolution it issued a decree calling on men and women between the ages of 17 and 25 (those born between 1922 and 1930) to service. On 22 January 1948, the Jewish leadership ordered that all those born between 1931 and 1932 were not to leave the country; a month later all those born between 1908 and 1932 were ordered to come forward and enlist. On 3 February, all Jews aged between 19 and 23 (born between 1925 and 1929) were called to serve. The new recruits were not ordered to join a specific underground organization – this could have caused an immediate controversy – rather to enlist to *Sherut Ha'am* (literally: 'Service of the Nation').

The Arab force in the civil war was made up of four components. First was the Arab Liberation Army (ALA), which had around 4,000 volunteers from Palestine and the neighbouring Arab countries, mainly Iraq and Syria.[35] The ALA was organized and equipped by the Military Committee of the Arab League and was trained at the Syrian training centre, Katana. It marched into Palestine on 20 January 1948 from Jordan, and operated from two locations: Galilee, where it had two battalions comprising between 1,500 and 2,000 men; and Samaria, just west of the Jordan river, where it deployed about the same number of men.

The second element of the Arab force consisted of between 1,000 and 1,500 volunteers from the 'Moslem Brothers' and Egyptian youth organizations who had crossed from Egypt to Palestine, and operated in the southern part of the country and in and around Majdal (now called Ashkelon) and Yibne (now called Yebne).

The third element, some 5,000 men, was led by Abdall Quader Al-Husseini, a relative of the Mufti of Jerusalem and perhaps the most charismatic and ablest Arab leader in Palestine; he was operating in the Jerusalem, Ramallah and Jericho areas. Husseini's force comprised irregular bands and masses of villagers – the Palestinian element was strong – and it also had some European elements, that is volunteers from Britain, Yugoslavia and Germany who had joined the Arab Palestinians in their fight against the Jews. Another Arab group, 3,000 at most, was led by Hassan Salemeh, who had been trained in Germany, had been parachuted into Palestine, and was operating in the Jaffa-Lydda-Ramleh area. All in all, the number of Arab para regulars, irregulars and volunteers can be estimated at 25,000–30,000 men; their weakness, though, was a lack of cooperation and central control.[36]

Aims and fighting

The principal aim of the Jews in Palestine in the period immediately after the UN resolution to partition Palestine, was to gain effective control over the territory allotted to them by the UN and to secure communication with thirty-three Jewish settlements which, according to the UN plan, fell outside the proposed Jewish state. For although the UN had partitioned the land between Jews and Arab Palestinians, there were still Jewish settlements which were to remain within the Arab area and, on the other hand, Arab villages on land allotted to the Jews. In contrast to Arab villages within Jewish areas, which were self-reliant, the Jewish settlements relied heavily on outside supplies, which made the keeping open of routes a necessity for them. Another aim of the Jewish forces was to prepare the ground for what seemed to be an inevitable invasion of neighbouring Arab regular armies the moment the British left Palestine. The General Staff of the Jewish forces devised what became known as 'Plan Dalet' (*Tochnit Dalet*), the principal objective of which was to consolidate control over areas allotted to the Jewish State and also to seize strategic positions to make it possible to block regular Arab armies in case they marched into Palestine. What is significant about 'Plan Dalet' is that, apart from envisaging the occupation of strategic positions, it also allowed for the occupation of Arab villages, towns and cities and, where necessary, the expulsion of their inhabitants.[37] This, we should comment here, was a blank cheque for Jewish forces to expel Arab Palestinians, as indeed took place in the ensuing days of the war. The Palestinians' strategic aim during the civil war was negative in nature, namely to prevent the implementation of the partition plan by disrupting and strangling Jewish lines of communication, and by cutting off Jewish settlements from localities and positions that were already occupied. These opposing aims of Jews and Arabs led to the 'battle of the roads' which raged in Palestine during the first half of 1948, with Jewish forces attempting to gain control of the communications roads and the Arabs of Palestine seeking to prevent them from achieving this.

In the initial stages of the civil war the Arabs gained the upper hand and succeeded in dictating the pattern of the struggle. By March 1948 they had cut off the entire Negev – allotted to the Jews by the UN – from the coastal plain, as well as most of Western Galilee and the Jerusalem area; they also succeeded in isolating many of the Jewish settlements within these regions from one another. So successful were these operations that the Arabs of Palestine came close to reaching their principal aim when, in March 1948, British Colonial Secretary Creech-Jones told the British House of Commons that the Palestine situation was 'rapidly becoming insoluble' and on 19 March proposed that the UN rescind partition in favour of trusteeship. The US administration, too, frustrated by the deteriorating situation in Palestine, had joined the British call and declared, in mid-March, that since partition was hard to establish, a trusteeship should replace it; only the Soviet Union remained constantly in favour of partition.[38] The British-American view, aimed at replacing partition with trusteeship, dismayed the Jews, who saw their dream of establishing a state on the land allotted by the UN slipping away.

But soon the civil war began to take a new shape. In April 1948, with the war at its height, an attempt by the ALA to cut off the Haifa region and the Valley of Jezreel from the coastal plain failed (4 April) and Jewish forces proceeded with their own offensive, which proved to be eminently successful. In central Palestine, they broke open the road to Jerusalem ('Operation Nachshon', 3–15 April) and this allowed supplies of food and ammunition to get through to the Jews in the city. Elsewhere, all Arab towns and villages, and the mixed cities within the territory designated for the Jewish state, were overrun in rapid succession. Tiberias was captured on 18 April, and the vital port of Haifa fell into Jewish hands on 22–3 April. Most of Haifa's 70,000 Arabs fled, many to Acre, others to Lebanon.[39] Between 25 and 27 April, Irgun forces attacked the all-Arab town of Jaffa, which was meant to be included in the future Arab state; at first they were checked by British troops, but once the British had left, Irgun forces took the town (13 May 1948) whose original 90,000 inhabitants were reduced to only 5,000.[40] In northern Palestine, the town of Safad was occupied, and on the night of 13–14 May all Western Galilee came under Jewish control. The all-Arab town of Acre – like Jaffa it was meant to be included in the future Arab state – was besieged by Jewish forces and capitulated on 17 May. The Arab forces in Palestine were now bewildered by defeat, and retreated, with their leadership confused and disorganized.

Massacres and refugees

The civil war in Palestine was vicious, cruel and littered with atrocities. It involved immense human suffering and a degree of blatant brutality never before seen in Jewish–Arab relations in Palestine, which had usually seen the two peoples living side-by-side in relative peace. On 31 December 1947, taking revenge for the killing of six of their fellows by Irgun, Arabs attacked and killed thirty-nine Jews at the Haifa oil refineries.[41] The Hagana responded in kind, attacking the village of Blad-el-Shieke, where it killed more than sixty Arabs, including women and children. At the beginning of February 1948, more than ten Arabs and two British policemen were killed in an explosion near the Jaffa Gate in Jerusalem and, on 22 February, sixty Jews were killed by a car-bomb explosion on Jerusalem's Ben Yehuda street.[42] On 11 March, seventeen Jews were killed and forty were injured by a bomb in the courtyard of the Jewish Agency in Jerusalem[43] and, on 9 April, 110 Palestinians – men women and children – were killed by Jews in the small village of Deir Yassin just west of Jerusalem, at least twenty-five of them being massacred in cold blood. Four days later, on 13 April, the Arabs took revenge by attacking a Jewish convoy of medical staff on its way to Mount Scopes, leaving seventy-seven dead.

What is so significant about the civil war in Palestine is that it was then that what became known as 'the Palestinian refugee problem' started. With its leadership and the middle class – those who had the money to do so – leaving Palestine to take what they believed to be temporary refuge in neighbouring Arab countries, and with the Jews advising the poorer Palestinians to follow suit and using force to expel the others – the Arab Palestinians moved out of Palestine.[44] Exaggerations by Arab leadership of Jewish atrocities, as happened after the events at Deir Yassin, was also a catalyst, leading the Palestinians to flee whenever a Jewish soldier was seen approaching their village.[45]

The demographic scales were now tilting in favour of the Jews, and with the *en masse* departure of the Arabs, Jews became the majority in the land of Palestine. While there was no explicit decision by the Jewish leadership to expel the Palestinians, there was nevertheless a tacit agreement that this should be done.[46] In a meeting with military commanders, Prime Minister Ben Gurion said: 'In each attack [against Arabs] it is necessary to give a decisive blow, ruining the place, kicking away the inhabitants'.[47] It is estimated that about 750,000 Palestinians left Palestine during the war (160,000 remained behind) and their homes were taken by new Jewish immigrants; as Ben Gurion recorded in his war diary: 'New immigrants [we] put in Arab houses'.[48] This was the method the Jewish leadership employed to absorb the 5,500 new Jewish immigrants who, in spite of the ongoing civil war, poured copiously into Palestine.

Although highly successful, the period which had followed the UN partition resolution was for the Jews in Palestine, many of whom were European refugees, traumatic. During the six months from November 1947 to mid-1948, 1,308 Jewish soldiers and 1,100 civilians perished.[49] This is a very high toll, given the relatively low number of Jews in Palestine and the relatively short duration of the fighting.

Proclamation, end of British mandate and regional war

On 14 May 1948, Prime Minister David Ben Gurion recorded in his war diary: 'At four in the afternoon the Jewish independence was proclaimed and the state [of Israel] was established', and he added 'Its fate is in the hands of the armed forces'. From the thirty-two-minute ceremony where he had declared the establishment of Israel, Ben Gurion went straight to the 'Red House', the headquarters of the Israeli forces on Tel Aviv beach, to discuss with his military commander 'the deteriorating situation'.[50] Declaring a state was a bold and courageous move, given the threat of Arab neighbouring states to prevent by force the establishment of a Jewish state, even on that part of Palestine which had been allotted to the Jews by the UN. It also seemed, at the time, a suicidal move, given that US Secretary of State George Marshall had warned the Jews that America would not consider itself responsible for the consequences of their declaring a state and would not 'bail them out' if attacked by their Arab neighbours.[51]

That Friday night, just half an hour before midnight, Lieutenant-General Sir Alan Cunningham, the seventh and last British High Commissioner for Palestine, sailed in HMS *Euryalus* from the bay of Haifa for England.[52] The birth of the State of Israel and the end of more than thirty years of British rule in Palestine took place on a single day. These two events were significant for two main reasons. First, they came to symbolize the transformation of the status of Jews in Palestine from a community to an independent state, soon to be recognized by the international community. Second, these two events were the catalyst which transformed a strictly localized conflict – until the departure of the British and the proclamation of Israel the Jewish–Arab struggle had remained essentially a communal war – into a full-blown regional confrontation which also involved neighbouring Arab states and their regular armies.

That night, American President Harry Truman recognized the Jewish state. This was a major development, and vital for Israel, because neither the UN decision to partition Palestine nor Ben Gurion's unilateral declaration of independence gave any international status to the Jewish state. A recognition by a superpower – as the United States was after the Second World War – meant that, at least symbolically, the newly established state of Israel was accepted into the family of nations.[53] At five in the morning on 15 May, while giving his positive reaction to the American recognition in a Tel Aviv radio studio, Ben Gurion could hear the Egyptian bomber planes overhead.[54] By now the Arab Legion, consisting of four well-trained regiments, was already on the march into the West Bank, an area allotted to the Palestinians by the UN.[55] That day, which was a Saturday, the Egyptian government sent a telegram to the President of the UN Security Council, announcing that Egyptian armed forces had entered Palestine and were engaged in 'an armed intervention'. On Sunday 16 May the Arab League sent a cablegram making similar statements on behalf of the Arab states.[56]

By world standards the war which was now developing in Palestine-Israel was a small-scale, primitive confrontation conducted by poorly equipped and ill trained units. For his invasion of Russia – 'Operation Barbarossa' – in 1941, Hitler had assembled 160 divisions; in the Palestine war the biggest unit to take part in battle was a brigade, and actual fighting often involved smaller units. The German armoured strength in the Barbarossa invasion totalled 3,550 tanks; in the Palestine war the Israelis had no tanks at all and the Arabs had only a few primitive ones.[57] Nevertheless, for the parties involved, in particular for the Israelis, the war was perceived, rightly or wrongly, as a life-or-death struggle. It was a war fought all over the country in separate battles – a see-saw struggle with many changes of fortune.

It is worth looking at the forces, Israeli and Arab, which were now con-fronting each other in Palestine, to demolish what is perhaps the biggest myth with regard to this first all-out Arab–Israeli war.

Forces and weapons

Contrary to popular belief, the 1948 war between Israeli forces and the invading regular Arab armies was not one between 'the few [Israelis]' and 'the many [Arabs]', or, as it is often put, a clash between David (Israel) and Goliath (the Arabs). The root of this popular, though utterly erroneous, notion lay in the Israeli practice of referring to the potential of the Arabs rather than to the actual number of troops they put into the field. By confusing the issue, the Israeli leadership, in its war of words and attempts to gain the sympathy of the world and its own people, had for many years knowingly ignored the fact that ratios among adversaries do not merely reflect population ratios, and that a high degree of manpower mobilization can make up for the quantitative demographic inferiority of a small nation like Israel. Indeed, during the 1948 war, Israel had mobilized almost its entire resources and ablest population, while the more numerous Arabs had utilized only a small fraction of their huge potential.

The number of Israeli troops committed to battle on the eve of the Arab invasion was more or less equal to that of the Arabs, but then, while the number of Arab troops increased only slightly, the number of Israelis grew steadily and dramatically. A breakdown shows that the total strength of the invading Arab armies was about 23,500 troops, made up of 10,000 in the Egyptian army, 4,500 in the Arab Legion of Transjordan, 3,000 Syrians, 3,000 Iraqis and 3,000 Lebanese and ALA troops; there was also a token contingent from Saudi Arabia.[58] Compared with these numbers, Israel, as Ben Gurion notes in his diary of the war, had committed a total of 29,677 men and women to battle.[59] But then, with the progressive mobilization of Israeli society and the average monthly arrival of 10,300 new immigrants, the number of available fighters steadily grew.[60] On 4 June 1948, the number of Israeli troops was, according to Ben Gurion, 40,825; and on 17 July it grew to 63,586. On 7 October 1948, these numbers swelled to 88,033, and by 28 October reached more than 92,275.[61] On 2 December the number of Israeli soldiers on the field was 106,900;[62] on 23 December it stood at 107,652, and on 30 December the number had risen to 108,300 (10,259 of them women).[63] Jewish volunteers from abroad – *Mahal* – also joined, and although their number was relatively low, at most 5,000, they nevertheless provided valuable technical expertise. By the end of the war Israel's fighting force was larger in absolute terms than that of the Arabs, and as John Bagot Glubb correctly observed:

> the common impression that the heroic little Israeli army was fighting against tremendous odds (one army against seven armies was one of the expressions used) was not altogether correct. The Israeli forces were, generally speaking, twice as numerous as all the Arab armies put together.[64]

In weaponry and firepower, however, the Arabs had a clear edge. The total inventory of Hagana at the start of the war consisted of 22,000 rifles of various calibres, 1,550 light and medium machine guns, 11,000 largely home-made submachine guns, 195 three-inch calibre infantry mortars, 682 two-inch mortars, 86 PIAT (Projector Infantry Anti-Tank – a crude man-portable device of armour-piercing explosive charges) and five old 65mm field guns. A few tanks and aircraft still awaited shipment in Europe.[65] Egypt, according to Israeli estimates, had 48 field guns, 25–30 armoured cars, 10–20 tanks, and 21–25 aircraft. Iraq had 48 field guns, 25–30 armoured cars, and 20 aircraft. Syria had 24 field guns, 36 armoured cars, 10–20 tanks and 14 aircraft. Jordan had 24 field guns and 45 armoured cars; and Lebanon 8 field guns and 9 armoured cars.[66]

But as in manpower, so with weaponry; as the war progressed the balance steadily tipped in favour of the Israelis. A fund-raising mission by Golda Meir to America raised $50 million, which was used to buy arms, and ships loaded with weapons were purchased and sent to Israel by such people as Ehud Avriel.[67] In New York, a team headed by Teddy Kollek (later the long-serving Mayor of Jerusalem) bought aeroplanes, took them to pieces and, with the help of the Mafia, and under the nose of the FBI, shipped the precious weapons to Israel.[68] Israelis not only purchased weapons, but they also took measures to prevent the Arabs from adding arms to their own arsenals. In Bari, Italy, on 9 April 1948, Israeli agents executed 'Operation Shalal 1' and sunk the ship *Lino*, which was packed with 8,000 rifles designated for Syria.[69] Also in Italy, on 18 September 1948, Israeli agents broke into a garage where they destroyed four aeroplanes which were awaiting shipment to Egypt.[70] Additionally, Israel developed its own weapons industry, which included chemical and biological weapons.[71]

There were, apart from manpower and equipment, other factors which affected the character of the battle. The invading Arab armies had the advantage of being fresh in comparison with the Israelis, who were exhausted after five months of bloody civil war in Palestine. Moreover, the invading armies were relatively homogenous, with commanders and troops communicating in the same language, compared with the Israelis who suffered language difficulties. The weather also played an important part. The summer of 1948 was extremely hot and harsh, and Israeli troops, many of whom had just arrived from cold Europe, found it too oppressive.[72] While the invading Arab armies had the tactical advantage of surprise, the Israelis had the advantage of interior lines of communications and fortified settlements which provided useful bases of operations.

Turning to the fighting itself, we see not only that the Arab invaders were inferior in numbers to the Israelis, but also that they failed to coordinate their moves and to prepare themselves properly for war. They also underestimated the determination of their opponents, all of which explains their total failure to dislodge the Israelis.

Fighting

The invading Arab armies of Syria, Iraq, Lebanon, Egypt, Transjordan and a contingent force from Saudi Arabia had started from different directions, heading towards the heart of the Jewish state and the lands allotted to the Palestinians by the UN in November 1947. Had they coordinated their operations better and concentrated their offensive, the outcome of the struggle could have been different. In the event, however, there was coordination neither of operational plans nor of movement and concentration of forces, reflecting both the lack of common interest of the invaders and the divided purposes in the minds of the Arab leaders, who were suspicious of each other's intentions. All regarded Jordan's King Abdullah with intense suspicion, and rightly so, for the King was far more concerned to seize the land west of the river Jordan, which had been allotted to the Palestinians, than to destroy Israel.[73] The British commander of the Arab Legion later confirmed that the Jordanian troops were indeed instructed 'To occupy the central and largest area of Palestine allotted to the Arabs by the 1947 partition'.[74] This is a most significant statement, for it shows that rather than five Arab armies attacking the Israelis, there had been only four – Egypt, Syria, Iraq and Lebanon – and rather than intending to destroy the newly born state of Israel, the Arab Legion had crossed the Jordan river with the aim of partitioning the land by seizing the territory allotted by the UN to the Palestinians. Lack of coordination among the invading forces is reflected in testimonies of Arab troops who took part in this war. Mohsein Abdel Khalek, a captain in the Egyptian army and later a prime minister of that country, recalled how

> The Jews were attacking us from the flank that the Iraqis were supposed to be protecting. We discovered that the Iraqi army had withdrawn, without even telling us. We had to shorten our lines, else the Egyptian army would have been destroyed. It was the turning point in the war.[75]

Thus, although Israel suffered war on three fronts, she fought in effect separate enemies among whom there was little coordination. The invading armies also suffered from lack of preparation – they had simply neglected to prepare their armies for such an operation. The Egyptian army, for example, which was considered the most powerful of all Arab regular armies, had less than two weeks to prepare itself for the war and everything had to be improvised in haste. Abdel Ghani Kanout, an Egyptian officer during that war, recalled: 'We went to the front on horseback … we did not have enough food for the horses so we had to send them back during the war. So overnight my unit was transformed from a cavalry unit to an infantry unit'.[76] Worse still, the invading Arab armies had a poor opinion of the Jews and underestimated their strength and determination. Adel Sabit, a cousin of King Farouk and the liaison between the King and the Arab League, later recalled: 'We were complacently expecting the Jews to run away the moment they saw us … we thought it would be a pushover'. And Mourad Ghaleb, another Egyptian officer: 'We thought that the Jews were not courageous … not fighters'.[77] And Lieutenant-General John Bagot Glubb, the British commander of the Arab Legion: '[The Arabs] believed themselves to be a great military people, and regarded the Jews as a nation of shopkeepers. … [The Arabs] assumed that they would find no difficulty in defeating the Jews'.[78] The Israelis, however, determined to win the war – for they felt themselves with their backs to the wall – exploited the confusion on the Arab side, and after less than four weeks of fierce fighting they had managed to withstand the initial critical moments of the invasion.

While the fighting was still raging, important organizational and structural changes were taking place in the Israeli forces. Mobilization was completed, and on 31 May 1948 Prime Minister and Defence Minister Ben Gurion published an Order of the Day officially establishing the Israeli Defence Force (IDF, or *Tzhal* in Hebrew) as the sole armed force of the state.[79] This meant that Irgun and Lehi – the dissident underground groups led, respectively, by Menachem Begin and a committee of Lehi members, Nathan Yelin Mor, Yisrael Eldad and Yitzhak Shamir – had to disband and its men and weapons to be incorporated into the IDF, the nucleus of which was Hagana. Disarming the dissidents and restoring law-abiding habits – taking the law into one's own hands had become a custom hallowed by patriotism throughout the decades of British rule in Palestine – was not an easy task for Ben Gurion's government. Indeed, the attempt to dissolve the dissident groups and divert their weapons to the IDF led to a severe deterioration of relations between these organizations and the government, to the point where a Jewish civil war seemed imminent. But this was avoided thanks to the willingness of Irgun's commander, Menachem Begin, to call off his troops and agree to their complete integration with the IDF.[80]

The first three crucial weeks of fierce fighting between Arabs and Israelis ended in a truce which was negotiated by the Swedish UN mediator Count Folke Bernadotte. The Arabs had objected to stopping the fighting on the grounds that the Israelis might exploit the respite to regroup, strengthen their defences and obtain weapons. The Israelis, on the other hand, welcomed the possibility of a truce so that they could snatch a breathing space and reorganize themselves. Fearing UN sanctions, the Arabs reluctantly accepted the truce which came into effect on 11 June 1948 at 10 a.m.[81] Four days later Ben Gurion recorded in his war diary the arrival of ten 75mm guns, ten light tanks with 37mm guns, nineteen 65mm guns and four 20mm automatic guns.[82] During the truce a highly centralized command system was also set up, and from his office in Tel Aviv, Ben Gurion's orders passed through GHQ to the four regional commands – North, Centre, East and South – which were functioning as operational fronts.[83]

As the time approached for the truce to expire, the Arab League Political Committee met in Cairo and decided, under pressure from the Egyptian Prime Minister Nokrashy Pasha, to renew the fighting with the Israelis. Efforts by the UN mediator Count Bernadotte to renew the truce failed, and he recorded in his diary: 'They [the Arabs] totally rejected my proposal to agree to prolong the truce'.[84] Upon realizing that the truce would not be renewed, the Israelis took the initiative and struck on 9 July, two days before the ceasefire was due to expire. Now – as the Arabs rightly feared when they objected to having a truce – the Israelis were even better organized and equipped with new weapons.

Fighting raged for ten successive days, during which the battle clearly went in Israel's favour. Israeli operations were particularly concentrated in the area of Tel Aviv, and led by a young military commander, Moshe Dayan, later a chief of staff of the Israeli army and defence minister. Israeli forces occupied the Arab towns of Lydda (11–12 July) and Ramleh (12 July) – both of which had been alloted to the Arabs by the UN Partition Plan – expelling their 50,000 inhabitants and thus making more space for settling new Jewish immigrants.[85] This major expulsion of the Palestinians was carried out with the tacit approval of Israeli Premier Ben Gurion, as is recorded by Yitzhak Rabin – then a military commander who took part in the operation – in a piece which was censored from his published memoirs:

> We walked outside [the headquarters], Ben Gurion accompanying
> us. Allon [the commander of central command] repeated his ques-
> tion:'What is to be done with the [Arab] population [of Ramleh and
> Lydda]?' Ben Gurion waved his hand in a gesture which said:'Drive
> them out!' Allon and I had a consultation. I agreed that it was essen-
> tial to drive the inhabitants out. We took them on foot towards Bet
> Horon road. ... The population did not leave willingly. There was no
> way of avoiding the use of force and warning shots in order to make
> the inhabitants march the ten to fifteen miles to the point where
> they met with the Arab Legion.[86]

One of those expelled was George Habash – years later the leader of the
Palestinian terrorist organization PFLP:

> They directed us to a specific road ... there were road blocks
> manned by Israeli soldiers every 100 metres to make sure that no one
> diverted. This went on until we arrived at the outskirts of Lydda
> (now Lod). There we found a large number of [Israeli] soldiers. They
> put us in rows and started searching each person, a body search ...
> they were not just looking for weapons but also tried to take
> money.[87]

The expelled Arabs were not allowed back to their homes, for what the
Israelis wanted was to have the land without its inhabitants so they could
establish an exclusive Jewish community. In a meeting of the Israeli cabinet on
16 June 1948, Prime Minister Ben Gurion told the ten ministers who were
present:'War is war. We did not start the war. They did. Do we have to allow
the enemy back so they could make war against us? They lost and fled and I
will oppose their return also after the war'.[88]

On 19 July 1948, a second UN truce came into effect, but by this time the
Israelis were well on the offensive, while the Arabs were exhausted and
demoralized and had no alternative but to sue for a truce. Military
commander Rabin recorded in his memoirs: '[The Arabs] did not incline to
renew the war ... we estimated that the Egyptians were not interested in
renewing it'.[89] But to build on their previous successes, the Israelis now
wished to continue the struggle and to fight on, especially in the Negev,
which could provide Israel with much space to accommodate Jewish immigrants.

On the night of 15 October, under the command of Yigal Allon, an Israeli
army launched – in breach of the truce – 'Operation Yoav' which was aimed
at breaking into the Negev. Beersheva, the capital of the Negev, fell into their
hands on 21 October, and two months later, on the night of 22–3 December,
they attacked again; and later, on 5–10 March 1949, they attacked again in the
Negev, reached Eilat and occupied it.[90] This was significant for, by seizing

Eilat, Israel had driven a wedge between the east and the west Arab world, thus preventing Egypt from having a direct land bridge to Jordan. In the north of the country, during 29–31 October 1948, four Israeli brigades had penetrated into Lebanon – this was 'Operation Hiram' – and moved up to the Litani river, destroying on its way the ALA, as well as Lebanese and Syrian units.

All in all the war lasted one year, three months and ten days and cost Israel $500 million, compared with $300 million for the Arabs. There had been three separate rounds of fighting between December 1947 and March 1949, interrupted by two truces imposed by the UN. The Israeli forces occupied about 2,500 square miles of Arab land, which was added to the 5,600 square miles allocated to them by the UN in November 1947. According to the UN partition resolution, about 55 per cent of the land was to be given to the Jews and 45 per cent to the Arabs, but when the war ended Israel controlled almost 80 per cent of the land. Israel – odd though it seems – had managed to keep these occupied territories without serious protest or international outcry – this was not to happen again in future wars. Egypt retained the Gaza Strip, and Jordan's King Abdullah the West Bank of the river Jordan, which he annexed to his kingdom in 1950. For all practical purposes Palestine was partitioned; not, however, as the UN had envisaged, between Jews and Arab-Palestinians, but rather between the Israelis and the Arab states which had, apparently, invaded the land in support of the Palestinians. These last were the big losers in this war, for they had become refugees in camps in Gaza, the West Bank, and other neighbouring Arab states.

When the war ended, Israelis and Arab representatives of the invading armies met on the island of Rhodes where, as Moshe Dayan of the Israeli delegation later recalled, 'Good food, spring weather, enchanting scenery … hundreds of butterflies of all sizes and colours' lent a 'fairy tale air' to the tough negotiations on achieving armistice agreements between the opposing parties.[91] The talks were tough because there was no clear victor in this war. Israel had withheld the Arab invasion and beaten Lebanon and Egypt, but both Syria and Jordan had done well. The Syrian army had managed to cross the international border (agreed between France and Britain in 1923) and occupy land which had been allotted by the UN to the Jewish state. The Arab Legion, as has been shown, seized the West Bank and kept East Jerusalem. Thus in contrast, for instance, to the situation after the First World War, where the victors were able to impose 'peace' on Germany at Versailles, here there had been no clear winner, and reaching an agreement had to involve give-and-take between the parties.

Nonetheless, on 24 February 1949, Egypt was the first to sign an armistice agreement with Israel, and on 23 March 1949, after Israel agreed to pull out of fourteen Lebanese villages it had occupied during the last stage of the war, Lebanon signed on the dotted line. On 3 April 1949, after four weeks of negotiations, Israel and Transjordan signed an agreement. Negotiations between

Map 2 Israel 1949: armistice lines

Israel and Syria ended when, under international pressure, Syria was forced to agree to withdraw its forces from the land it had occupied west of the international border, which now became a demilitarized zone; Israeli and Syrian representatives signed on 20 July 1949. Iraq, however, refused to sign an armistice agreement with Israel, and its forces on the West Bank were replaced by those of the Transjordan Arab Legion.

The armistice agreements were seen as temporary settlements which would later be replaced by permanent peace agreements. But the conflict between Israel and the Arabs and Palestinians was bound to continue, for the great problem which had caused the war in the first place – the struggle between Jews and Arab Palestinians for mastery of the land – was still unresolved at the war's end. Worse still, the war had created a particular problem that was to fester and provoke unrest for more than fifty years: the Palestinian refugees.

The impact of war on the Israelis

'The War of Independence' or 'The War of Liberation', as the Israelis refer to the 1947–9 war, was perceived by them as a life-or-death struggle. But with the benefit of hindsight we can state that if any danger of extinction did exist – when the country's fate was still in the balance – it was only during the very short period between 15 May 1948, the day the regular Arab armies invaded, and 11 June, the day the first UN truce came into effect. This three-week period was the time when there was still a clear Arab superiority in weaponry and firepower – though as we have shown, not in manpower – and when it was also unclear how the freshly recruited Israeli soldiers, many of whom were newly arrived immigrants, would perform. However, once the Israeli forces had checked the Arab onslaught, absorbed new weapons, increased their own weapons production, and trained immigrants and volunteers, the worst was over and Israeli superiority in manpower and weapons combined with short internal lines of communication and high motivation to defeat the Arabs.

That said, this bloodiest of all Israel's wars was to have a most profound and longstanding impact on the psyche of the people of Israel. A particularly significant effect of the war on the collective spirit of the Israelis concerned the fact that it was fought only a short time after the terrible tragedy that had befallen the Jewish people in Europe, with the massacre of 5.4 million of them at the hands of the Nazis.[92] Moreover, in sharp contrast to most of Israel's future wars, the majority of the Israeli population was effectively on the front-line, facing war on its doorstep and exposed to bombardment by enemy aeroplanes; Tel Aviv was bombed fifteen times, with several hundred civilian casualties.[93]

The war cost Israel 5,682 dead, 20 per cent of them civilians and about 8 per cent women. This amounts to about 1 per cent of the total Jewish population in Palestine-Israel, and is indeed a high ratio if compared, for example, to the number of casualties in the First World War, where France lost 34 per thousand, Germany 30 per thousand, Austro-Hungary 10 per thousand, Britain and Italy 16 per thousand, and Russia 11 per thousand.[94] Taking into consideration that the First World War was nearly three and a half times as long as the 1948 war – 51 months compared with fifteen – then it can be said that the ratio of Israeli dead compared with the population was more than Germany's and closer to France's. There were 1,260 women widowed, 2,290 children orphaned and 3,000 soldiers wounded, of whom as many as 360 became mentally ill.[95]

The loss of so many young men – the fittest of their society – was perhaps the main feature of this war, but ironically, it had very little long-term effect on the growth of the Israeli population. A war like this, in which many perish, often causes a reduction in the number of marriages and inevitably leads to a sharp dip in the birth rate. But in Israel, the destruction of an entire generation did not lead to what had happened in Europe after the First World War – a 'surplus of women', or rather a 'deficit of men'. The reason for the absence of this problem after the 1948 war was that the death of so many men was compensated for by the waves of new immigrants arriving in Israel, which in 1948 amounted to 118,000, in 1949 to 239,000 and in 1950–1 to 343,000. In crude terms, for every Israeli killed, several more Jews had come. And thus although in 1948, the most hard-fought year of the war, the number of marriages went down to 10.85 per thousand – compared with 12.98 per thousand in 1947 – it went up (and again in spite of the sheer number of young men who died) in 1949 to 13.40 per thousand (even higher than in 1947!), and up again to 14.54 per thousand in 1950. The annual birth rate, which between 1947 and 1948 went down from 30.55 per thousand to 26.31 per thousand, had risen in 1949 to 29.95 per thousand and went up further in 1950. The young Israeli nation demonstrated its resilience, and a closer look shows that in all walks of life there had been little change, even during the most intensive months of the war. The number of deaths in the Jewish population (excluding deaths resulting directly from the war) was stable: 6.36 per thousand in 1946; 6.58 per thousand in 1947; 6.46 per thousand in 1948; this shows that in spite of the dreadful war the standards of medical care remained intact. Jerusalem was under siege, but there was no hunger, and social life continued to function more or less normally.

Nevertheless, the war provided succeeding generations of Israelis with plenty of material for mythology and legend with which to nourish their future. But not all that was told was strictly true. The Israeli soldier emerging from this war was portrayed as a fighter always playing a fair game – a sort of an English gentleman who even in the heat of the battle never stabs his enemy in the back. In reality, however, the Israeli soldiers, contrary to the myth, had behaved no differently from many other armies – they looted, expelled, massacred and raped. In Acre a group of Israeli soldiers raped an

Arab woman, killed her father and injured her mother; and this, as we learn from the war diary of Prime Minister Ben Gurion, was not an isolated case.[96]

The experience of the war stamped a sense of unity and common destiny on the psychic fibre of the Israelis, who had emerged from it with a new national consciousness, a unity of purpose overriding party conflict and internal feuds. What further cemented unity and emphasized the common destiny of the people of Israel was the huge effort which had followed the war to commemorate those who had died. The Ministry of Defence assembled details of those who perished and produced 4,520 obituaries, collected in a book entitled *Yizkor* ('Remembrance'). Another official memorial was *Gevilai Esh*, which included 455 items: poetry and stories written by those who had died. It was after this war that the term *Mishpachat Ha'schol*, meaning 'The family of mourning', was coined to emphasize that the entire nation was one family grieving its dead. The number of memorials erected to commemorate the dead had reached 1,321 by the mid-1950s; at least one out of every three dead soldiers was individually commemorated.

Gunther Rothenberg, in *The Anatomy of the Israeli Army*, summarizes the story of the 1948 war of independence in a fine passage: 'Both the realization that his life and that of his family literally were at stake ... fuelled by the pronouncements of Arab politicians about a "war of extermination" stiffened the will [of Israelis] to fight'.[97] And this will to fight was further strengthened by the dominant presence of the Holocaust generation. For as Bernard Lewis correctly observed in *Semites and Anti-Semites*:

> For most Jews, that genocide was the most shattering event in their history ... the central experience of their personal lives, and their thoughts and actions are dominated by the knowledge that what has happened once can happen again, and by the determination that it must not.[98]

Indeed, feeling that they were with their backs to the wall facing enemies determined to destroy them, and with the experiences of the Holocaust still fresh in mind, Israelis in the coming years would continue – as they had done during the first war with the Arabs – to rally behind the flag and its leadership, to take up arms when asked, and to fight with determination and desperation, believing themselves to be fighting for their very survival.

CHAPTER TWO

A nation-in-arms

1949–67

In the days, months and years that followed the 1948 War of Independence, the Israeli government had to face two supreme tasks. The first was to absorb the tide of destitute, physically and mentally handicapped Jewish immigrants, who poured copiously into the country following the British departure and Ben Gurion's announcement that the 1939 White Paper and all immigration laws based upon it were null and void.[1] Ben Gurion's statement was reinforced by the 'Law of Return' which was passed by the Knesset on 5 July 1950 and said, among other statements, that: 'Every Jew has the right to immigrate to the country'. This became one of the most important laws ever passed by the Israeli parliament, for it opened the gates of Israel and enabled every Jew to come and join in the attempt to build a nation and a state and to become automatically one of its citizens.[2]

During the first seven and a half months of the state's existence, 101,819 Jewish immigrants arrived, and they were added to in 1949 by 239,076 new arrivals, in 1950 by 170,597, in 1951 by 172,245 and between 1952 and 1955 by 92,204 Jews; in addition there were 88,338 Jewish births during these last four years.[3] Entire Jewish communities had left their homes and countries of origin and immigrated to Israel. But rather than being a voluntary step, it was often one of desperation, for the truth is that the majority of these Jews, especially those living in Middle Eastern countries, were pushed out of their native countries by outraged Arabs humiliated by the victory of the Jews in 1948, rather than being attracted by the newly established Jewish state. Thus the entire Yemenite Jewry, a total of 49,000, was transferred to Israel in 'Operation Magic Carpet' in 1949, and the majority of Iraqi Jewry, a total of 100,000, were airlifted to Israel in 'Operation Ezra and Nehemiah' between May 1950 and December 1951.[4] The Jews of Iraq formed a unique case, for they were harassed not only by the Iraqi authorities but also by Israeli agents who, in April 1950, pretending to be anti-Jewish Iraqis, threw hand grenades at the Dar al Bayda coffee house where Jews used to meet, then repeated the same exercise at the US Information Centre where young Jews often came to read, and in March 1951 struck again just outside the Masuda Shemtov synagogue. This unusual method of frightening away the Jews so that they would leave Iraq and immigrate to Israel seemed justified at the time, giving that the *raison d'être* of a Jewish state and one of its paramount goals was to gather the Jews from all over the world and bring them to *Eretz Yisrael*.[5] Survivors of the European Holocaust also arrived in Israel after being held in internment camps in Cyprus, because the British, as long as they were still in Palestine, would not grant them entry visas. Others had arrived from Eastern Europe, where, unlike Western Europe, the post-Nazi era did not bring a decline in anti-Semitism through compassion for the victims, but rather an increase directed principally against those Jews seeking to return to their homes.[6] By 1951, 100,000 Jews from Poland and 120,000 from Romania had settled in Israel in addition to the Jewish communities of Bulgaria (37,444 had arrived between 1948 and 1955), Czechoslovakia (18,297 had arrived between 1948 and 1955), Yugoslavia, and the greater part of Turkish Jewry.[7]

Yet these Jews, coming from the four corners of the world, had little in common – their diets were different, their cultures unique, and they used different languages, one group often unable to communicate with the other.[8] Together they formed a very fragmented community, and while absorbing and providing them with the barest necessities of life – food, housing, clothing – was the government's main task, transforming them from individuals and close-knit communities into a cohesive Israeli society was also of paramount importance.

The other task of the Israeli government was to reorganize the Israeli army[9] and transform it into an efficient, professional body capable of defending the fledgling state. In fact it was necessary to build it from scratch, for when hostilities ended most of the forces that had won the 1948 war, about 100,000 troops, were demobilized and the armed forces had now effectively ceased to exist.[10] Worse still, weapons and ammunition were in short supply, the remaining forces were under-equipped and military standards were appalling.[11] Rebuilding and equipping the IDF was an urgent task, and there was no time to indulge in leisurely preparations for war because a renewal of hostilities with the Arabs seemed inevitable. The General Staff – led in the postwar period by Chief of Staff Yigael Yadin – had predicted that Israel 'should expect [another] war [with the Arabs]',[12] and Premier and Defence Minister Ben Gurion agreed with this assessment, recording in his diary: 'The Arab states were beaten by us. Could they forget that? 700,000 [Jewish] men had beaten 30 million [Arabs]. ... Could they forget such a humiliation?'[13] In the Foreign Ministry a file named 'The renewal of war' was opened as early as July 1949.[14]

These two tasks – absorbing and transforming the people of Israel from individuals into a cohesive society, and building a new army – were interconnected. A healthy, cohesive society was needed in order to provide the resources – both human and material – to build a highly motivated armed force capable of winning future wars, and armed forces, in turn, seemed at the time to be the best instrument to turn a fragmented community into a nation and society. 'Even the English nation', Ben Gurion observed, '[was no more than] tribes [which were] different from each other. ... And only after hundreds years of evolution did they become one nation ... we [Israelis] do not have hundreds of years and without this instrument – *the army* – we will not become a nation'.[15] What Ben Gurion had in mind was an army which should be a school for society, namely an organization which would be 'not only the fortress of our security', as he put it, 'but also [serve as] an educational force for national unity' where Jews from different cultures would mix together and become 'friends and partners with the native born'.[16]

Building an army – creating a melting pot

The civilian is a soldier on eleven months' annual leave.
(Chief of Staff Yigael Yadin)

Ben Gurion's notion of an army which was an instrument to build a nation and cement the fragmented Israeli society can best be illustrated if the army is seen as a bottleneck through which almost all Israeli citizens, including women, must pass during a compulsory military service. While undergoing this experience Israelis live together, learn to know each other and about each other, communicate in the same language – obviously Hebrew – and are all indoctrinated with the common and ultimate goal of defending their homeland, Israel, from enemies bent on destroying it. Furthermore, the 'bottleneck experience' is reinforced when Israelis, after experiencing compulsory military service, continue to see and meet each other when they are called every year for routine security duties, training and wars. For even after becoming civilians, the Israelis, as Chief of Staff Yadin once put it, remain 'soldiers on eleven months' annual leave'. Such a life experience – it has been calculated that almost every Israeli male devotes at least six full years of his life to military service and almost every woman between one and two full years – inevitably creates a strong bond between society and the military to the point where the society is the army and the army is a mirror of society, or as it is often put: 'the IDF is the people of Israel in uniform'.[17]

In attempting to create a military system based on almost the entire Israeli society, Ben Gurion opted for the Swiss model. In this, a small nucleus of regular and conscripted personnel trains, maintains depots and command structures, and carries out routine security duties. This nucleus is also available in the event of an emergency, and is the body responsible for holding the ground and absorbing a potential surprise attack by the enemy until the main bulk of the armed forces which consists of reservists, namely civilians who were previously trained as conscripts, takes over.[18] The advantage of this system which so attracted Ben Gurion is that it both provides for an adequate defence of the state in times of war, and allows an ordinary functioning of the economy in peacetime.

The new IDF, which was reorganized after the 1948 war and which was modelled closely on the Swiss military system, was established with three tiers. The first tier, the standing army, contains 30 per cent of the total available manpower and is composed of conscripts subject to universal and compulsory military service. During this period of service, conscripts are trained and specialize in specific areas: armour, artillery, air force, navy, and so on. In times of war, this component is given, as in the Swiss system, the mission of absorbing an enemy's first strike and if necessary of being the first to move into enemy territory. The second tier of the new IDF is the reserve body. Composed of civilians who have completed their period of compulsory service, the reserves provide the quantitative component of the IDF, which reverses the numerical advantage of the Arab troops in favour of the Israelis and bridges the gap between peacetime and wartime manpower requirements. In fact, the main feature and also the object of this new military system is the production of a huge reserve with which to expand the active army in war. The third tier of the military system is the professional component composed of career personnel, most of whom serve in the air force and the navy. It was clear from the start, that if this system, which is based overwhelmingly on civilian reserves, was to function properly, it would have to rely heavily on a first-rate intelligence service which was capable of providing an alert early enough for reserves to be called up, mobilized and join the regulars; a big investment was therefore put into creating an effective army intelligence service. Chief of Staff Yadin who, under the close supervision of Ben Gurion, had carried out the task of building the new IDF, often compared it to an iceberg with only its tip, namely its regular and the professional components, visible, while the iceberg itself, namely the reserve component, based on almost the entire society, was hidden.[19]

To enable the government to mobilize the entire society – for this was the implication of having a military system based on civilian reserves as the main component of the wartime order of battle – in June 1949 the Knesset passed 'Chok Sherut Bitachon Leumi'. Under the provisions of this law, which has been amended throughout the years but basically remains unchanged, men and women who were found physically and mentally fit were liable to service at the age of eighteen; the period of service to be modified in accordance with defence requirements. The law also stipulated that upon terminating a period of compulsory service the authorities could call men and women to serve in the reserve force, either to be trained in new methods or to participate in military actions. The law also allowed a semi-military framework called *Gadna* ('youth brigades') to prepare boys and girls of 14–18 to become soldiers. Thus by law almost the whole of Israeli society between the ages of fourteen and fifty-five was enlisted.

There were, however, a few exemptions. The law stipulated that Arab citizens living in Israel – meaning those who had not left during the 1948 war and were living under Israeli military rule until after the 1967 Six Day War –

should be exempted. The reason for that was that the makers of the law felt they had to keep guns away from a potential fifth column, and also to absolve the Arabs of Israel from a dual loyalty to the Jewish state and to their fellow Arabs. That said, Christians and Bedouin were allowed to volunteer, and indeed many of them chose to serve in the IDF. Responding to political pressure from orthodox religious parties and a demand to replenish the pool of Torah scholars after the Holocaust, Ben Gurion also agreed to exempt 400 top students of religious institutions (called *Yeshivot*).[20] In addition, girls of orthodox background were allowed to sign a declaration stating that military service was incompatible with their upbringing.

To the Knesset, which had voted overwhelmingly for this law, Ben Gurion explained that it aimed 'to prepare the entire people for defence; to give the youth – Israeli born and immigrant – pioneering and military training, to maintain a permanently mobilized force adequate to withstand a surprise attack and hold out until the reserves were mobilized'.[21]

Arming the IDF and perfecting the system

Equipping the new IDF, though crucial, was no easy task given the stress and burden caused by the need to absorb the massive influx of immigrants.[22] But then, as we have already noted, a 'second round' with the Arab world seemed certain, and the Israeli government felt obliged to make its first priority the buying of arms and equipping the IDF. Thus, in the period between March 1949 and December 1951, it procured some 216 planes, 21 tanks, 46 naval vessels, 19 armoured vehicles, 102 half tracks, 591 cannons, 23 torpedo boats, 403 heavy machine guns, 11 medium machine guns, 5,135 rifles, 7 sub-automatic rifles and 3,453 pistols. At the beginning of 1952 the IDF had a total of 420 planes, 61 tanks, 85 naval vessels, 221 half tracks, 19 armoured vehicles, 1,007 canons, 24 heavy mortars, 23 torpedo boats, 561 heavy machine guns, 1,428 medium machine guns, 6,039 automatic rifles, 57,526 rifles, 530 sub-automatic rifles and 5,208 pistols.[23] This might appear to be an unimpressive arsenal, but compared with the tiny stockpile of arms the Israelis had only four years earlier, it was indeed a most impressive amount of weapons to have been assembled within a relatively short period of time.

As with arms, so it was with training – expensive but essential. Mobilization in future wars, so the Israeli planners had stipulated, would have to be very different from the way it was carried out during the 1948 war, when mobilization was gradual and months had passed before the army reached full strength. In future wars Israeli society would have to mobilize much more efficiently – reserves moving quickly to the battle fronts and the rapid transference of cars, vehicles and other resources from the citizenry to the IDF. Those segments of society which did not join the front-line fighting force, mostly women, the young and the old, were to flock into factories, offices and voluntary services, to hospitals and to schools in order to take the place of men so that mobilization would not wreck the economy.

Military manoeuvres and training got under way immediately after the 1948 war, and this was regularly reported in the papers – which were tightly controlled by the state – presumably in order to induce a sense of belonging among the Israelis and also to make a show of strength and deter potential adversaries. The IDF magazine *Ba'machane*, reported, on 17 October 1949, that 'When the men were called up to take part in the summer military manoeuvres ... they were not the only ones who were called to the flag. Recruitment calls were also issued for animals'. It was, in other word, almost the entire society which was called to serve – even animals.

In spite of the hardships and austerity and the fact that the economy was in a desperate condition, Chief of Staff Yadin was able to hold three large-scale manoeuvres involving more than 100,000 reserves. The first major exercise, which was called 'Manoeuvre A', took place in 1950 and was aimed at testing the call-up system by using two types of calls up – 'silent calls' in which officers called up reserves by telephoning them; and an open mobilization where reserves were summoned to join their units by codes broadcast over the radio. In 1951 two other extensive exercises, 'Manoeuvre B' and 'Manoeuvre C', took place, in which reserve formations were physically deployed and took up positions to test the system under two different scenarios: one in which Israel had suffered a surprise attack, and another in which Israel had itself launched a pre-emptive strike. For although the Israeli doctrine of warfare based on pre-emptive strike and the transfer of war into enemy soil was developed only after the 1956 Sinai campaign, in the early 1950s the advantages of this method for a small state like Israel were already becoming clear.

The manoeuvres had proved beyond any doubt that the new IDF functioned properly and its reserve component – that is, the society as a whole – had cooperated fully. This was crucial, given that for such a system to function properly – with men leaving their jobs and other obligations and also transferring their private cars to the army – full public cooperation was essential.

A sense of insecurity and public cooperation

After the 1948 war the government of Israel could count on the public to rally behind it and cooperate fully, both in paying high taxes for defence and also in devoting much time to carrying out routine military duties. What ensured the public's full cooperation was its strong sense of insecurity, caused partly by Arab actions, which seemed to be aimed at harming Israel, and partly by the tendency of the Israeli leadership to exaggerate the external danger posed by the Arabs.

Palestinian infiltration, for example, had strongly affected the public mood. Palestinians, now living as refugees in camps in the Gaza Strip, Jordan, Syria and Lebanon, would enter Israel through its penetrable borders. These incursions, especially in the early 1950s, were not, however, aimed at re-occupying the land these people had lost a few years earlier, but rather at returning to villages and homes in order to collect possessions and crops in abandoned fields, and also to steal from Israeli farms.[24] In fact, much of this non-violent Palestinian infiltration was encouraged by Israel's policy of repatriation, which extended rights to close family members separated by the war to return home. Since, in order for a person to be eligible for this scheme, there had to be some member of their family remaining in the country, a method was developed by which Palestinian women and children infiltrated Israel and thereafter applied for permission for members of their families to join them.[25] IDF figures show that in 1952, 16,000 cases of Palestinian infiltration occurred; in 1953 there were 7,018 cases; in 1954, 4,638; in 1955, 4,351; and during the first months of 1956, 2,786 cases.[26] Israel's policy was determined and ruthless – its armed forces shot the infiltrators. This policy was aimed at deterring Palestinians from attempting to return to their homes, thus preventing a trickle of return turning into a flood which would then endanger the Jewish character of Israel.

But not all Palestinian infiltration was non-violent, and there were infiltrators who sought to carry out acts of sabotage and kill Israelis. IDF figures show that in 1950, 19 Israelis were killed and 31 were injured by Arab marauders. In 1951 the figures were 48 and 49 respectively; in 1952, 42 and 56; in 1953, 44 and 66. Palestinian violent actions had gathered momentum from April 1955, when groups of fedayeen were established in the Gaza strip under Egyptian intelligence supervision, with the aim of striking at Israel.[27] All in all, between 1949 and 1956 Israel lost 486 lives, including 264 civilians; and 1,057 were injured, including 477 civilians.[28]

In absolute terms this was surely not a heavy toll for a country whose population exceeded 1.5 million, but as Avner Yaniv rightly observed in *Deterrence without the Bomb*:

> The damage was perceived as extensive … in terms of people's state of mind. Incidents leading to death and injury of Israelis by Arabs who had crossed over from the neighbouring countries created a pervasive sense of insecurity. People became afraid to travel at night – even, in certain areas, in broad daylight.[29]

Israeli leaders often exaggerated the danger of Arab infiltration, as did, for example, minister Yitzhak Ben-Aharon when declaring that Arab infiltration 'Endangers our very existence'.[30] Inevitably, such statements increased rather than eased the public's sense of insecurity, and as Sir John Bagot Glubb, the British commander of the Arab Legion, the army of the state of Transjordan, correctly observed:

> One of the most dangerous aspects of this unrestrained [Israeli] propaganda was the effect which it seemed to be having on the Israeli public. They [the Israeli government] complained that the inhabitants of their frontier colonies could not sleep at night. This is scarcely to be wondered at, if they read the Israeli Press, which daily described the most bloody (but fortunately often fictitious) battles [between Israeli forces and the infiltrators].[31]

Was the Israeli government exaggerating the external danger in order to rally its people behind it? This is hard to answer and we have not a scrap of evidence to show that this was indeed the case, but such an unofficial Israeli policy of frightening its own people so that they would rally behind the flag should not be ruled out automatically.

To counter Palestinian violence, the Israelis devised a policy which became known as the 'doctrine of retaliatory action'. One of the features of this policy was to hit hard in response to even a small provocation, and also to strike at the countries from which the perpetrators had come so as to put pressure on hosting Arab governments to prevent incursions of Palestinian fighters into Israel.[32] The killing, for instance, of an Israeli mother and her two young children in Yahud in 1953, led to a massive Israeli retaliatory action in Kibia which resulted in the deaths of sixty-nine Arab civilians.[33] The killing of an Israeli cyclist near Rehovot led to an equally massive Israeli retaliatory action against the fedayeen in Gaza on 28 February 1955, in which thirty-eight Egyptian soldiers were killed and thirty-two wounded.[34] An Egyptian attempt to demolish Israeli water devices near the border with Gaza led to Israeli retaliation against the Khan Yunis police fort on 31 August 1955, in which seventy-two Egyptians were killed and fifty-eight wounded. When Syrians fired at Israeli fishermen on the Sea of Galilee, the Israelis retaliated on 11 December 1955, killing fifty-four Syrians, wounding nine and capturing thirty.[35]

Israel's retaliatory doctrine neither curbed infiltration nor eased public insecurity. In fact it achieved precisely the opposite effect for, by reacting massively and disproportionately to even minor Palestinian provocations, the Israeli leadership instilled in the public a mistaken impression that a big and continuous war was being waged between Israeli troops and the fedayeen.[36]

Another reason for a growing sense of insecurity among Israelis was what seemed to be an Arab intention to strike at and destroy Israel. While true at times, this has not always reflected reality. In fact in the early 1950s, Arab leaders were less concerned with their struggle with Israel than was reported at the time. In Egypt, for example, the Free Officers who overthrew King Farouk in July 1952 did not even mention Israel in their manifesto, which dealt only with social reforms.[37] Nevertheless in the mid-1950s, policies taken by Egypt which had little to do with Israel were often seen by the Israelis as aimed at harming them. On 27 September 1955, for example, Egypt's

President Nasser concluded his arms deal with Czechoslovakia under which Egypt was to receive huge amounts of weapons.[38] At first this failed to make an impression on the Israelis, and Prime Minister Moshe Sharett did not even bother mentioning it in his personal diary, where he would record almost every event. It took Sharett no less than three days to convene a special session of the government to discuss the matter.[39]

But soon the arms deal was causing considerable panic, with every paper in Israel running headlines such as 'A time of danger, a time of opportunity' and 'Anything could now happen along Israel's borders'. In *Ma ariv*, Azriel Carlibach, a senior journalist, published an editorial warning of Egyptian aggression.[40] *Davar*, the paper controlled by the Labour movement, declared in its 2 October editorial that 'The arms were purchased solely for planned aggression against Israel. … The Egyptian ruler and the other Arab rulers believe it their right to foreclose Israel's possibility of self-defence, just as they deny the very existence of our state'.[41] In the Knesset Ben Gurion, now a defence minister under Sharett, announced that

> The rulers of Egypt seem to have concluded that it is easier to win victories on the foreign policy front than to reform the unfortunate and shameful domestic situation, and in order to gain Arab hegemony the tyrants of Egypt have apparently decided that the easier and cheapest way is by attacking Israel.[42]

On 10 October, Ya'acov Meridor of Herut declared that the Czech arms deal 'put into question the future of our nation here, our very existence and well-being'. Prime Minister Sharett announced from the podium of the Knesset: 'From here in this house, in this our capital, we call on the citizens of Israel, to the Jewish people throughout the Diaspora, and to the entire world for weapons for Israel', and elsewhere he said 'We [Israelis] must now pull together to mobilize all our capabilities which may be limited but are not insignificant … to take a stand and defend the ramparts'. The Knesset declared its concern about the large quantities of weapons supplied to Egypt which 'will be directed by Israel's enemies against her. … The Knesset charges the government with mobilizing the people and the state against the dangers'.[43]

The view that Nasser meant to attack Israel at that time was, in my judgement, mistaken. Nasser had no precise plans of aggression; at best he had an *intention* of doing so, which he held in common with most Arabs. And while such an arsenal in the hands of an Arab state undoubtedly presented a potential threat to Israel, we now know – and it is likely that the Israeli leaders knew at the time – that Nasser's arms deal was more a protest against the Baghdad Pact than against Israel. This pact, of 24 February 1955, of mutual cooperation between Iraq and Turkey, in which Britain and Iran joined and the US supported with arms and money, was part of American Secretary of State John Foster Dulles' policy of containing Soviet expansion by clear contractual deterrents that would prevent Soviet penetration of the Middle East. Nasser, who saw himself as the leader of the Arab world, regarded the pact as an attempt to divide the Arabs. Hence, as the Israeli diplomat Abba Eban observed, the acquisition of weapons was 'above all Nasser's response to the Baghdad Pact', and agression against Israel was 'at most, a subsidiary motive'.[44]

Was the Israeli government exaggerating the danger of weapons in Nasser's hands in order to rally its people behind it? This is hard to answer. It is probable that it was assumed by Israeli leaders that almost any jet could take off and bomb towns in Israel, and that all these weapons could be used against Israeli targets, and that they *would* be used. But it also might well be that in addition to this, Israeli leaders assumed that exaggerating the external danger was not a bad idea after all, for it would rally the nation behind it. Indeed, on the day of the Knesset debate on the Egypt–Czechoslovakia deal, a young boy came to the Ministry of Defence offices in Tel Aviv asking to see the Minister. When he was directed to one of the clerks, the boy gave him a handful of small coins that he had been saving for his *Bar Mitzvah*, to buy defensive weapons for Israel; the next day an old woman appeared offering her own contribution of a gold bangle.[45] Former Chief of Staff Yadin added to the sense of urgency when he called on Israeli parents to 'buy an iron cloth for the defence of your children'.[46] Soon, prices of weaponry systems were published in the daily papers and the public was invited to 'buy' them for the IDF. The Israeli Teacher Association donated money to 'buy' a jet plane and a tank, while Haifa Council 'bought' a torpedo boat for the navy. Ramat-Gan Council 'bought' a transport plane and 100 parachutes and the Discount Bank of Israel collected money to 'buy' a tank, as did representatives of the public in the town of Ramleh, who called the tank they had 'purchased' 'Ramleh I'. And with the public fully cooperating, the government moved to consolidate the donations by establishing the 'Voluntary Defence Fund' into which old and young poured money. Calls on the public to help in order to face the Egyptian threat had gathered momentum with Prime Minister Sharett's announcement that 'The decisive military advantage which will soon be held by a nation intent on laying Israel to waste, endangers the state and each and every one of us ... it is time to work for the defence of Israel'.[47] Playing the Holocaust card, the leadership went so far as to announce that the lesson of Jewish history, reinforced by the experience of the Holocaust, was simple – a Jewish state must be able to protect itself. Defence Minister Ben Gurion told the public that President Nasser's aim was to strike at Israel because he had been humiliated in 1948, and Chief of Staff Moshe Dayan called the Egyptian leader 'a military dictator'. In ten days, IL5 million had been collected to buy arms for the IDF.

Mordechai Bar On, an intelligent and well informed observer, who served as Moshe Dayan's head of bureau, wrote in a fine passage:

For most Israelis, the conflict shaped since the War of Independence had limited their perspective. Their images had crystallized during the hostilities of 1948; if this was how one began reckoning history then the conflict in the mid-1950s could only be seen as one between a defensive Israel, protecting its very existence and the belligerent Arabs, intent on Israel's destruction. This view provided Israel's security establishment with two important assets: a wide public consensus on security issues and total civilian willingness to fight in the wars.

Indeed, a wide public consensus on security enabled the Israeli leadership to channel substantial sums of money into defence and spend increasing proportions of the national income on armaments, without raising any significant opposition from taxpayers. In 1950 the defence budget amounted to $87.6 million; in 1951 it was $151.5 million; in 1952 it was $75.5 million; and in 1953 the figure was $68.8 million. Defence expenditure as a percentage of government expenditure grew dramatically from 23.0 per cent in 1952 to 34.9 per cent in 1956.[48] That the government could spend so much on arms, while at the same time demanding that the public 'tighten its belt' and live an almost Spartan life, is a clear indication that it had strong public support. Furthermore, as Bar On correctly observed, given the Israeli sense of insecurity, the government could be sure that if called to the flag, Israelis would cooperate fully and take up arms to defend themselves. Indeed, this proved to be the case in the autumn of 1956.

A major test

The 'Kadesh War', or as it is better known, the 'Sinai Campaign', was the largest military operation undertaken by the IDF since the 1948 war.[49] It was sparked by President Nasser's announcement on 26 July 1956 that his government had decided to nationalize the Suez Canal Company. Nasser offered to compensate the company's shareholders, mainly France and Britain, and said he would use the income from the canal to build the Aswan Dam, at an estimated cost of $1.3 billion, a project that Egypt needed for irrigation and for power. Nasser's announcement came in response to American Secretary of State John Foster Dulles' announcement, made on 19 July, that no American aid for the building of the Dam would be forthcoming, and that American and British participation in financing the High Dam of Aswan through the World Bank was not 'feasible in present circumstances'. This meant that Washington had reversed its previous pledge to support the project. It had done so, among other reasons, because of Nasser's growing links with the Soviet Union and his fierce campaign against the Baghdad Pact.[50]

Nasser's nationalization of the Suez Canal drew together two previous colonial powers – France and Britain – who resented the idea that with

Nasser's nationalization of the Suez Canal Company they would be dependent for their major supplies, especially of oil, not on an international waterway over which they had direct control, but on Nasser's goodwill.[51] In London and Paris, Nasser's action was seen as a major threat to their far-flung maritime economic interests east of Suez.

Soon after Nasser's announcement, France and Britain began considering the use of force to regain control of the Suez Canal. Israel – odd as it seems – was also invited to join the anti-Nasser coalition, and saw in the possibility of war against Egypt an opportunity to achieve its own aims, which were not at all, however, connected with the Suez Canal, but rather with the Straits of Tiran.

The Straits of Tiran were Israel's primary route to East Africa and Asia, but for several years had been blocked by Egyptian batteries deployed at Sharm el-Sheike. Troubles had started in 1953 when Egypt had detained, for the first time, a Danish cargo ship en route to the Israeli port of Eilat. In September 1953 the Egyptians treated a Greek vessel in the same way, and on 1 January 1954 they opened fire on a small Italian cargo vessel en route to Eilat. For the Israelis, interference with freedom of navigation through the Straits posed not only an economic but also a political danger. For the Israelis were haunted by the fear that the West, in its anxiety to lure Egypt into a pro-Western alliance, would force Israel to cede the Negev so as to facilitate territorial continuity between Egypt and the Fertile Crescent.[52] Settling the Negev and keeping the port and town of Eilat bustling with activity might have prevented such demands, but for this to succeed Israel needed the Straits to remain open. On 6 May 1955, Ben Gurion had declared that blocking the Straits was for Israel a *casus belli*, and when the blockade continued he went so far as to threaten, in an interview given to the *New York Times* on 29 September 1955, that if Egypt failed to lift the blockade within a year, Israel would use force to open the Straits. And now, following Nasser's nationalization of the Suez Canal and the building of an anti-Nasser alliance which contemplated military action, Israel saw an opportunity to achieve this aim.[53] Military action against Nasser could also be beneficial to Israel for two further reasons: first, it would enable Israel to strike at the Egyptian army before it assimilated the weapons Egypt had acquired through the September 1955 deal with Czechoslovakia. Second, it would enable Israel to hit and destroy the fedayeen bases in the Gaza Strip, which had been their jumping-off points for attacks on Israel.

A period of consultation and planning involving Israeli, French and British representatives had resulted in a simple military plan: Israel, as the eastern flank of a Franco-British attack, would provide a pretext for a French and British intervention by attacking Egypt towards the Suez Canal. On being appraised of this, the British and the French governments would make two appeals to the governments of Egypt and Israel. To Egypt: '(a) halt all acts of war. (b) withdraw all its troops ten miles from the Canal. (c) accept temporary occupation of key positions on the Canal by the Anglo-French forces to guarantee freedom of passage through the Suez canal'.[54] To Israel: '(a) halt all acts of war (b) withdraw all its troops ten miles to the east of the Canal'.[55] It was obvious that Israel, which was party to this plan, would agree, though it was stipulated that Nasser might refuse to withdraw, in which case France and Britain would use force to take over the Suez Canal.

On 22 October, Prime Minister and Defence Minister Ben Gurion, accompanied by his two principal lieutenants, Chief of Staff Dayan and director of the defence ministry Shimon Peres, flew to Sèvres in France to finalize the joint military plan. On 25 October, Dayan recorded in his diary:

> We can sum up the situation today as follows: 1. The prime minister and defence minister, David Ben Gurion, has given approval in principle to the campaign and its aims. 2. Our forces will go into action at dusk on 29 October 1956, and we must complete the capture of the Sinai Peninsula within seven to ten days. 3. The decision on the campaign and its planning are based on the assumption that British and French forces are about to take action against Egypt.[56]

To the Israeli cabinet, on 28 October, Ben Gurion presented Israel's aims as follows:

> We are interested, first of all, in [opening] the Straits of Eilat [to Israeli shipping] and the Red Sea. Only through them can we secure direct contact with the nations of Asia and East Africa. ... The main thing, to my mind, is freedom of navigation in the Straits of Eilat. As far as the Gaza Strip is concerned. ... If I believed in miracles I would pray for it to be swallowed up in the sea. All the same, we must eradicate the fedayeen bases and secure peaceful lives for the inhabitants of border areas.[57]

The Israeli forces for the campaign, as detailed by Chief of Staff Dayan, comprised an armoured brigade – the 7th, with two tank battalions; two mechanized armoured brigades – the 27th and 37th; a paratroop brigade – the 202nd, and six infantry brigades – the 1st, 4th, 9th, 10th, 11th and 12th. Except for the 7th and 202nd, all were reserve formations.[58] Given that the majority of forces were reservists, this campaign was to be a major test for the new IDF. To maintain security, Dayan delayed mobilization for most units until the last moment, and the initial mobilization which had begun on 26 October was carried out by messengers. Two days later on 28 October, an open mobilization was ordered, and once the radio call-up was used, units rapidly filled up and moved to the front.

The attack on Egypt was launched at 4.59 p.m. on 29 October, with Israeli aircraft dropping 'out of the blue' 385 parachute troops of the 890th battalion at the Israeli end of the Mitla Pass, some 30 miles east of the Suez Canal.

Simultaneously, the rest of the 202nd paratroop brigade, under the command of Ariel Sharon, had embarked on an overland advance of 190 miles across central Sinai towards Mitla to link up with its parachute battalion twenty-eight hours later.[59]

The campaign was quickly and easily won by the Israelis, who had managed to occupy the entire Sinai Peninsula within 100 hours, and reach and open the Straits of Tiran to Israeli shipping by occupying Sharm el-Sheike.[60] Israel had destroyed the Egyptian forces in Sinai at a cost of 172 killed, 700 wounded and four prisoners of war. Egypt suffered thousands of deaths, great numbers of wounded and 5,581 prisoners of war.[61] The IDF, and particularly its reserve component, seemed to have conclusively proved its efficacy. The scores of thousands of civilians, who in the years preceding the war had trained within the constraints that a reserve system involved, in particular the limiting of training time, did not seem to have affected adversely the IDF's performance in battle. An army of civilians had proved itself capable of fighting a brief, intensive war. The logistical system, too, had withstood the demanding conditions of such a war.[62]

The Sinai campaign proved that the panic caused in Israel by the Egyptian–Czech arms deal was premature; the Egyptians had failed to assimilate the weapons, and Israel had captured great quantities of them. While this brief war was a major test for the armed forces as far as mobilization and fighting practices were concerned, it had little impact on Israeli society as a whole. This was because it was called a 'campaign' and perceived as such by the Israelis, and was seen as not much different from the major large-scale retaliatory actions which had taken place against Egypt and Jordan in the period leading up to it. More importantly, the campaign was short, decisive and successful, and as the old proverb goes, 'nothing succeeds like success'.

After the storm came a strange calm. Israel withdrew from the territory it had occupied, including Sharm el-Sheike, and, in general, the next decade or so was a period of relative peace and tranquillity, especially along Israel's border with Egypt. It was a period in which Israel had the time to devote to producing some order from the chaos of war and social upheaval. Israeli society after the Sinai campaign became much more cohesive and self-assured, and was able to concentrate on consolidating its position in world affairs and at home.

That said, the consciousness of a severe external threat to its very existence remained. Nasser, after what seemed to be a victory over France and Britain, became much more confident, and also felt growing resentment towards Israel for having attacked him. As a result, his anti-Israeli declarations became more pronounced than in the early 1950s, although, as we have seen, he avoided unrest on his border with Israel. On 4 October 1958 Nasser endorsed the anti-Semitic *Protocols of the Elders of Zion*, which was the spiritual basis of European and especially Nazi anti-Semitism, thus arousing the deepest fears of the Israelis, many of whom were Holocaust survivors.[63] Five years later in

1963, Nasser joined Iraq's President Abdul Salam Arif in signing a communiqué proclaiming that 'The aim of the Arabs is the destruction of Israel'.[64] On 11 July 1965, Nasser declared: 'The final account with Israel will be made within five years if we are patient. The Moslems waited seventy years until they expelled the Crusaders from Palestine'.[65] With such threats and intimidating declarations, and with the warnings of Israeli politicians that such statements should be taken very seriously indeed, the Israeli public rallied behind its leadership and was willing to carry on the burden of paying high taxes so that there would be no cuts in the defence budget, to leave jobs and families to take up routine training, and to agree to serve for long periods. For as one observer put it:

> Rightly or wrongly, most Israelis were convinced that the Arabs were bent on destroying their state and that they were fighting with their backs to the wall. For them there could be no retreat because there was no place to retreat to and in every war the individual soldier believed that he was fighting for the life of his family, his home, and his nation.[66]

CHAPTER THREE

The six bad years
1967–73

A powder keg

The outbreak of war in the spring of 1967 shocked Israelis to the core, for it came, to speak bluntly, as a bolt from the blue. And it is only because this war was so remarkably successful that no demand was ever made – as was to be the case after the 1973 war – to investigate the politico-military establishment, whose superficial optimism and complacency had led Israelis to believe that war was a remote and unlikely event. That the Israeli leadership was totally relaxed about the security situation in the period just before this war, is well illustrated in the following extract from a report written by Walt Rostow, National Security Adviser in Lyndon Johnson's administration, of his meeting with Israeli Ambassador Abraham Harman on 31 January 1967:

> Israeli ambassador Harman came in yesterday ... to share his observations on the mood in Israel. His theme was basically that Israel faces an economically difficult situation over the next three years or so ... he said most Israeli leaders feel the long-term security situation is under control.[1]

The view in Israel in the first half of 1967 was that its most implacable foe, President Nasser of Egypt, was unlikely to embark on a full-scale war. This opinion rested upon a theory that proved to be utterly erroneous; it was that as long as *la crème de la crème* of Nasser's forces, eight brigades in all, was still involved in the civil war in Yemen, he would not dare to attack Israel.[2] Complementary to this assessment was the view that neither Syria nor Jordan would open fire without the active participation of Egypt, which not only had the most powerful army but which was also in a geographical position to impose on Israel its traditional nightmare – a war on more than one front. And because the Israeli theory that war was remote was based heavily on the continuing Egyptian presence in the Yemen, the eyes of its intelligence services were fixed on airfields in Yemen and Egypt to check whether Egyptian troops were being brought back home, for their return to Egypt would be a strong indication that the prospects of war were higher than before. But in the first half of 1967 the Egyptian elite forces were still bogged down in the Yemenite civil war – they would return to Egypt only *after* the 1967 war – and in Israel it seemed as if the relatively calm situation along the Israeli–Egyptian border would continue unabated.

In stark contrast with the relatively calm relations between Egypt and Israel, the latter's relations with Syria were volatile and, in the period up to the 1967 war, characterized by a series of mounting tensions and skirmishes. There were three bones of contention between Israel and Syria. The first of these was over water. Israel wished to divert water from Lake Kinneret (also known as the Sea of Galilee) down south to the Negev desert where water was scarce. It was vital for Israel to develop the Negev, because this was its most unpopulated area, and it contained valuable resources such as uranium. Perhaps more important was the fact that a Negev which was dotted with Jewish settlements and factories would, so the Israelis hoped, put an end to the persistent calls on Israel to cede parts of the desert to the Arabs and allow Egypt to establish a land bridge with Jordan. But without water Israel could not develop the desert, and this is why she built a pipeline, partly open, called *Ha'movil Ha'artzi* to divert water from the north to the south. The Syrians, however, objected to this project – their aims, after all, were opposite to those of Israel – and as the water sources, mainly from the Hatzbani and Banyas rivers, were in their territory, they attempted to divert the water before it reached Israel. This in turn had led to exchanges of fire in which Israeli tanks and aeroplanes hit and destroyed Syrian tractors and other machinery assembled to divert the water.[3] Israel did manage to transfer water to the Negev, but the water project was a constant source of tension between the two countries.

The second bone of contention between Israel and Syria, and a persistent source of trouble in the region, was the support which the Syrian regime was giving to Palestinian paramilitary groups to cross into Israel and terrorize its citizens. This often led to Israeli military retaliatory actions against Syria, aimed at forcing her to curb these incursions from her territory. But while the authorities in both Jordan and Lebanon had taken tough measures to curb such infiltrations from their own countries into Israel, the Syrian leadership had extended its support to the Palestinian paramilitary groups. This led Yitzhak Rabin – he had taken over as Israel's Chief of Staff in January 1964 – to state on 12 May 1967 that the retaliatory actions Israel had directed against Jordan and Lebanon to force them to curb terrorist attacks on Israel, were not an effective measure as far as Syria was concerned because, as Rabin put it, 'In Syria ... the authorities themselves activate the terrorists'. He went on: 'therefore, the aim of any [future Israeli military] action against Syria will be different from the actions which Israel has taken against Jordan and Lebanon'.[4] This statement – although given to the small and unimportant IDF Magazine *Ba'machane* – was regarded in Arab circles as an Israeli intent to harm Syria. As Nasser later put it: 'Israeli commanders [meaning Rabin] announced they would carry out military operations against Syria in order to occupy Damascus and overthrow the Syrian government'.[5] Although Premier and Defence Minister Levi Eshkol – he had taken over from Ben Gurion in June 1963 – criticized Rabin for issuing statements which increased tensions in the region, he had himself fuelled Arab anxiety by issuing similar declarations (Nasser: 'on the same day … Eshkol made a very threatening statement against Syria'). Eshkol's bizarre behaviour had little to do with Israeli–Arab relations, but rather with his own relationship with Chief of Staff Rabin and the attempts of each of them to outdo the other and impress upon the Israeli people that they were tough on the Arabs.[6] Such declarations put President Nasser under strong pressure because of the defence pact between Egypt and Syria – signed on 4 November 1966 – which committed Egypt to helping Syria if it was attacked by Israel.

The third bone of contention between Israel and Syria was over control of the demilitarized zones (DMZs). These were three areas west of the international border (agreed in 1923 between French mandatory Syria and British mandatory Palestine) which Syria had occupied during the 1948 war. Under intense international pressure, the Syrians were obliged to withdraw and to agree to these lands to becoming demilitarized zones without defining their sovereignty.[7] The Israelis – who had signed up to this arrangement voluntarily rather than under a *Diktat* – later regretted this, and attempted to regain control over these lands by provoking the Syrians and then taking advantage of military clashes to expand control over the DMZ. In a candid interview, former Chief of Staff Moshe Dayan had openly admitted that Israel, rather than Syria, was responsible for 'at least 80 per cent' of the clashes that had occurred in the DMZ between 1949 and 1967.[8] Perhaps the most serious clash between Israeli and Syrian forces just before the June 1967 war occurred on 7 April 1967. On that day an exchange of fire in the DMZ escalated into an air battle in which Israeli planes shot down six Syrian Mig fighter planes, two of them on the outskirts of the capital Damascus.[9] This was a humiliating defeat for Syria and, again, it put Nasser of Egypt under intense pressure to come to Syria's assistance.

To sum up, in the spring of 1967 Israeli–Egyptian relationships were relatively calm, in contrast with the tense Israeli–Syrian situation. As we shall now see, what ignited the Israeli–Syrian powder keg into a full-blown war which would also involve other Arab states, notably Egypt, was a Soviet lie.

The spark – a false Soviet report

In the literature, there are two competing views on relationships between the superpowers – the USSR and the USA – and the local states in the Middle East during the period of the Cold War (1945–89). One view maintains that throughout these years the local states had their own domestic and regional agendas which they tried, in their different ways, to make the Cold War serve. The other view is that the Middle Eastern powers had been mere pawns in a game played by the superpowers.[10] The 1967 war has often been explained in terms of the first view, and the answer to the question of who first raised the storm and launched the march of events which ended in the short but decisive confrontation between Israelis and Arabs and which almost led to direct US and Soviet intervention, was clear: it was Nasser. New evidence, however, shows that this was not the case, and in fact what really sparked this confrontation was a Soviet attempt to exploit the local states in order to score points in its confrontation with the US.[11]

To understand how this came to happen we should go back to 13 May 1967, the date on which Anwar el-Sadat, speaker of the Egyptian parliament, was on an official visit to Moscow. When the visit was over Sadat was seen off at Moscow airport by Vladimir Semnov, the Soviet Deputy Foreign Minister, and it was then that Sadat heard from Semnov that according to Soviet intelligence, 'Ten Israeli brigades had been concentrated on the Syrian border' ready to strike at Syria; in Cairo the same message was delivered to President Nasser by the Soviet ambassador.[12] Against mounting tension between Israel and Syria – which, as we have seen, was caused by statements from Israeli leaders and troubles in the DMZ, notably the shooting down of six Syrian fighter planes on 7 April – the Russian information was taken very seriously indeed. Nasser now felt he had to act, for he had long been under intense pressure and criticism from Jordanian and Saudi Arabian radio stations for not doing enough to support fellow Arab states.[13] This is why, at a late-night meeting with his deputy and commander of the Egyptian armed forces, Field Marshal Abd el-Hakim Amer, and Sadat, who had just returned from Moscow, Nasser ordered the dispatch of two divisions across the Suez Canal and into the Sinai, with the aim of distracting Israel from what seemed to be, according to the Soviet report, an imminent strike at Syria. It is important to note here that Sinai was Egyptian territory, and although the move was unusual there was nothing wrong with sending Egyptian troops there. In fact, seven years earlier, on 18 February 1960, Nasser had taken similar action in dispatching an armoured division and three infantry brigades – quite a substantial force at the time – into the Sinai to hint to the Israelis that they should leave Syria alone after they had attacked it at a place called Tawfik. But the difference between the two occasions was that in 1960 the Egyptian mobilization into the desert had been quiet and secret, whereas this time Egyptian troops on their way to Sinai marched through the streets of Cairo shouting: 'We are off to Tel Aviv'.[14]

In addition to dispatching troops into the desert, Nasser sent his Chief of Staff Mohammed Fawzi to Damascus, entrusting him with two missions: first to confirm the Soviet information about the apparent Israeli mobilization, and second to coordinate moves with Damascus. In Syria, Chief of Staff Fawzi went with Syrian General Anwar Al-Kadi to inspect the border, but found nothing unusual; he also examined aerial maps which indicated no unusual movement of Israeli troops.[15] The Syrians – they too had been informed by the Russians of the apparent Israeli mobilization – had sent reconnaissance planes which reported back that 'there was no massing [of Israeli troops] on the border [with Syria]'.[16] The Israelis, in turn, dismissed reports of mobilization as false, and Prime Minister Eshkol even suggested that the Soviet ambassador in Tel Aviv, Leonid Chuvyakin, join the head of Mossad, Meir Amit, in touring the border between Israel and Syria to see for himself that the Soviet allegations were unfounded; Chuvyakin, however, declined the offer.[17] Neither in Israel nor in Syria had the foreign press reported any mobilization, which, as Abba Eban, Israeli Foreign Minister at the time, found odd, for:

> The mobilization of 'Eleven to thirteen Israeli brigades', to say nothing of their concentration on a narrow front, would have had a conspicuous effect on Israel's life. No newspaperman or foreign mission in Israel could have been unaware of it. The disruption of normality in so many families would have been registered in all the chanceries and newspapers of the world.[18]

Israel, as everyone now knows, did not move any forces to its border with Syria, and it is widely acknowledged that the Soviet report, which for a long time has been one of the most puzzling features of the run-up to the 1967 war, was false. An explanation of Soviet motives in issuing a false report is now possible, thanks to recent testimonies of such people as Evgeny Pyrlin, head of the Egypt department in the Soviet foreign ministry at the time the report was released. According to Pyrlin the reason why this crucial and most damaging report was issued was because the Soviets wanted to spark a war between Israel and its Arab neighbours, believing that

> even if the war was not won by our [the Arab] side a war would be to our political advantage because our side would demonstrate its ability to fight with our weapons and with our military and political support.[19]

That this was all part of the ongoing Cold War between the superpowers is also confirmed by the extraordinary report of a CIA agent, who had heard from a KGB agent that by releasing the report and instigating a full-scale Arab–Israeli war,

> The USSR wanted to create another trouble spot for the United States in addition to that already existing in Vietnam. The Soviet aim was to create a situation in which the US would become seriously involved economically, politically, and possibly even militarily and

would suffer serious political reverses as a result of siding with the Israelis against the Arabs.[20]

This evidence provides striking proof that, contrary to popular belief, the 1967 war was not instigated by the local states – neither Egypt nor Israel – but rather by the USSR as part of its competition with the US for world influence and supremacy.

Oddly enough, and in spite of Fawzi's findings that Israel had not mobilized troops on its border with Syria, Nasser did not call his divisions back from the Sinai – in fact he went so far as to reinforce them by dispatching more troops to the desert. Furthermore, on 16 May he instructed UN troops, which since the 1956 war had been deployed on the Egyptian side of the border (Israel would not allow them to deploy on her side of the border) and in Gaza and Sharm el-Sheike, to leave their posts. Even though these UN troops were not strong enough to prevent either Israel or Egypt attacking the other, they were a symbol of non-belligerence and their removal was seen, and rightly so, as a further escalation of an already critical situation. We should point out, however, that Nasser's action was qualified, for what he did was order the removal of UN troops solely from their positions along the Egypt–Israel border, and not from Gaza or Sharm el-Sheike, which controls passage through the Straits of Tiran. As Nasser put it in a later interview: 'I did not ask U Thant [the UN Secretary General] to withdraw UN troops from Gaza and Sharm el-Sheike ... but only from a part of the frontier from Rafah to Eilat'.[21] Here, however, U Thant acted hastily and foolishly, insisting that either *all* UN troops remain in their positions, or that they leave altogether.[22] Nasser – he could not back down on the UN issue without loss of face in the eyes of the world and his own people – took the latter option.[23]

A week later, on 23 May, Egypt's president took yet another step, which raised the temperature of an overheated situation to boiling point, by ordering the closure of the Straits of Tiran to Israeli shipping. At a meeting with pilots at Bir Gafgafa air base, Nasser said:

> The armed forces yesterday occupied Sharm el-Sheike ... under no circumstances will we allow the Israeli flag to pass through the Gulf of Aqaba ... if Jews threaten war we tell them 'you are welcome, we are ready for war. Our armed forces and all our people are ready for war'. ... This water is ours.[24]

As has already been shown,[25] the Straits of Tiran were perceived by Israel as a vital interest, and closing them meant bottling up Israel and hampering both vital imports – mainly oil from Iran – and exports. Closing the Straits, as we have made clear, also threatened Israel's ability to develop the Negev. The issue, however, was not only economic but also political, for the Straits had become a test of prestige for both Israel and Egypt. We should recall that after the 1956 campaign in which Israel occupied Sharm el-Sheike and opened the blocked Straits, it was forced to withdraw and return the territory to Egypt. At the time, members of the international community pledged that Israel would never again be denied use of the Straits of Tiran. The French representative to the UN, for example, announced that any attempt to interfere with free shipping in the Straits would be against international law, and American President Dwight Eisenhower went so far as publicly to recognize that reimposing a blockade in the Straits of Tiran would be seen as an aggressive act which would oblige Israel to protect its maritime rights in accordance with Article 51 of the UN Charter.[26] Reluctantly, Israel accepted these diplomatic guarantees as a bad second-best substitute for the material security of actual occupation of the Straits. But on 1 March 1957, prior to the withdrawal of Israeli troops, Foreign Minister Golda Meir stated Israel's position before the UN General Assembly in unmistakably clear terms. She said:

> interference by armed force, with ships of Israeli flag exercising free and innocent passage in the Gulf of Aqaba and through the Straits of Tiran will be regarded by Israel as an attack entitling it to exercise its inherent right of self-defence under Article 51 of the Charter and to take all measures as are necessary to ensure the free and innocent passage of its ships in the Gulf and in the Straits.[27]

Yet in May 1967 Nasser ignored all this, and in the full knowledge that the Israelis were likely to react violently, he declared the Straits closed to her shipping. That he did so with open eyes we know from Anwar Sadat, who later testified how Nasser had said to his colleagues, whom he had brought together to decide on the closure of the Straits: 'Now, with the concentration of our force in Sinai the chances of war are fifty–fifty but if we close the Straits, war will be 100 per cent certain'.[28] What is also puzzling is that Nasser took such a drastic move without consulting either Syria or Jordan.

A. J. P. Taylor once said that 'the greatest decisions are nearly always the ones most difficult to explain', and indeed, Nasser's fateful decision to close the Straits will long remain one of the most puzzling features of the 1967 war, and it may never be possible to learn for certain what his motives were.[29] Nevertheless, two possible explanations can be offered to the question why he had decided on this action in the knowledge that for Israel this was a *casus belli* and the Straits represented a supreme national interest, their use being a right which it would assert and defend whatever the sacrifice. The first explanation, simple and straightforward, was probably best stated by Sadat – he would succeed Nasser in 1970 – who wrote that 'Nasser was carried away by his own impetuosity'.[30] Yet there may be a deeper explanation, and that is that in a matter of days Nasser's motive had changed from that at the start of the crisis, which was, following the false Soviet report, the attempt to distract the Israelis from attacking Syria, to a totally different aim, which was to take advantage of the growing crisis to reverse the post-1948 situation in the southern Negev and Eilat.

We should remember that at the end of the 1948 war, and after armistice agreements between Israel and Egypt (but not with Jordan) were concluded and signed, Israel breached these agreements by sending troops to Eilat and occupying it.[31] This was significant, for by seizing Eilat Israel prevented Egypt and Jordan from having direct land access to each other. In *Al-Aharam* on 7 January 1966, Mohamed Hassanian Heikal, a versatile journalist and intimate of Nasser whose writing frequently reflected the thinking of his president, wrote that it was most regrettable that in 1948 Israel had taken Eilat and thus created a 'wall' between the east and the west Arab world. He then added that in any future war with Israel, Egypt must attempt to pull down this wall and restore the pre-1948 situation in the vicinity of Eilat.[32] It seems that now, with a crisis under way, Nasser decided to take advantage of the situation and achieve his long-held aim of reversing the situation in Eilat. What supports this interpretation is that the specific deployment of Egyptian forces in the desert appear instrumental to achieving such a task. We shall now examine this.

On the brink of war: the opposing forces and their objectives

By 1 June – roughly two weeks after Nasser's first mobilization of troops into the desert – the Egyptian forces in the Sinai comprised seven divisions and a strength of 100,000 men. In addition, an infantry brigade was deployed at Sharm el-Sheike, in control of the Straits of Tiran but not physically blocking it. It is a puzzling but little-known fact that Egyptian troops never blocked the Straits, which remained open before and throughout the crisis.[33] As regards weaponry, the Egyptian forces were equipped with nearly 1,000 tanks, 900 guns of various calibres, 419 aircraft, four missile boats and two submarines. Yet contrary to popular belief, these forces were not deployed in attacking positions but rather on strictly defensive lines.[34] That said, the one force which was ready to strike in the event of war, and thus was deployed in jump-off places, was Saad el-Shazli's, which was not, however, aimed at moving on Tel Aviv, but rather at striking in the direction of the southern tip of the Negev and Eilat in order to pave the way to establishing a land bridge between Egypt and Jordan. All other Egyptian forces in the Sinai were required to seal and isolate the operational area by blocking potential Israeli thrusts and thus enabling the Shazli force to accomplish its mission.

The Syrian army, which was also now fully mobilized, comprised between 50,000 and 60,000 men with at least 200 tanks of operational capacity and 100 Soviet aircraft, including thirty-two modern Mig 21s. The military aim of the Syrian forces was to occupy eastern Galilee and defend the Golan Heights from any Israeli attempt to seize them.

Jordanian forces were also fully mobilized and deployed. King Hussein's army was 56,000 strong and its main strength lay in its two armoured brigades – the 40th and 60th – mustering some 200 Patton tanks. These were deployed in a counter-attack role in the Jordan valley around the Damiya bridge in the north and near Jericho in the south; their aim was to defend the West Bank and East Jerusalem.[35] A Jordanian–Egyptian force was also deployed in the salient of Latrun, just west of Jerusalem on the way to Tel Aviv. On 30 May, the King and President Nasser signed a joint defence pact. It meant that an attack on one country was seen as an attack on the other, which was required to come to the rescue. The King and the President also agreed that, in the event of war, Jordan's forces would be placed under Egyptian command.[36]

Other Arab forces which were assembling against the Israelis included an Iraqi division, which took up positions on Jordanian territory and two Iraqi squadrons which were advanced towards the Jordanian border and were thus closer to Israeli territory. Small token forces from other Arab countries, including Algeria and Kuwait, were sent to Egypt, and a small Lebanese army was also deployed.

Israel – whose main strength was its reserve force – had started mobilizing on 16 May and moved to full mobilization on 19 May; this was completed by the 20th. The forces were deployed in line with operational plan 'Sadan', which was a defensive posture, but one also designed for a speedy switch from defence to counter-offensive. Regarding Egypt as its main adversary and hoping that both Syria and Jordan would keep out of the battle, Israel had concentrated the bulk of its armed forces in the desert, leaving only scanty forces to fend off any attack on other fronts.

Israel's forces in the Sinai were organized into three divisions; the most northern was commanded by the diminutive Yisrael Tal, and consisted of two armoured brigades in which there were between 250 and 300 tanks. Also under Tal's command and led by Colonel Rafael ('Raful') Eitan was a paratroop brigade supported by a battalion of Patton tanks. The second Israeli division in the Sinai, based entirely on reserves, was commanded by the veteran Abraham Yoffe and consisted of two armoured brigades equipped with Centurion tanks. The third and most southern division was a mixed force which included an armoured brigade, two paratroop battalions, an infantry brigade, six battalions of artillery and a combat engineer battalion. It was commanded by the robust Ariel Sharon. In addition to these forces there were several independent combat groups: a mixed infantry armoured brigade in the rear of El Kuntilla; the 55th paratroop brigade headed by Mordechai Gur, and a naval task force. Totting up the balance sheet (Table 3.1), it can be seen that the Arab armies had clear superiority both in human and material resources.[37]

Table 3.1 Comparison of IDF and Arab forces

	IDF	Arabs
Armoured brigades	10	18
Paratroop brigades	9	53
Tanks	1,300	2,500
Artillery pieces	746	2,780
Fighter jets	247	557
Ground-to-air missiles	5	26

The crux of all Israeli military operations in the desert was the offensive, for the strength of the Israeli Defence Force – despite its name – was in attack. Since the 1956 campaign, the IDF had been trained as an assault force whose doctrine of warfare was based on two principles: first, a pre-emptive strike by the air force, and second, the transfer of the war into the enemy's territory.[38]

The first military plan, drawn up immediately after Nasser's closure of the Straits of Tiran, visualized the movement of Israeli troops into the Gaza Strip with the aim of seizing it and then using it as a bargaining card to compel Nasser to open the Straits of Tiran.[39] But opinions were divided as to the merits of such a plan. Moshe Dayan – he would later become Defence Minister – strongly opposed it on the ground that the Gaza Strip was not important enough for Nasser to be willing to trade it for ending the blockade of the Straits. In a private meeting with the Chief of Staff, Dayan told Rabin that the plan to capture the Gaza Strip in order to compel Nasser to open the Straits would not work, and added 'What will we then do with all these Arabs [meaning the Palestinian refugees of the Gaza Strip]?'[40]

Under Ezer Weizman – he was then Chief of Operations, and on 24 May temporarily replaced the sick Chief of Staff Rabin – this plan was substantially modified. Now codenamed 'Atzmon Murchav', it visualized the occupation of the Gaza Strip and from there an advance of troops to occupy El Arish, and thence along the northern coastal axis to reach the Suez Canal.[41] When Rabin returned to full service – he was absent for forty-eight hours and rumours said he had suffered a nervous collapse under the intense strain of the previous few days – he ordered the war plans to be recast. The air force was now to launch a pre-emptive strike to be followed by a simultaneous thrust of the three divisions in the northern part of the Sinai, in the area between Rafa and Umm Kataf, to break through into the desert and engage the Egyptian forces. Tal's forces operating in the northern sector were to occupy Gaza, El Arish and Rafa, which – controlling a natural passage of approximately ten miles between the sea and the dunes to the south – was considered a critical location as the jumping-off point for other forces into the heart of the Sinai. In the southern sector, Sharon's forces would take Abu Ageila and the Kuseima strongholds, two separate but mutually supporting bases. Sandwiched between Tal's forces in the north and Sharon's in the south, Yoffe would advance over dunes that had been considered to be almost impassable for tanks, and engage the major Egyptian armoured formations in central Sinai before moving deeper into the desert to seal the Mitla and Giddi passes against retreating Egyptian forces. From there the divisions would be ready to move up to the Suez Canal upon receiving new orders.

Israel – a society under pressure

In Israel, meanwhile, the danger of war aroused increasing anxiety, and what came to be known as the 'waiting period', where forces were fully mobilized and the country came almost to a standstill, was nothing but a war of nerves. With news of the closure of the Straits of Tiran, anxiety turned to panic because after years of warnings by its leaders that a closure of the Straits meant war, Israelis could expect nothing but war. Threatening declarations by Arabs fuelled Israeli anxiety. In a speech before unionists on 26 May – just three days after the closure of the Straits of Tiran – Nasser declared: 'The battle [with Israel] will be a general one and our basic objective will be to destroy Israel', and later:

> I was told at the time that I might have to wait seventy years. During the crusaders' occupation, the Arabs waited seventy years before a suitable opportunity arose and they drove away the crusaders. ... The whole question then, is the proper time to achieve our aims. We are preparing ourselves constantly.[42]

Nasser was not one to declare his total objectives. In Damascus it was announced that the time was ripe 'to liberate Palestine', and a Syrian delegation was reported to be heading to Cairo to coordinate military plans.[43] The defence pact signed between Egypt and Jordan on 30 May – despite the inveterate hostility between the two countries – indicated to the anxious Israelis that this time the Arabs meant war and that Israel was totally isolated and faced a disaster. This all had a strong effect and awakened old memories of the Holocaust; as military commander Uzi Narkiss – he would later lead his forces to occupy Jerusalem – recalled: 'Auschwitz [the death camp where Jews were executed] came up. It never happened before. [Israelis] said ... "we are surrounded, no one will help us, and God forbid if the Arabs armies invade, they'll kill us" '.[44] Such was the panic that it was reported that Holocaust survivors were rushing to pharmacies to buy poison tablets lest they fell into the hands of the enemy.[45] Rumours were rife, and we now know that these were based on fact, that the authorities had estimated 10,000 dead and, as we also now know, the Chief Rabbi, Shmuel Goren, demanded the preparation of coffins and sent his men to inspect public parks which would potentially become huge cemeteries in the event of war.[46] In *My Country*, Abba Eban describes the mood in Israel at that moment in time: 'A sense of vulnerability penetrated every part of the Israeli consciousness like an icy wind. As Israelis looked around, they saw the world divided between those who were seeking their destruction and those who were doing nothing to prevent it'.[47]

With tensions mounting and the mood becoming desperate, there was strong public pressure on Premier Eshkol to allow Ben Gurion back as either Prime Minister or Defence Minister. This was because Ben Gurion, the father of modern Israel, had led Israel through the 1948 and 1956 wars and was considered an expert in military affairs, while Eshkol was more of a finance expert. It did not matter to the Israelis that by now Ben Gurion was relatively out of touch, for what they sought was a strong, charismatic leader, and it seemed that Ben Gurion was the right man for this role. But relationships between Eshkol and Ben Gurion were at a low ebb, and Eshkol – an earth-bound man and realist by nature, who had invested heavily in buying arms for the IDF in the years before this crisis – bitterly opposed having his prede-cessor in the cabinet. He said to those who pressurized him to invite Ben Gurion into his cabinet: 'These two horses can no longer pull the same cart'.[48]

But on 28 May came an event which forced Eshkol to give way to public demand and political pressure. That Sunday he personally took to the airwaves to address the nation, and as he delivered his speech and as Israel heard it over the radio – there was not yet television in Israel – Eshkol stumbled over the words.[49] He read his speech so badly and gave so poor a performance that it left the worst impression. It should be pointed out, however, that Eshkol's was more a failure of presentation and delivery than of substance, for there was nothing wrong with the speech itself – but such was the national mood that the effect of such a poor delivery was devastating. After his speech, which came to be known as *Ha'neum Ha'megumgam* ('the stammering speech'), Eshkol was widely criticized.[50]

Now under growing pressure, Eshkol had no other option but to relin-quish the defence post and offer it to Moshe Dayan, former chief of staff of the IDF and now a politician in Ben Gurion's small Rafi party. With the nomination of Dayan, it seemed as if the brake had been released and that the IDF – it could not remain mobilized indefinitely without wrecking Israel's economy – would be ordered to take action.

The eve of war

On 2 June, Dayan met the IDF high command, and after being presented with the latest war plans he introduced three changes; the first related to the Straits of Tiran. We should recall that the last straw for Israel had been Nasser's decision to close the Straits to Israeli shipping; therefore Dayan held that in the event of a war breaking out, the Straits of Tiran must be opened. His instructions were that while the decisive thrust should be – as already planned by the military – in the direction of the heart of the Sinai desert, there should also be a thrust towards Sharm el-Sheike to open the Straits.[51] It was necessary to give such an instruction, for although the Straits were the main issue during the 'waiting period', by now the military planners preferred to concentrate on deciding how to engage the bulk of the Egyptian army in the desert and break its backbone. Dayan's second change to the operational plans dealt with the Gaza Strip. According to the military plans which were originally approved by Eshkol before the nomination of Dayan to the post of Defence Minister, Israeli forces were tasked with occupying the Gaza Strip. It was, in fact, Minister of Labour Yigal Allon – who was normally on the worst of terms with Dayan – who persuaded Eshkol that Israel 'should take the Gaza Strip and plan the transfer of its Palestinian refugees to Egypt'.[52] But to this Dayan objected strongly, for he held that the entire international community would turn against Israel if it attempted to transfer the Palestinians. Perhaps more importantly, he considered the Gaza Strip to be a place that 'bristled with problems ... a nest of wasps', a place which Israel should not occupy if it did not want to be 'stuck with a quarter of million Palestinians'.[53] Therefore, in this crucial meeting with the military High Command, Dayan ordered that the Gaza Strip should not be occupied, and as he later wrote in his memoirs: '[the plan] now before us received my approval ... there would be no conquest of the Gaza Strip'.[54] It is of historical interest to note here that Dayan was not the first to warn of the danger of occupying the Gaza Strip. In 1956, after Israeli troops had occupied the densely populated Strip, Prime Minister Ben Gurion said that he regarded Israel's rule over this compact mass of 'unreconciled people' as being 'as dangerous as dynamite placed at the foundation of the state'.[55] The third element in the war plan which Dayan recast was the Suez Canal. Dayan held that if Israel occupied the Canal and deployed its forces on its eastern bank, a mere 180 metres from Egyptian troops, Nasser would not operate the Suez Canal and he would resume the war against Israel; Dayan therefore gave orders that the troops should stop short of the Suez Canal. The restrictions which Dayan had imposed with regard to the Gaza Strip and the Suez Canal were clear and precise; as Aharon Yariv, then director of military intelligence later recalled: 'Dayan said to the General Staff: "I give you now the instruction of the defence minister: 1. To hit the Egyptian army. 2. *Not* to reach the [Suez] Canal. 3. *Not* to enter [the] Gaza [Strip]" '.[56] Dayan's observation that if Israel occupied the Suez Canal the war would continue and if it took the Gaza Strip it would 'be stuck' with too many Palestinian refugees was, as we now know, a deadly accurate forecast of the shape of things to come. One wonders why no one other than Dayan had similar insights, and furthermore how, given such a prophetic sense, Dayan later, as will be shown, gave way and agreed to allow the generals to occupy Gaza and reach the bank of the Suez Canal.

But still, on that crucial night of 2 June 1967, in the light of Dayan's instructions, a new plan codenamed 'Nachshonim' was prepared and its object was defined as 'Occupying Sinai up to the line El Arish–Jabel Libini–Bir Hasna–Kuseima … eliminating the Egyptian forces in this zone and being ready to continue development of the offensive into the area of the Sinai'.[57] From this newly devised plan two previous military aims were omitted: occupying the Gaza Strip and reaching the Suez Canal.[58]

Back to the superpowers

On 25 May, Nasser dispatched his Minister of War, Shams el–Din Badran, to Moscow to head an Egyptian delegation. Its mission was to obtain Soviet approval for Egypt to strike at Israel, and also to request a supply of war material.[59] Nasser rightly assumed that whoever struck first would enjoy the advantage of surprise and hold the initiative, but he also recognized that acting without Soviet permission to do so would be risky; Moscow might refuse to restock his arsenal after the war, and might also refuse to extend much needed political support. Badran and his delegation met Prime Minister Alexei Kosygin and explained that Egypt wished to strike at Israel. To this Kosygin replied: 'We, the Soviet Union, cannot give you our consent for your pre-emptive strikes against Israel. … Should you be the first to attack you will be the aggressor … we are against aggression … we cannot support you'.[60] It is indeed puzzling that the Soviets, who had instigated the crisis in the first place by spreading the lie that Israel was mobilizing its forces on its border with Syria, were now attempting to control the situation and rein back Egypt.

On his return to Cairo, Badran reported to Nasser that the Soviets would not allow Egypt to strike and would not provide it with much-needed war material, but would intervene in the war on Egypt's side if America were to intervene on behalf of Israel.[61] Nasser was careful to abide by the Soviet instructions and told his military commanders that Egypt would have to absorb a first strike by Israel. He insisted on this in the face of strong opposition, especially from the commander of the air force, General Sudki Mahmoud, who pleaded with him that such a policy 'will be crippling. … It will cripple the armed forces'.[62]

Israel also sent a special emissary to its 'patron', the USA.[63] This was the former general and head of Mossad, Meir Amit, who flew to Washington on 31 May. His mission was to see how Israel's view of the crisis compared with that of the American intelligence community (mainly the CIA), to see what would be Washington's response if Israel took action, and also to find out if any preparations had been made to put together an international armada – this had been proposed by British Prime Minister Harold Wilson – which would attempt to sail through the Straits of Tiran in defiance of Nasser's blockade. By this time the sole chance of preventing a general war lay in such an action, and given that, as we have already mentioned, the Straits were declared closed but were not in fact physically blocked (this of course was not known at the time), it might well be that such an armada could have passed without being fired on or even stopped, and war could have been averted. But this was a vain hope. In Washington, Amit found that the plan to set up a joint task force, composed of the principal maritime powers committed to the freedom of passage through the Straits of Tiran, had not even reached the launching stage. He also met Dean Rusk, American Secretary of State, who 'could not agree more' with Amit's assessment of the gravity of the situation.[64] Amit also had three private meetings with James Angleton, the CIA's longtime liaison with Mossad, from whom he learnt that the Americans would welcome it if Israel were to 'strike [at Egypt]'.[65] To Robert MacNamara, Amit said that he intended to recommend to his government that they launch an attack, to which the American Secretary of Defence replied: 'I read you loud and clear'.[66]

Thus it all came back to the superpowers. The USSR, which had instigated the crisis in the first place by issuing a false report, now showed the 'red light' to the Egyptians, warning them not to be the first to strike, though promising to intervene if America joined the war. As for the Americans, they had shown a 'yellow light' to the Israelis ('I read you loud and clear'), which was interpreted by the head of Mossad as a 'green light' to go to war. Following Amit's report, the Israeli cabinet decided to order the IDF to attack Egypt.

The attack on Egypt

A successful air strike was crucial for the overall victory of the Israelis. This was aimed at curbing Egypt's capability to strike at Israeli cities and, perhaps more importantly, to achieve air supremacy over the desert, which would make Egyptian defeat certain. The air operation, codenamed 'Moked', began at 7.45 a.m., as Egyptian pilots were having their breakfast, on Monday 5 June 1967. The air strike took a very roundabout approach, flying via the sea and coming in from the west. While the first wave of Israeli aeroplanes – 183 in all – was making its way to Egypt, the entire command of the Egyptian armed forces, including Marshall Amer and Minister of War Shams el-Din Badran, were also in the air on their way to inspect Egyptian units in the Sinai; to ensure their safe passage and that they were not fired at by their own people, the radar system in Egypt was shut down. This tragi-comic episode, in which the Egyptian command is airborne, the radar system is shut down and Israeli fighter-bombers are on their way to targets in Egypt, symbolizes, perhaps more than anything else, the inefficiency of the Egyptian command, and demonstrates that part of Israel's stunning success resulted from the recklessness, blind folly and ineptitude of the enemy's political-military leadership.

'Operation Moked' was extraordinarily successful and led to a sensational and dramatic victory for the Israeli Air Force (IAF). Within 190 minutes the backbone of the Egyptian air force was broken – 189 Egyptian aeroplanes were destroyed, mostly on the ground, in the first wave of attack, and by the end of the first day of war a stunning 298 Egyptian planes lay in ruins. Back in his headquarters Marshall Amer was trying to piece together a new plan from the wreckage. He ordered the air force to hit back at the Israelis, but the reply he received was that the little that remained of the air force was unable to carry out any meaningful operation. Nasser was later to complain bitterly that the Israeli air strike eventually came not from the direction his guns were pointing, but from behind: 'They came from the west', he said, 'when we expected them to come from the east'.[67]

Backed by complete air superiority, the three Israeli divisions thrust into the desert to engage the Egyptian forces, which were incessantly pounded by Israeli planes and were no match for the Israeli ground forces. Meanwhile, the spokesman of the IDF announced that since the early hours of the morning Israeli forces had been engaged in fierce fighting with Egyptian forces which had started 'advancing towards Israel'; this was not quite true for, as we now know, the Israelis rather than the Egyptians were the first to open fire.[68]

The retreat of the Egyptian army, though unavoidable, was hasty and chaotic. A skilfully conducted step-by-step withdrawal could have saved lives, or at least proved less costly, but in the event the retreat was very disorderly, with small and uncoordinated groups of troops trying to escape on foot through the desert dunes in the direction of the Suez Canal. The end result was disastrous – for while 2,000 Egyptian troops were killed fighting the Israelis, 10,000 perished in the retreat.

As Israeli forces gave chase in an attempt to cut the Egyptian lines of retreat, they drew closer to the Suez Canal, which Defence Minister Dayan had on the eve of the war ordered them not to occupy. At one point Dayan, thinking that his troops had already reached the Canal, issued orders to pull back. But then, under strong pressure from his Chief of Staff, who argued that militarily it was better to stop at the Canal, Dayan reversed his decision and allowed the troops to resume their advance and reach the bank of the Suez Canal.[69] Furthermore, following the shelling of the Israeli settlements of Nachal Oz, Kisufim and Ein Ha'shlosha from inside the Gaza Strip, Dayan was requested to allow troops to enter the Strip and silence the enemy's fire. Again, Dayan gave way and allowed a force to enter the Gaza Strip, even though a few days before he had said that it 'bristled with problems', was 'a nest of wasps', and was a place which Israel should not occupy if it did not want to be 'stuck with a quarter of million Palestinians'.

Why Dayan gave way and allowed the armed forces to dictate the stopping line is a question to which there will never be a definite answer. But any clues may lie more in the character of Dayan than in any strategic consideration. For although Dayan was renowned as a brave soldier and almost a prophet because of his foresight, he was, on the other hand, too much the pessimist, often failing to fight for his ideas with colleagues or to impose his will on his subordinates; as was the case in the war in the Sinai, where he allowed short-term tactical considerations to disrupt his realistic policy.

Jordan and Syria

On the Jordanian front war started at 9.45 a.m. on 5 June, as King Hussein's guns opened fire along the border with Israel and Jordanian troops attempted to occupy the United Nations headquarters and other positions in Jerusalem. On this morning the Israelis delivered a message to the King, saying: 'This is a war between us and Egypt. If you stay out we will not touch you'.[70] Upon receiving this message, the King — he was at air force headquarters — said: 'Jordan is not out. Jordan is already engaged'.[71] This is understandable, for with Palestinians making up half of his population, if Hussein had stood aside his kingdom could have disintegrated.[72] In addition, the King may have feared that he would miss the boat if he did not join the war, for in the early hours of 5 June, a message was received from Marshall Amer, saying: 'approximately 75 per cent of the enemy's aircraft have been destroyed or put out of action ... UAR troops have engaged the enemy and taken the offensive on the ground'.[73] This of course was a lie, but the King could not have known that. After all, Nasser had also called to say that Egypt was doing well. He said to the King — and we know exactly what he said because his conversation was intercepted and recorded by Mossad — 'We have sent all our aeroplanes against Israel. Since early this morning our air force has been bombing the Israeli air force'.[74] This too was a lie, for while talking with King Hussein, Nasser already knew that his air force was totally destroyed. We know this because just *before* calling the King, Nasser had talked with President Boumedienne of Algeria, to whom he announced that the Egyptian air force was totally destroyed, and asked if he could spare a few aircraft. In his talk with the King, Nasser also urged that he join him in publishing 'an announcement concerning the British and American participation' in the war. This was clearly aimed to drag in the Soviets, for, as we should remember, the USSR had promised Egyptian Minister of War Badran that, if America joined the war, Russia would come in on Egypt's side.

Israel's response to the Jordanian attack was immediate and devastating — it destroyed Jordan's two air force bases and in fifty-one sorties totally crippled its small air force, before moving to occupy the West Bank and Jerusalem.

Elsewhere, on the Golan Heights, war did not start until 8 June. In fact the Syrians, after perceiving the fate of Egypt and Jordan, preferred to keep out of the battle, and when asked by the King of Jordan to provide air support they replied that: 'all their aircraft were on training missions and not a single aircraft was available'.[75]

At first Israel refrained from attacking Syria because Defence Minister

Dayan felt that if Israel struck, the Soviets might intervene on behalf of the Syrians. He also felt that if Israel occupied the Golan Heights it would never be willing to give it back and the conflict with Syria would continue for years.[76] In the end, however, Dayan gave way, reversed his previous order not to attack, and authorized the occupation of the Golan Heights; in fact he did not even contact the Chief of Staff, who was sleeping at home in the belief that the war was over, but picked up the phone and issued an order to strike. We will probably never know why Dayan reversed his decision; it may be that he feared that after the war he would be blamed for not taking advantage of the situation to hit at Syria, with whom Israel had hostile border relationships. According to Dayan, his change of policy was made following intelligence information indicating that the Syrians would not resist if Israel struck. We now know what was not known even to Dayan at the time – that his prediction, that the Soviets might intervene alongside the Syrians to stop the Israeli advance on the Golan, almost materialized; Soviet planes in the Ukraine were preparing to attack Israeli military targets and Soviet submarines were approaching the shores of Israel.[77] We do not know why they did not attack.

With Egypt and Jordan crippled, the IDF could concentrate all its strength on Syria, which was clearly no match for the Israeli air and ground forces. 'We dropped everything on the Golan Heights', recalled former IAF commander Mordecahi Hod: 'In two days we dropped more that we had dropped on all Egyptian airfields [throughout the war]'.[78] According to Syrian General Abdel Razzak Al-Dardari, who commanded four Syrian brigades on the Golan Heights,

> On that morning the Israelis moved ahead. ... There was a sudden panic and there was an order to withdraw to the south. The pull-out was done in total chaos ... the retreating soldiers had left their weapons behind and were almost running home. Some were running home even before the Israeli soldiers had come anywhere near their positions ... there was no air cover nor an Egyptian front to distract the Israelis.[79]

In spite of UN pressure on Israel to stop the war, and rising tensions between Washington and Moscow – the latter threatening to 'take any measures to stop Israel, including military' – the Israelis had managed to occupy the Golan Heights.[80]

Euphoria and division

The speed of the operation staggered the world, and the Israelis, whose immediate reaction to the stunning victory was euphoria and jubilation as a spontaneous expression of relief that the worst – what seemed to be an imminent second Holocaust – had not materialized and instead Israel had gained a victory with relatively few casualties. Indeed, in six days the battle was over, and by then Israeli troops were less than 50km from Amman, 60km from Damascus and 110km from Cairo. Israel now controlled an area of 88,000 square kilometres compared with 20,250 before the war, or eighteen times the area which was allotted to the Jews by Lord Peel in the first partition plan for Palestine of 1937. The Sinai desert, the Gaza Strip, the Golan Heights and the West Bank now provided Israeli cities with a buffer zone, dramatically reducing the danger of Israel's extinction by a surprise Arab attack.

The victory had a special historic meaning because of the capturing of territories central to the religious mythical past: the Old Town of Jerusalem with the Western Wall, which is the remnant of the ancient Jewish temple destroyed by the Romans; and the West Bank, which is part of biblical *Eretz Yisrael* and where such sites as Machpela are situated. For Israel's religious community, the occupation of these territories established the relationships between what they define as 'People, God and Promised Land', strengthening their sense of Jewish identity.

But the occupation of Arab land also sowed the seeds of conflict and division within Israeli society; this was apparent immediately after the war, when a fierce debate regarding the future of the occupied lands broke out. A society, which only three weeks before was huddling together and fearing for its very existence, was now beginning to split between those who wished to cling to the occupied land and those calling for it to be given back in return for peace and reconciliation. But it was more than a debate regarding the occupied territories, for in the postwar era, with what seemed to Israelis to be a reduction of external danger because of their newly acquired strategic depth, a whole range of problems began to surface. As Abba Eban, a diplomat and a good observer, has written:

> As the pressure of war ... died down, some of the latent tensions in Israeli society came to the surface. The turbulence took many shapes and expressions but the common factor was the growth of dissent ... [Israelis now] rejected the idea that external dangers justified inertia or apathy towards domestic imperfections.[81]

What became crystal clear in the post-1967 war period was that Israeli society was essentially a diverse, turbulent organism which tended to have a monolithic aspect only when facing urgent external danger. And this is precisely what made the 1967 war such a turning point in the life of the Israeli nation and society. For while the war seemed to remove a great external danger to Israel – whose cities were now far from the front – it also, ironically, removed the cement which had kept the people of Israel together. And although, in the postwar era, opinion polls indicated the overwhelming popularity of the national leaders, with those in charge of defence policies supported by staggering percentages, the government was challenged as never

Map 3 The 1967 Six Day War: Israel's conquests

before by its citizens. This criticism quickly gathered momentum and reached an unprecedented peak during the War of Attrition along the Suez Canal.

'The forgotten war of attrition' 1968–70

The Egyptian army, we should remember, though badly beaten and crippled, had not been destroyed in the 1967 war, nor did the Egyptian leadership lose the appetite to reorganize itself to hit back at the Israelis, who were now deployed on the other side of the Suez Canal. In this regard, Defence Minister Dayan's observation, made on the eve of the 1967 war, that occupying the Suez Canal would mean the continuation of war with Egypt, proved prophetic.

On 22 June 1967, less than two weeks after war ended, President Nasser told the Soviet President: 'Because the Israelis are now in Sinai, we are building our defences on the west bank of the [Suez] Canal. If the Israelis refuse to leave peacefully, sooner or later we'll have to fight them to get them out'.[82] Moscow was sympathetic, promising Nasser: 'Soon you will have a larger number of fighter aircraft than you had before the [1967] invasion'.[83] In fact, by the second day of the 1967 war, Moscow was supplying both Egypt and Syria with weapons; 544 airlifts and fifteen cargo ships transferred nearly 48,000 tons of military equipment to both countries.[84] Egypt, whose air force was in ruins, had received twenty-five Mig-21 aircraft and ninety-three Mig-17s, followed by another transfer of forty Mig-21s and six Mig-21s equipped for training purposes; it also received thirty-eight Sukhoi aircraft, as well as 100 tanks. Between 1,000 and 1,200 Soviet advisors also arrived in Egypt to help assimilate and indeed operate the new weapons.[85] As early as February 1968, General Fawzi, the new commander in chief of the Egyptian army, announced that the armed forces had reached 70 per cent of their strength before the outbreak of the June 1967 war.[86]

The first major incident between Egypt and Israel after the Six Day War took place on 21 October 1967, when an Egyptian destroyer torpedoed and sank the Israeli destroyer *Eilat* in international waters off Port Said. Israel retaliated by shelling Egyptian oil refineries close to the city of Suez and setting alight the adjoining oil storage tanks. Clashes along the Suez Canal had developed into artillery duels between 8 September and 26 October 1968, where in two massive barrages Egyptian artillery inflicted heavy casualties on the Israelis.[87] Israel's ground forces retaliated both along the Canal and deep into Egyptian territory. The air force blew up several bridges on the Nile, and paratroops, landing deep inside Egypt, destroyed the electricity transmission station at Naj Hamadi.[88] By carrying out raids into Egyptian territory Israel signalled that it would not confine its retaliations to the Canal area. To some extent these raids compelled the Egyptians to call off their attacks, and led to a relatively calm period from November 1968 until March 1969.

It is important to note here that these clashes, the majority of which were initiated by Egypt, were not random incidents caused by local trigger-happy military commanders, but rather part of a well-planned Egyptian military programme which envisaged a total war against Israel in three main phases. The first of these was called the 'holding out' or the steadfastness stage; the second was the 'state of deterrence' and the third was to be a total 'war of attrition' against Israel.[89] In a speech on 21 January 1969, Nasser explained: 'The first priority, the absolute priority in this battle, is the military front, for we must realize that the [Israeli] enemy will not withdraw unless we force him to withdraw through fighting'.[90] A month later, in February 1969, Nasser said to the council of ministers:

> We should go ahead this year and escalate the situation with Israel and in particular step up the commando operations in Sinai because, as part of the War of Attrition, such operations have a significant impact on the enemy's military deployment and morale. Operations of this sort will force the enemy to keep large numbers of troops under arms, which runs counter to his military policy and stretches his capabilities.[91]

In military terms, the first priority of the Egyptian armed forces, to put it in crude terms, was to cause Israel to bleed to death. As General Fawzi explained to the council of ministers:

> [Our intention is] first to provoke bloody clashes with the enemy with the aim of killing the largest possible number of enemy personnel; that is to say, priority will be given to [weakening] Israeli manpower in preference to weapons and equipment, because loss of lives causes greater concern to the Israeli military command.[92]

To impose on Israel what came to be known in Egypt as *Hareb el Istinzaf*, namely the 'War of Bloodshed', was a shrewd way to tackle the Israeli occupation of the Sinai, for Nasser was right in assuming that the close-knit, highly-sensitive-to-casualties Israeli society could hardly sustain a long and bloody contest – a war of positions – in which it would lose soldiers on a daily basis. The Egyptian plan was to hit at the Israelis not only militarily, but also psychologically: to hit the soft spots of Israeli society.

The Bar Lev line

Indeed, as the war dragged on and the number of casualties mounted, the Israeli General Staff was obliged to seek ways of protecting the troops along the Suez Canal. This led to the construction of a defensive line of fortifications named after the then Chief of Staff Haim Bar Lev. The line was a chain of thirty-two strongpoints (*Ma'ozim*) stretching 180km from Ras el-Eish in the north to Port Tawfik in the south. Each fort had firing positions, as well as a courtyard big enough to hold a few tanks and allow soldiers enough space to carry on with their daily lives and routines. A paved road linked the strongholds, and a sand ramp was built between it and the canal to prevent the Egyptians from observing the movements of troops inside the forts. Between the fortifications there were observation posts and tank emplacements. Bunkers were built which were covered by thick layers of fill and stones. Between 7 and 12km east of the line, eleven big strongholds (*Ta'ozim*) were constructed. The Bar Lev line on the edge of the water, as Haim Bar Lev explained, was 'only one component of a system which relied on defence in depth'.[93] Troops stationed in the line had to serve as the eyes and ears of this system and, in case of emergency, to summon tanks and activate other resources which were deployed behind them in the depths of Sinai.

IDF opinion was divided regarding the idea of constructing a line of defence along the Suez Canal, and it is curious to see how closely this debate resembled that which had taken place in France regarding the construction of the Maginot line. In the French case it was the young Charles de Gaulle and a few other military commanders who attacked the idea of the Maginot line, saying that tanks and warplanes, armoured divisions and fleets of bombers had revolutionized warfare and that the advantage would in future lie with the state that could concentrate highly mechanized and fast moving strike-power.[94] Within the Israeli command, it was mainly Generals Sharon and Tal who strongly opposed the building of the line, arguing similarly to De Gaulle, that the advantage would lie with those armies that could manoeuvre and concentrate forces at crucial point in the battlefield, and that the offensive was more in tune with Israel's character and its forces. They also argued that the depth of the Sinai desert occupied in the previous war would enable the IDF to sell ground to gain time, practise shock-absorbing tactics and delay any offensive until the reserves were mobilized. Their bottom line was that the Bar Lev line would force Israel to fight positional warfare, which would be catastrophic to her. But then, what Bar Lev had in mind was not a Maginot line of defence, with a braking function, but rather a line to offer cover to troops under bombardment and reduce the number of casualties.[95] Bar Lev then enforced his will and the line of defence was built and completed in March 1969.[96] We now know that the objectors to the line were probably right, for the Bar Lev line played into the hands of the Egyptian army, which was thus able to proceed with Nasser's plan and impose an all-out war of attrition on the Israelis.

In March 1969, after a relatively calm period, Egypt resumed the war and carried out massive barrages of the Bar Lev line, with 35,000 shells being fired between 8 and 10 March. To this attack and those which followed, Israel's response was to send ground forces to carry out deep penetration raids. On 28 July paratroopers and naval commandos captured the rock fortress of Green Island, the southern hinge of the Egyptian air defence network, and destroyed its radar and anti-aircraft installations; this opened the way for Israeli aircraft to bomb Egyptian positions. On 9 September 1969, an Israeli seaborne force crossed the Gulf of Suez and landed not far from the Egyptian port of Zafarana, from where it moved for almost ten hours along the coastal road towards Suez, destroying installations on its way before re-embarking.[97] On 26 December, Israeli forces carried out an operation against a new P-12 radar installation to detect low-flying planes, some 250 miles south of Suez; Israeli technicians dismantled the radar and a helicopter carried it back to Israel for examination.[98] But all this was to no avail – the war continued with undiminished fury, the number of Israeli casualties mounted, and uneasiness mounted within Israeli society.

The strategy of deep penetration

Unable to put an end to the War of Attrition, and under strong public pressure to stop the bloodshed caused by this static war of positions, the IAF was dispatched to execute 'Operation Boxer', a massive air bombardment of Egyptian positions along the Suez Canal.[99] This was no more effective. Egyptian shelling of the Bar Lev line continued, and the black announcements, often carrying a photograph of a young soldier, continued to appear daily in the Israeli press. This lowered morale and spurred the Israeli military-political leadership to look for other ways of ending the war. The military command then devised a new strategy of deep penetration by the air force, aimed at bombing positions deep within Egypt, thus relieving pressure on Israeli troops along the Canal.[100] As Defence Minister Dayan put it: 'The first and foremost aim of the deep penetration strategy is to make it easier for the [Israeli] defence forces to hold the cease fire line'.[101] The plan to bomb deep into Egypt was much helped by Israel's recent purchase of Phantoms and Skyhawk fighter jets.[102]

The IAF began its bombardment on 7 January 1970 by attacking Egyptian military camps, including the Headquarters of the Suez Canal, some 30km northeast of Cairo.[103] Throughout January and February 1970, raids were focused on military targets near the cities of Ismailia, Cairo Insha and Hilwan, and between 1 January and 18 April 1970, the period of the bombing campaign, the IAF flew 3,300 sorties and dropped 8,000 tons of munitions on Egyptian positions.[104] No civilian targets were deliberately attacked, but there were human errors which resulted in civilians being killed. On 13 February 1970 a Phantom bombed an Egyptian factory, killing seventy civilians,[105] and on 9 April a hit on a primary school killed forty-six Egyptian children.[106] The pressure on the Egyptians was such that they were forced to reduce resources along the Canal in order to protect its interior, which in turn eased pressure on the Israelis along the Bar Lev line and reduced casualties. But Israel also suffered heavily, because the Egyptian anti-aircraft defence system, thirty times as powerful as it had been before the 1967 war, hit hard at the IAF.[107] In

August 1970 a ceasefire was agreed, and until the 1973 war the front was more or less calm.

The Queen of the Bathroom

The War of Attrition – often termed 'the forgotten war' – rarely hit the international headlines, and there are only a few studies of this relatively long and bloody conflict.[108] But it did make a major impact on Israeli society. The decision of Israel's leadership to construct the Bar Lev line, to send troops on raids across the Suez canal, to bomb along the Canal, and finally to dispatch fighter-jets between January and April 1970 to bomb deep into Egypt, were all desperate attempts to respond to public demand to put an end to an immensely unpopular war. After the euphoria of the 1967 victory there could be nothing as disappointing and frustrating for the Israelis as the War of Attrition. And although Prime Minister Meir claimed 'Never before has our situation been better', this was not what the ordinary Israeli felt. What Israelis saw was bloodshed on the bank of the Suez Canal – between March 1969 and August 1970 alone, 138 soldiers were killed and 375 wounded; and a total of 400 Israelis were killed and more than 2,000 wounded between the end of the 1967 war and August 1970, the day a ceasefire between Israel and Egypt came into force.[109] The Israeli public reacted strongly to the costs both human and material. The play *The Queen of the Bathroom* offered perhaps the strongest condemnation, and it was an expression of the Israelis' fatigue with wars and sacrifice. A satirical show, it attacked the 'joy' over war and the 'cult of fatalities'. And although there were some interest groups which boycotted the show and called for it to be stopped, it nevertheless attracted thousands of Israelis and was a novelty in a society which until then had showed itself willing to sacrifice without protest. Worse still, young pupils, on the eve of being recruited into the IDF, sent a letter to the Prime Minister saying 'We don't know if we will be able to do what we have to do in the army'. Such a protest would have been unthinkable before the 1967 war.

It was also a costly war, and defence spending had to rise – in 1965 defence consumption as percentage of GNP was 9.5; it went up in 1966 to 10.4, reached 17.7 in 1967, in 1968 it rose to 18.2, a year later it was 20.2, in 1970 it was 25.7 and in 1971 a staggering 26.3. per cent.[110] While previously there had been hardly any protest against high spending on defence, this was not the case after the 1967 war and during the War of Attrition. Non-European Israelis, mainly of North African origin, had rioted in Jerusalem in March 1971, challenging the government's priorities that seemingly placed social services, housing and other social concerns on the back burner and clearly secondary to spending on defence. Thus, with the approach of a critical year, 1973, Israeli society was deeply divided on a range of issues, and was becoming much more critical of its leadership insofar as military matters were concerned.

CHAPTER FOUR

War and peace

1973–9

Anwar el-Sadat, who succeeded President Nasser in September 1970, was perhaps the most dynamic political leader in the Middle East between 1970 and 1979; he made war (1973) and peace (1979), forcing the Israelis to respond to his initiatives. With hindsight we can say that Sadat, more than any other Middle Eastern leader at that time, transformed the international relationships of the region, and also – though indirectly and unintentionally – altered the political situation in Israel itself. By taking Israel by surprise and successfully launching an attack across the Suez Canal on 6 October 1973, he managed to put in train events which eventually resulted in Israelis turning against their leadership and voting for a right-wing Likud government under Menachem Begin, with whom Sadat eventually signed a landmark peace accord on 26 March 1979.

Arab politics is not the subject of this book, but it is undeniable that the initiative throughout these critical years was firmly on the Arab side – mainly Egypt – and it therefore makes sense to begin the discussion of the 1973 Yom Kippur War, the peace which followed it and the impact of these events on Israeli society, in Egypt.

The dark donkey

When Sadat became President of Egypt upon the death of Nasser, he was not taken seriously by his colleagues, who had chosen him for the top job because they considered him to be a front man who would do as he was told and continue Nasser's Arab nationalism and pro-Soviet policies. Nor did Sadat impress the Israelis, who nicknamed him 'the dark donkey' and regarded him as a transitional leader and little more than a figurehead.[1] The Americans regarded Sadat as 'a semi-comic figure'.[2] Indeed, at the time of his appointment to the top job, there was little to indicate that Sadat would become the leading figure in making war and peace in the Middle East in the 1970s.[3] But soon after his accession to power, Sadat began showing his true colours, purging his opponents – mainly the group around Ali Sabri, a pro-Soviet Vice President – and taking bold initiatives in foreign policy.[4]

As early as 1971, Sadat announced that this year would be 'the year of deci-sion' – surely, hardly anyone understood what a 'year of decision' meant – but in an interview with Arnaud de Borchgrave of *Newsweek*, he declared that he would be prepared to recognize Israel and live in peace with her.[5] Soon after-wards, on 4 February, Sadat dropped a 'peace bombshell', announcing in the Egyptian parliament an entirely new initiative. 'If Israel withdrew her forces in Sinai to the [Mitla and Giddi] Passes' (about 48km east of the Suez Canal), he declared,

> I would be willing to reopen the Suez Canal; to have my forces cross to the East Bank [of the Suez Canal] … to make a solemn, official declaration of a cease-fire by six, rather than three, months; to restore diplomatic relations with the United States; and sign a peace agree-ment with Israel through the efforts of Dr Jarring, the representative of the Secretary General of the UN.[6]

As Sadat later remarked: 'None of my opponents had foreknowledge of my initiative … they were surprised, indeed dumbfounded, to hear me declare it to the world'.[7] It is hard to say, even with hindsight, whether Sadat's initiative had any chance of succeeding and the prevailing view is still that 'No compromise could have been reached on the basis of what Sadat was willing to offer in exchange for Israel's withdrawal from the Suez Canal. Neither side was ready at the time'.[8] Sadat's insistence on an unequivocal Israeli under-taking to withdraw completely from Sinai was also not helpful in convincing the Israeli government to accept his proposals. Nonetheless, the fact remains that in the early 1970s and well before his decision to launch a war against Israel, Sadat was willing to open a dialogue with her, and he did offer a programme to achieve this aim. The problem, it seems, was more on the Israeli side, where Prime Minister Golda Meir – she had been recalled from retirement to succeed Eshkol, who died in March 1969 – failed to show any flexibility. As a former foreign minister in Ben Gurion's government, she presided, most reluctantly we should say, over the withdrawal of Israeli troops from the Sinai and Sherm el-Sheike, the base commanding the entrance to the Gulf of Aqaba which Israel had occupied in 1956. Yet the return, under intense international pressure, of this occupied land to Egypt in 1957 did not lead to peace, and in May 1967, as we have already shown, President Nasser dispatched forces to Sherm el-Sheike and declared a maritime blockade on the Straits of Tiran, to be closed to Israeli shipping. With this in mind, Meir was adamant and firm in her opposition to the return of occupied land for less than what she considered to be a genuine peace and recognition by the Arabs of Israel's right to live peacefully in the Middle East.

It is important to note, however, that within Meir's cabinet there was a group of ministers which did favour a limited withdrawal from the Suez Canal. Notable among them was Defence Minister Moshe Dayan who, as we have shown in the previous chapter,[9] had objected in 1967 to the occupation of the Suez Canal, and as early as August 1970 had made the suggestion 'to pull back a little way from Suez [so that] the Egyptians could then resume navigation and rehabilitate their canal zone cities [which in turn] would weaken their desire to make further war upon us'.[10] Dayan's proposal that Israeli forces withdraw a short distance from the Suez Canal – he envisaged a retreat of some 35km – was a realistic policy based on the argument that Israel would be in less danger of war if it pulled back from the Canal so that Nasser could operate it. For with ships sailing to and fro there would be little incentive for Nasser to resume war, since this would prevent international shipping from using the Canal and would result in Egypt losing much-needed revenues. But as we have already seen, in spite of his pluck, prowess and originality, Dayan was no fighter for his ideas and was not someone to impose his will on colleagues, so that when Meir objected to his plan – she saw in it the beginning of an Israeli withdrawal to the old boundaries without the equivalent of a peace treaty – he simply gave way to the Prime Minister.

Meir's reply to President Sadat's offer came on 9 February 1971 in a speech to the Knesset in which, as a certain foreign ministry official put it, 'She extended him a finger – not a hand'.[11] In retrospect, this was a colossal missed opportunity for, if Israel had only been willing to negotiate an unequivocal withdrawal from the bank of the Suez Canal, the Yom Kippur War might well have been averted. But Dayan's typical reluctance to fight for his realistic policies and Meir's uncompromising personality combined to pave the way for the immobilism which was a main feature of Israel's policies in the early 1970s, and was eventually to lead to the outbreak of hostilities more devastating than those of any previous war, except for that of 1948. We now know that, in fact, Meir had failed to comprehend the line of thought behind Dayan's proposal to withdraw, and as she frankly put it to a meeting of the central committee of the Labour party on 5 December 1973:

> I admit and confess that when the defence minister [that is Dayan] proposed a few years ago that we agree to withdraw from the Suez Canal, in order that the Egyptians open it to shipping and rehabilitate their canal zone cities, I failed to understand what he was talking about. Just like that to suggest that we withdraw from the Canal [without the Egyptians giving us something in return]?[12]

Sadat's offer to open a dialogue with the Israelis was taken much more seriously by American President Richard Nixon who, in the summer of 1971, sent Under-Secretary of State Joseph Sisco – a highly qualified professional and a skilful diplomat – to the Middle East to try and break the impasse by convincing Prime Minister Meir to agree to a withdrawal from the Suez Canal. What very much encouraged the President was the fact that, privately, Israeli Defence Minister Dayan let Washington understand that he was in favour of a withdrawal from the Canal. Nevertheless, the President said to his emissary: 'Press Golda but if she reacts negatively, don't press it to a confrontation ... between Israel and the United States'.[13] We should remember that at that time – and especially after the crucial role it played in saving King Hussein in September 1970 ('Black September') – Israel was considered by the American administration to be a reliable strategic asset in the region, and Washington had no stomach to impose on Israel policies which might endanger the special relations between the two countries. So with a presidential mandate to talk but not to exercise too much pressure, Sisco travelled to Israel and met with Meir's cabinet. But soon he returned to Washington empty-handed and downhearted, and as he later recalled: 'After two days of in-depth discussion, it was clear we weren't making much progress ... the reaction of the Prime Minister was a negative one'.[14]

In an attempt to persuade the United States that he was serious about opening a dialogue with Israel, and to hint that the key for such a dialogue lay in Washington rather than in Moscow, Sadat took a bold step, and on 18 July 1972 expelled from Egypt 15,000 Soviet advisers.[15] These advisers, who had arrived in Egypt following Sadat's predecessor's visit to Moscow in January 1970, played a crucial role in the Egyptian army, and even took direct part in fighting against the Israelis. But if by taking this step Sadat had hoped that the American administration would react by pressurizing 'Israel to accept withdrawal' he was due for a disappointment.[16] As we have already said, Israel was at that time a strategic asset in the Middle East, and the US administration would not challenge Meir's insistence on not yielding an inch of occupied land for less than a full recognition and acceptance of Israel by the Arabs in the Middle East. Nonetheless, Sadat remained undeterred, and in a further attempt to persuade Washington to help him open a dialogue, he dispatched his national security adviser, Hafez Ismail, to meet President Nixon and his national security adviser Henry Kissinger. Ismail met the President in the White House on 23 February 1973, and he then had three secret meetings with Kissinger on 24–5 February, but it came to nothing, mainly because Washington would not believe Sadat, whose 'zig-zag' foreign policies confused both them and the Israelis. For, at the same time when he was hinting that Egypt was in the American camp, Sadat also signed a fifteen-year 'Treaty of Friendship and Cooperation' with the Soviets, and when asked by the Americans about this he flatly replied that Egypt was free to make her own decisions.

Back in Cairo, Ismail reported to Sadat on his meetings in Washington and, according to the then Chief of Staff of the Egyptian army Saad el-Shazli, declared that Kissinger had said to him: 'I cannot deal with your problem unless it becomes a crisis', which according to el-Shazli was regarded by Sadat as a sign that 'Kissinger was encouraging him to go to war. That war was the only option'.[17] It is interesting to note that at about this time, April 1973, Kissinger said in an interview to Arnaud de Borchgrave of *Newsweek* that he

'Expects something to happen which can be very serious [in the Middle East]'.[18]

Meanwhile, Sadat was also growing depressed because of the improvement in US/USSR relations which meant, as he saw it, that the superpowers were unlikely to embark on a major initiative in the Middle East lest this put a strain on their improving relationship. *Détente*, in Sadat's eyes, was a new situation likely to reduce the Middle Eastern problem to a minor item on the international agenda and freeze the status quo, leaving Arab-populated territories in Israeli hands.[19]

Sadat was disappointed. His initiatives had run aground, his approaches to Washington had failed to produce practical results, he had failed to dislodge Israel from its entrenched positions, and he had become a laughing stock in the eyes of his own people, to whom he had repeatedly promised that the 'year of decision' was around the corner.

A major shift in policy

The record clearly shows that quite independently of his diplomatic initiatives, Sadat also gave orders to prepare a plan of campaign for operation against Israel. He summoned a meeting with the Army High Command on 24 October 1972. At this, he explained that 'it is clear that there is no hope of Egypt's liberating its land through political methods' and he went on to instruct his commanders to step up preparations and be ready to launch a limited war against Israel.[20] This was a startling turn-about, a radical departure from previous policies, because until then Egypt had clung stubbornly to a policy of total, all-out war against Israel, aimed at freeing all the Sinai which Israel had occupied in 1967. But why did Sadat so dramatically change Egypt's policy from total to limited war, which he knew could only lead to the freeing of part of the Sinai? The reason is as follows.

When the 1967 war ended, Sadat's predecessor Nasser came to the conclusion that for Egypt to be able to embark on an all-out war to liberate all the land it had lost in the 1967 war, two preconditions must be fulfilled. The first was that Egypt obtain Scud missiles so that she could threaten Israel's population centres. The second precondition was that the Egyptian air force be equipped with advanced long-range fighter-bombers to enable it to penetrate deep into Israel and strike at airports, communications centres and other strategic installations. Indeed, during his visit to Moscow on 22 January 1970, Nasser, according to Chief of Staff Mohammed Fawzi who had accompanied him, 'Repeated his demand for [long-range] fighter-bombers because the range of our bombers does not enable us to reach deep into Israel'.[21] Sadat, like his predecessor, also recognized that without these weapons – long-range fighter-bombers and Scud missiles – Egypt would not be able to liberate its occupied lands; and therefore, in a secret letter, dated 30 August 1972, which he sent to Soviet President Leonid Brezhnev, he said:

I mentioned in our frequent discussions that we needed a *retaliatory weapon* which would deter the enemy ... because of his knowledge that we would then be able to retaliate in kind and attack his inland positions. *It was obvious, and still is, that, deprived of such a retaliatory weapon, we would remain incapable of taking any kind of military action.*[22]

The 'retaliatory weapon' to which Sadat referred was the Scud missile.

Moscow, however, consistently refused to supply Egypt with advanced fighter-bombers and with 'retaliatory weapons', presumably because it had realized that for Egypt to be in a position to strike at Israel was not in Moscow's interest at this time in the early 1970s, because of its improved relationships with Washington. That Moscow refused to supply offensive weapons to Egypt – it only provided it with arms for defence – we know from Sadat's own letter to Brezhnev, where he mentions the 'embargo you have imposed on us for the last five years, in regard to "retaliation weapons"'. That this embargo also included long-range fighter-bombers, which Egypt so desperately needed if it was to embark on a war to liberate the whole of the Sinai, we know from a recent testimony of Pavel Akopov, a Soviet diplomat who was present at meetings in which the supply of weapons to Egypt was discussed. According to Akopov:

I was present at negotiations [regarding the supply of weapons to Egypt] with Nasser, and afterwards the same issues were raised by Sadat all the time ... Sadat was always putting the question of supplying him with this sort of armament which we could not give them: say, aircraft that could fly from Cairo to Tel Aviv, and he was always asking for them so that he could bomb Tel Aviv.[23]

In this lies the reason for Sadat's decision to abandon the aim of embarking on a total, major war to liberate the Sinai and to concentrate instead on a more limited war. For his realization that Moscow was unlikely to provide him with the long-range fighter-bombers and Scud missiles which had been seen by his predecessor and himself as the preconditions for a total war against Israel, brought him to the conclusion that he should try to achieve a more limited objective and hope that this would break the political impasse and result in his regaining the Sinai through political negotiations.[24] As Egyptian General Mohamed Abdel Ghani Gamassy put it: 'The idea of a limited war came from the fact that we did not have enough equipment to go into a general war; the Soviets would not give us enough arms'.[25]

As the meeting with his military command progressed, Sadat came to realize that there was strong opposition within the armed forces even to a limited war. General Abdel Kader Hassan, for instance, protested and expressed doubts about the possibility of winning a war against Israel, arguing that Egypt was not yet prepared for such a conflict and was not strong enough to challenge the Israelis, and that:

> We might succeed in the initial phase of our attack, but then we would undoubtedly be forced on to the defensive by the enemy. The upshot could be that the Israelis would be in a stronger position than they are now. And what of us? We have to consider that most of our interior has no proper defences against air attacks. … We do not want to find ourselves screaming once more for the help of the Soviet Union.[26]

A long and acrimonious debate followed, in which other commanders too expressed their reservations and opposition to launching a war, arguing that Egypt lacked basic equipment and was not yet ready to strike at Israel.[27] But Sadat was adamant, for he had already made up his mind, and because he was not proposing a full-blown major war but a limited one it did not matter that he was not equipped for a total war. He thus curtly told his military commanders that the decision whether or not to embark on war rested with him and not with them. He also said: 'We are confronted with a challenge. To be or not to be. We will simply have to use our talents and our planning to compensate for our lack of some kinds of equipment. God bless you'.[28] On the basis of Sadat's instructions, the Egyptian High Command began drawing plans for a limited war against Israel, and also embarked on frequent false mobilizations to deceive the Israelis; twenty-two mobilizations would take place between 1972 and 1973, and not until the twenty-third would the attack on Israel be launched.[29]

Sadat wished to attack Israel simultaneously from two directions in order to compel her to split forces and be weakened by having to fight on two fronts. To this end he invited President Assad of Syria to come to Egypt, and they met at Bourg el-Arab in the western desert in April 1973, where Sadat explained that he had: 'decided to fight my battle this year and have issued the relevant instructions to [Minister of War] Marshal Ali'. Sadat then asked Assad 'What do you say to this?'[30] Wishing to regain the Golan Heights which he had lost to Israel in 1967, Assad replied: 'I'll be with you. We're going to fight and are preparing for it'.[31] Proceeding with military preparations, the presidents decided to set up the 'Higher Council' of Egyptian and Syrian generals, which was tasked with cooperating and drawing up final plans for war against Israel, and with working out the detailed arrangements of a deception programme aimed at catching Israel off guard.

A double agent[32]

Much has been written about how Egypt, and to a lesser extent Syria, deceived the Israelis by constantly mobilizing forces, bringing the situation along the borders to the brink of war and then demobilizing in order to reduce Israel's alertness, until the moment came to strike on Yom Kippur, 6 October. That the Israelis were caught napping, off-guard and with no mobilized forces adequate to repel the invaders was often explained in terms of the failure of AMAN, Israeli Military Intelligence, to predict that hostilities would break out, and its insistence on a low probability of war in spite of a stream of information which was flowing in and showed that the enemy was already in jump-off points and strong enough to launch a massive attack. The view that the failure to predict the outbreak of hostilities and as a result to mobilize the reserves on time to repel the invaders was solely due to AMAN, was later supported by the Agranat Commission which investigated the failures of the IDF in the initial phases of the war, and whose brutal verdict, published in 1974, put the blame for the failure mainly – though not exclusively – on AMAN.[33] But we now know that crucial information was concealed from the Agranat Commission, and what is now available clearly indicates that responsibility for the failure to see that war was on Israel's door step and that mobilization of reserves was urgently needed, rested not only with AMAN – it has been done less than justice – but also with the politicians and, in particular, Mossad which, ironically, was praised by the commission.

To understand fully how and why Israel stumbled into the trap and was caught off-guard on Yom Kippur 1973, we should go back to the days after the 1967 war. In 1969, Mossad recruited a top Egyptian official. In fact, he recruited himself, knocking on the door of the Israeli embassy in London and volunteering to work for Mossad. This man, although only in his mid-twenties, was very close to President Nasser and later became the right-hand man of Nasser's successor Sadat. In *Israel's Secret Wars*, Ian Black and Benny Morris quote an Israeli intelligence officer who said of this Egyptian Mossad agent that he was: 'The best agent any country ever had ... a miraculous source'.[34] Indeed, the man was held in high esteem in Israel, and the documents he had turned over to Mossad were read – as raw material – by the Prime Minister, Defence Minister, Chief of Staff and Director of Military Intelligence. The Agranat Commission, which would later investigate Israel's failure in the Yom Kippur War, referred to the information provided by this agent as 'unique material from an especially important Mossad source'. In return, this agent received a generous fee – more than £100,000 for each meeting he held with his Israeli contact.

Perhaps the most important document ever handed over by Mossad's Egyptian agent was the transcript of a conversation President Nasser had in Moscow on 22 January 1970, where he, as shown above, 'repeated his demand for [long-range] fighter-bombers because the range of our bombers does not enable to reach deep into Israel'. Another crucial document which this agent turned over to Mossad was the secret message addressed by President Sadat to President Leonid Brezhnev, on 30 August 1972, in which Sadat, as we showed above, asked for 'a retaliatory weapon' (meaning Scud missiles) adding that 'It was obvious, and still is, that, deprived of such a retaliatory weapon, we would remain incapable of taking any kind of military action'.[35] The Egyptian Mossad agent not only handed over these two (and other) documents, but he also explained to his Mossad contact that for both Nasser and Sadat, having long-range fighter-bombers and Scud missiles was a precondition for embarking on war, and that without these weapons Egypt would not attack Israel.

On the basis of this dramatic written and verbal information, the entire Israeli pre-Yom Kippur War strategy was recast – it became known as the 'Conception' – and in a nutshell, it assumed that Egypt would make war on Israel only after it had obtained advanced fighter-bombers and Scuds.[36] Israel began to monitor Egyptian airfields for evidence that these weapons had arrived in Egypt, for if they were to, and if the Sinai were still in Israeli hands, then after a period of training and assimilation, Egypt would be prepared for a military attack and would most likely strike.

However, what the Israeli leadership failed to realize was that the man they considered to be their top Mossad agent in Egypt was, in fact, a double agent also working for President Sadat.[37] And while the information he supplied which suggested that Egypt would not attack without fighter-bombers and Scuds was indeed true at the time, this position was later abandoned by Sadat who, as shown, came to the conclusion that Moscow was unlikely to provide him with these crucial weapons, and that he had no other option but to embark on a limited rather than a total war against Israel. Clearly, Mossad's Egyptian agent knew about Sadat's new policy, for he was the President's henchman, but he failed to notify the Israelis of the change in policy. For Israel, the unfortunate result of this was that she continued to believe that Egypt was holding to its previous policy.

Furthermore, parallel to providing the Israelis with critical information, this spy also embarked on a campaign of misinformation. He warned of an imminent war in 1972 which never happened, but when he did it again in the spring of 1973 he really did cause difficulties for the Israelis. That spring, he told his Mossad contact that Sadat was mobilizing forces and would attack Israel on 15 May. The arrival in Egypt on 7 April of a squadron of sixteen Iraqi Hunters and sixteen Mirage planes had strengthened the view in Israel that Egypt would indeed strike.[38] To respond to this warning, the IDF High Command drew up a plan codenamed 'Blue-White' which was aimed at mobilizing and deploying reserve forces, speeding up military purchases and crystallizing preparations for war.[39] But views differed within the Israeli military establishment regarding the way Israel should respond to the agent's warning; director of military intelligence Eli Zeira insisted that the probability of war was remote, and he also argued that the Egyptians were resurfacing some of their airports (he mentioned Mansmara) and would not embark on war while the work was in progress. But Zeira was overruled by Chief of Staff Elazar and Defence Minister Dayan, who decided that what Mossad's Egyptian agent had told them about an imminent attack was probably true and that, although it contradicted his previous written information, it should be taken seriously.

On 19 April, 'Blue-White' was implemented; but the Egyptian attack did not materialize, and on 12 August 1973 the forces were dispersed (this was just seven weeks before the Yom Kippur War).[40] This futile mobilization cost Israel a fortune – $45 million – and irritated many, particularly the Minister of Finance, who complained that the country was needlessly wasting much money. We now know that Sadat did not intend to attack Israel in April–May 1973 and that the Mossad double agent's report was intended to cause a false alarm as part of his misinformation campaign. 'I had no intention of starting a war in May' Sadat wrote in his memoirs 'but as part of my strategic deception plan I launched a mass media campaign then and took various civil defence measures which led the Israelis to believe that war was imminent'.[41] General Gamassy, the Egyptian director of operations, also said, referring to the April–May Egyptian mobilization, that the actions were: 'Something we did ... to deceive the Israeli intelligence'.[42] And General Fuad Awidi of the Egyptian army intelligence service said in an interview to an Israeli newspaper: 'The exercises and mobilizations in May 1973 were part of our deception plan'.[43] In fact, as we shall soon see, it was only in August 1973 that a final decision regarding the date of an attack on Israel was made in Alexandria, and that, therefore, 15 May could never have been a D-day for war, as reported by Mossad's Egyptian double agent.

It is fairly clear, then, that the Egyptian Mossad agent – the double agent – played a crucial part in the Egyptian deception plan, and that what he reported was taken very seriously indeed by the decision-makers in Israel. Although AMAN did indeed fail to interpret Arab intentions, it was Mossad and the politicians who were so hypnotized by Sadat's right-hand man, who was their top agent, that they failed to realize two crucial things. First, that the agent's information that Egypt would not attack before obtaining Scud missiles and advanced fighter-bombers ('The Conception') was no longer valid in the spring of 1973 and therefore the Israeli strategy based upon it was erroneous, and war was to be expected even without the fulfilment of the previous Egyptian preconditions. Second, that the man they considered to be their best agent in the Arab world was, in fact, hiding crucial information from them while simultaneously feeding them false information regarding Egyptian intentions, as he had explicitly done late in 1972 and, in particular, in April–May 1973, when his false warning caused a purposeless mobilization in Israel. This latter major call-up had adverse long-term implications for Israel; for it evoked such criticism that when later that year war was just around the corner and a mobilization of the reserves was urgently needed, the Israeli political-military leadership hesitated, fearing that it was yet again a false alarm.

Final preparations in Egypt and Syria

As we have seen, a final decision by Egypt and Syria to embark on war was not made before the summer of 1973. At a meeting on 22–3 August, in what was once Ras el-Tin Palace in Alexandria, the 'Higher Council' of Egypt and Syria met, and as the Syrian chief of operations Abdel Razzak Al-Dardary later recalled: 'We agreed on the last points of cooperation between the two fronts, we put the final touches. We finalized the deception plan'.[44] After two days of secret talks, the military planners were ready to inform their political leadership – Presidents Sadat and Assad – that two time periods in the coming months, 7–11 September and 5–10 October, would be suitable for launching an attack on Israel, and all the military required was an advance warning of fifteen days.[45]

On 28 August, Sadat flew to Saudi Arabia to inform King Feisal that he intended to strike at Israel and to ensure the King's financial support during and after the war. It should be mentioned here that Sadat was accompanied, among others, by the associate who had been providing misleading information to Mossad. This man was present at a meeting between the President and the King in which Sadat confirmed that he was to embark on an all-out war against Israel. After this meeting, however, this Mossad agent would falsely report to the Israelis that Sadat had decided to postpone the war – a lie, and unequivocal proof that he was deliberately misleading the Israelis.[46]

Sadat also visited Qatar and Syria, and discussed the final war plans with President Assad, after which Assad convened the regional leadership of the Ba'ath Party, to whom he said: 'It seems that our Egyptian brothers have decided that the political path is no longer getting them anywhere ... if Egypt goes to war and we decided against war, that would be bad for our image before the Arab world'.[47] One of the participants, George Saddeqni, who became Minister of Information on 26 September, later recalled that 'This statement made us feel that the decision had already been made and that the president was consulting us as a formality'.[48]

In Cairo on 13 September, Presidents Sadat and Assad and King Hussein of Jordan convened for a summit meeting. In fact, neither Sadat nor Assad wished to meet the King, who had been ostracized by the Arab world because of his harsh treatment of the Palestinians during 'Black September' in 1970, and his expulsion of them in July 1971 after continued fighting. Egypt had, in fact, severed diplomatic relations with Jordan in March 1972 because of Hussein's attempts to unite Jordan with the West Bank after an Israeli withdrawal which implied peace between Jordan and Israel. But now under pressure from King Feisal of Saudi Arabia, whose financial support was essential for the implementation of the campaign, Sadat agreed to mend fences with Hussein and invited him to join the summit in Cairo. Yet nothing was said to him about the possibility of war against Israel, and as Zeid Rifai, Jordanian Prime Minister, later testified: 'The discussions did touch on the

Arab–Israeli conflict but neither one, Sadat or Assad, mentioned anything about the vague possibility of a war. Never, never was the topic mentioned'.[49] But through their own contacts the Jordanians discovered that there was a joint Syrian–Egyptian plan to attack Israel, and as the King was against war – for he did not want Israeli or Syrian troops to cross his territory, nor to be forced to join the battle by domestic pressure as was the case in 1967 – he decided to warn the Israelis. A meeting was arranged for him with Israel's Prime Minister Meir – the strictest secrecy was kept – and on 25 September 1973 he flew his helicopter to Israel where he met the Prime Minister in the *Midrasha*, Mossad's HQ in Hertzelia just north of Tel Aviv. This is what he told Golda Meir (their exchange is presented here verbatim):

KING HUSSEIN From a very very sensitive source in Syria, that we have had information from in the past and passed it on, in terms of preparations and plans, actually all the units that were meant to be in training and were prepared to take part in this Syrian action are now, as of the last two days or so, in position of pre-attack. That were meant to be part of the plan, except for one minor modification – the 3rd division is meant also to cater for any possible Israeli movement through Jordan on their flank. That includes their aircraft, their missiles and everything else, that is out on the front at this stage. Now this had all come under the guise of training but in accordance with the information we had previously, these are the pre-jump positions and all the units are now in these positions. Whether it means anything or not, nobody knows. But I have my doubts. However, one cannot be sure. One must take those as facts.

GOLDA MEIR Is it conceivable that the Syrians would start something without full cooperation with the Egyptians?

KING HUSSEIN I don't think so. I think they would cooperate.[50]

This was an extraordinary event – King Hussein, whose country was officially at war with Israel, flew to the enemy to warn it of an imminent invasion by his Arab brothers. We will never know why Meir did not ask the King the crucial question: '*When* will they attack?', but she did call her Defence Minister Dayan, notify him of her meeting with the King and tell him of the warning. As the conversation between Meir and King Hussein was secretly taped by Mossad, Dayan also received the transcript, which was in English, and which he passed over to the Chief of Staff who, on the next day, 26 September, discussed the matter with his colleagues. As extracts from this discussion are now available, it is shocking to realize that the Israeli High Command, and Defence Minister Dayan himself, simply failed to understand what the King was saying to the Prime Minister. For while, as the above extract shows, the King's warning was that '[Egypt and Syria] would co-operate [in their attack]', Chief of Staff Elazar said in the meeting that: 'It is not known if [Syrian preparations to open fire] are in cooperation with the

Egyptians'. He also said – disregarding the fact that according to the transcript the King's was a clear warning of a *joint* Egyptian–Syrian attack – that 'There could be nothing more idiotic for Syria than to attack on its own'. Dayan also failed to understand what the King was saying, and commented that the Syrians 'will find it difficult to go to war without Egypt'.[51] Thus, ironically, Prime Minister Meir, whose English was perfect – she grew up in America – failed to grasp the importance of Hussein's warning, while Dayan and the military command, probably because of their poor command of the English language, simply failed to understand that the King was giving warning of a joint Egyptian–Syrian attack. The end result was that the crucial warning – just ten days before the war – was not heeded; no reserves were mobilized to deter the assembling Syrians and Egyptians or to block them when they started moving.

All this time the build-up of Egyptian and Syrian forces steadily continued. In Egypt mobilization was announced on 27 September, but to lull suspicion and to camouflage its intention the Egyptian High Command ordered, on 4 October, the demobilization of 20,000 men of the 27 September intake. Furthermore, instructions for officers desiring to leave during the course of the exercise to take part in the *Umra*, the small pilgrimage to Mecca, were announced in *Al-Aharam*.[52] On 1 October the Egyptian 'strategic exercise' called 'Tharir 41', which included massive movements of troops and armour and was to last until 7 October, had started; on the 6th the exercise maps would be replaced with the genuine war maps. In Syria, in order to lull Israel's suspicion, the new Minister of Information George Saddeqni had announced that, in the week of 6 October, Assad would be visiting the faraway provinces of Deir Al-Zour and Hasaka.[53]

On 3 October 1973, a three-man Egyptian delegation – Minister of War Ahmed Ismail, intelligence officer Hassan Gretly and Chief of Staff of the Federal Operation General Staff Bahey Edin Noufal – flew to Damascus on a secret special mission. Noufal later recalled:

> We went on a cargo plane and no one knew we were going. We had to deliver the final order of war to the Syrians by hand. Ahmed Ismail joked while we were sitting uncomfortably in the cargo plane, saying 'What happens if the Israelis catch us and they find us with the order of war?' I said: 'I will simply eat the piece of paper, it is small and easy to swallow'. We asked to see [Syrian Minister of Defence] Mustapha Tlas. When we arrived Tlas was very surprised because he didn't know we were coming. He quickly gathered all the top brass at headquarters. We discussed the date again; the Syrians were unhappy because they wanted more time to empty their oil refineries [at Homs, which would be a certain target for Israel]. We couldn't agree on this.[54]

They fixed 6 October as the date of war, though there was an argument about the timing of the attack. The Egyptians wanted to start it in the late afternoon, so that the sun would be in the eyes of the Israelis and Egyptian engineers could build bridges over the Suez canal under cover of darkness. The Syrians, on the other hand, wanted a dawn attack so that the sun rising from the east would blind the Israelis; the two sides settled on 2 p.m.[55]

That day, President Sadat called in the Soviet Ambassador Vladimir Binogradov, to whom he said: 'I'd like to inform you officially that I and Syria have decided to start military operations against Israel so as to break the present deadlock'.[56] In spite of the July 1972 expulsion of the Soviets, there were still a few hundred in Egypt (and also in Syria) whom the Soviet authorities now decided to evacuate. The next day five giant Antonov-22s landed to pick up Russian families from Syria, and six arrived in Egypt.[57] Additionally, Soviet ships began steaming out of Alexandria to the open sea, and a Soviet ship carrying supplies wandered around in the Mediterranean, not entering the port of Alexandria.[58] All this traffic was picked up by AMAN, Israel's military intelligence.

On Friday at 11.30 a.m., Prime Minister Golda Meir convened her cabinet – there were five ministers in addition to herself – to discuss the situation.[59] The Chief of Staff and Director of Military Intelligence described the situation at the fronts. The Syrians and Egyptians, they reported, were ready at jump-off points, which served well for defence and equally well for launching an attack. The evaluation of the Director of Military Intelligence, which was accepted by the Chief of Staff, was that an attack was not likely and the assumption was that if war was imminent, there would be further indications and intelligence reports to this effect. The cabinet decided to entrust the Prime Minister with the authority to mobilize the reserves if this should be necessary the next day (the next meeting of the cabinet was scheduled for Sunday).[60]

Had mobilization been ordered on Friday – for according to Israeli doctrine of warfare such a concentration of enemy troops along the borders did indeed merit a mobilization – history might have taken a different turning, but this was not to be the case. It seems that those present at this crucial Friday meeting – just a day before war broke out – believed, wrongly as we shall soon see, that even if attacked, Israel's regular forces and the IAF could check the invaders and at least impose a delay on their advance until the arrival of the reserves; at the same time they grossly underestimated the enemy's strength. What also deterred them from authorizing all-out mobilization was a fear that an increase in the fighting forces might be seen as a threat and so accelerate the danger of war and even spark a clash of arms.[61] Of course, the false mobilization of April–May 1973 which had cost Israel a fortune and led to heavy criticism was still fresh in their minds, and they hesitated to call up the reserves lest this should turn out to be yet another false alarm.

Let us now turn to the forces concentrated on both sides of the borders and examine their military aims.

The opposing forces and their aims

Sinai

Egypt's combat force on the eve of the war comprised nineteen infantry brigades, eight mechanized brigades, ten armoured brigades, three airborne brigades, an amphibious brigade and an R–17E SSM brigade. In terms of weaponry these forces had about 1,700 tanks, 2,000 armoured vehicles, 2,500 artillery pieces, 1,500 anti-tank guns, 700 anti-tank guided weapons, several thousand RPG-7 portable anti-tank projectiles and more than a thousand RPG-43 anti-tank grenades. The equipping of Egyptian troops with a massive number of anti-tank guns was an important development missed by the Israelis, and was to cause them great damage, particularly in the initial phases of the war. The Egyptian air force had 400 fighter-bombers, seventy transport aircraft and 140 helicopters, and in the air defence 150 SAM battalions and 2,500 anti-aircraft guns. The SAM missile umbrella, which the Egyptians had advanced closer to the Suez Canal bank after and in breach of the Israeli–Egyptian ceasefire agreements of 7 August 1970, would totally neutralize the IAF in the initial phase of the war and would prevent it from striking at Egyptian troops and supporting Israeli ground forces. In their navy the Egyptians had twelve submarines, five destroyers, three frigates, twelve submarine chasers, seventeen CSA and Komar class missile patrol boats, thirty Shershaen and P-6 motor-torpedo boats, fourteen minesweepers and fourteen landing craft. This substantial force was reinforced by other Arab contingency forces: from Algeria a Mig-21 squadron, an SU-7 squadron, a Mig-17 squadron and an armoured brigade; from Libya two Mirage III squadrons and an armoured brigade; from Iraq a Hawker Hunter squadron; from Morocco and Sudan each an infantry brigade; from Kuwait and Tunisia each an infantry battalion.

The Egyptian military plan named 'Operation Badr'[62] was straightforward, incorporating a thrust by five infantry divisions – the three northern divisions constituted the 2nd army and the two southern divisions the 3rd – across the Suez Canal on the widest possible front, virtually the entire length of the Canal. Such a wide invasion would not give the Israelis any clue as to the main thrust of the attack, and thus confuse and prevent them from concentrating forces for a counter-attack.[63] To enable the Egyptian troops to hold their bridgeheads, they were each reinforced with an armoured brigade, a battalion of self-propelled SU-100 anti-tank guns and an anti-tank guided weapon battalion. The Israelis knew the finest details of the Egyptian military plan; a document of some forty pages setting out the plan and including detailed maps had been supplied to them by the CIA on 16 April 1972.[64]

As already explained, the essential feature of the Egyptian military plan was that it was intended as a limited operation: after crossing the Suez Canal and gaining a foothold on its eastern bank, forces were to penetrate no more than 10–15km into the desert and then dig in.[65] This was a logical way to proceed, because a limited move across the Canal and into the desert would enable the Egyptian forces to remain under the protection of the SAM missile umbrella, thus deterring the IAF from harassing them.

However, during the planning phase, the Syrians insisted that the Egyptians move deeper into the Sinai in order to pin down Israeli forces and ease potential pressure on Syria. To please the Syrians and in order not to lose them as crucial partners in the war, the Egyptians tricked them by drawing a false attack plan which indicated deeper penetration into the desert in the direction of the Sinai passes, some 48km east of the Canal. Chief of Staff of the Egyptian army el-Shazli later said of this bluff: 'We made this other plan extending our advance all the way to the passes only in order to show it to the Syrians'.[66] The latter, in turn, swallowed the bait, and as Syrian Minister of Defence Mustapha Tlas later recalled: 'So it was agreed that the Egyptians would advance to the [passes] ... and meanwhile we would occupy the Golan Heights'.[67]

The Israeli defence plan against any potential Egyptian offensive was basic and unimaginative. Called *Shovach Yonim* ('Operation Dovecote'), it was drawn up by the IDF in August 1970. Under it, the 180km front – 160km along the Suez Canal and 20km along the Mediterranean – was divided into three sectors: northern, central and southern. The northern sector was to resist any potential attack in the direction of Kantara-El Arish; the central sector opposed a potential offensive from Ismailia in the direction of Abu Ageila, and the southern sector was to repel any potential thrust from Suez in the direction of the Mitla and Giddi passes. Within each sector there were three lines of defence: the front line comprised the Bar Lev line, which together with the Suez Canal formed a formidable barrier 180m wide, on the eastern side of which and rising to a height of 20m stood a gigantic sand dune, sloping in places at 45–65 degrees, which ran so close to the Canal that its face merged with the steeper gradient of the concrete banking. The second Israeli defence line was 5–8km behind the Suez Canal and comprised three battalions, forty tanks to a battalion, with a battalion assigned to each sector. The third line of defence, between 19km and 32km behind the Canal, was based on reserve forces and comprised three armoured brigades, 120 tanks to a brigade, less the battalions forward in the second line. The Israeli plan was that, if attacked, the second line of defence should move up to its firing position at the water's edge or to the ramps just behind it, and the third line move up to the second line in order to create a front line of defence made up of a brigade of infantry in the Bar Lev line plus 120 tanks in three tank battalions.[68]

On the eve of the Yom Kippur War the entire Israeli line of defence was held by a mere ten infantry platoons, twelve artillery batteries (fifty-two cannons), 290 tanks, two ground-to-air missiles (Hawks), and six anti-aircraft batteries. This very thin shield of 450 troops was deployed in sixteen strongholds and four observation points. The reason why there were so few troops along the Suez Canal and why only about half of the Bar Lev line positions were manned, was that Ariel Sharon, OC Southern Command until a few weeks before the war, did not believe in the concept of the Bar Lev line, but after failing to persuade his superiors that a line of defence would crumble in war and therefore Israel's strategy should be mobile – in which he was to be proved right – he retained the line but shut down sixteen out of its thirty strongholds.[69] The result was that the fortifications were too far apart to give each other effective fire support and, when war broke out, the Egyptian troops after crossing the Canal were able to move into the desert mainly through the wide gaps between these fortifications.

The Golan Heights

On the Golan Heights, a Syrian force of three infantry divisions and a strength of 45,000 men was deployed, with each division made up of two infantry brigades, a tank brigade and a mechanized brigade. The 7th division with its 68th and 85th infantry brigades was in jump-off positions in the northern sector; the 9th division with its 52nd and 33rd infantry brigades was deployed and in jump-off points in the central sector; and the 5th division, which included the 112th and 61st infantry brigades, also in jump-off places and deployed along a line stretching from Rafid to the Yarmouk. In addition to 540 tanks which were with the front-line forces, the Syrians had an extra 460 tanks in reserve just behind the first line. Additional Syrian forces included the Republican Guard, a brigade in strength which was equipped with T-62 tanks and whose mission was to protect the regime in Damascus, and two armoured brigades and some 200 static tanks in the line, making a total of approximately 1,500 Syrian tanks ready for battle; this formidable force was supported by 942 pieces of artillery.[70] Other Arab countries sent forces to help the war effort; Iraq sent to Syria three Mig-21 squadrons, a Mig-17 squadron, its 3rd armoured division and an infantry division. Morocco sent to Syria a tank regiment, and Jordan sent its 40th and 3rd armoured brigades; the latter, however, did not arrive until 22 October and so did not take part in fighting. The Syrian forces were concentrated under an umbrella of thirty-six ground-to-air missiles which were deployed on the Golan Heights and close to the capital Damascus. This missile system covered an area stretching 8km into Israel's territory and was capable of detecting anything flying under 500ft. This was an immense problem to the Israelis, for it denied the IAF freedom of movement even on its own land. This threat seemed so formidable that in the summer of 1973, Deputy Chief of Staff Yisrael Tal proposed that it be destroyed. However, his proposal was rejected and, as we shall see, later in the war the IAF would pay a heavy price for this.[71]

The Syrian war plan was called *Mashrua 110* ('Operation 110') and it envisaged the occupation of the Golan Heights, the establishment of bridge-heads west of the Jordan river, and then movement towards Nazareth in Israel's Galilee. Syrian troops were also to seize the Israeli Hermon foothold, which at a height of 2,100m above sea level had provided the Israelis with an ideal observation point into the adjacent territories of Syria.[72] As with the Egyptian war plan, AMAN knew the Syrian war plan down to its finest operational details.[73]

The Israeli forces facing the Syrians comprised ten infantry platoons, 178 tanks, and eleven artillery batteries with a total of forty-four pieces. This force was much bigger than the standard force deployed on the Heights, the reason being the rising tensions between Israel and Syria following a major air battle on 13 September 1973.[74] That day, two Israeli Phantoms and four Mirages had flown over Syrian territory on a photo-reconnaissance mission, and when the Syrians dispatched Migs to deflect them an aerial battle ensued in which the Israelis shot down eight Migs, losing one Mirage of their own. An attempt by the Israelis to rescue their Mirage pilot, who had ejected, led to a second dogfight and ended in the shooting down of another four Migs, bringing the total Syrian losses to twelve and so causing them a major humiliation. In the past, the Syrians had reacted massively to incidents of such gravity, but on this occasion days had passed without a reaction, which caused suspicion and uneasiness on the Israeli side, and apprehension that the Syrians were planning a large retaliatory action. At a General Staff meeting on 24 September, Defence Minister Dayan agreed to demands made by Yitzhak Hofi – he had taken over as GOC Northern Command in 1972 – to reinforce his forces on the Golan Heights and strengthen the front line.[75] This reinforcement was backed up by a visit made by Dayan on 26 September, which was the eve of *Rosh Hashana*, the Jewish New Year, to the Golan Heights, where he also issued a firm warning to the Syrians.[76] As we will see, this reinforcement was crucial, and when war broke out a few days later, Israeli forces on the Golan Heights performed better than those in the Sinai.

The Israeli military plan to meet any potential challenge from Syria was called 'Operation Chalk' and its sole aim was 'to destroy [any] enemy forces' attempting to retake the Golan Heights.[77]

War

Saturday 6 October: in Israel Yom Kippur, the most sacred day in the Jewish calendar, and in the Arab world the tenth day of the month-long fast of Ramadan. This is what happened in Egypt, Syria and Israel between 1 and 2 p.m. of this day.

In Egypt President Sadat arrived in Centre no. 10, the headquarters from where he was to direct the war; he was wearing his uniform, as the President of Egypt is also the supreme commander of the armed forces. Just before 2 p.m., 222 Egyptian bombers took off from seven airfields and flew low on bombing missions against Israeli military targets in the Sinai. The opening gambit of the Egyptians in 1973 was similar to that of the Israelis in 1967 – a massive air strike. Soon after, Egyptian guns began a tremendous bombardment and in the first minute of the attack 10,500 shells landed on Israeli positions at the rate of 175 shells per second.

In Syria   In the operations room, a bunker two floors underground, President Assad arrived wearing his military uniform. Then, according to the testimony of former Minister of Information George Saddeqni:

> A few minutes before 2 o'clock there was silence. There was this big white clock on the wall and everyone was staring at it in complete silence. At 2 sharp, the telephone rang and Assad picked it up. The war had started. Then the telephones started going wild and there was a lot of commotion in the operations room.[78]

Sixty Syrian aircraft – part of the combined Egyptian–Syrian air attack which was called *Awasef* ('Storms') – flew to bomb Israeli targets, and Syrian guns opened a fierce and intense barrage to soften up Israeli positions.[79]

In Israel   Ministers and military personnel were at an emergency meeting at the office of Prime Minister Meir in Tel Aviv. A final confirmation that war would break out was given in person to head of Mossad Zvika Zamir by Sadat's henchman who, as we have already mentioned, was an agent of Mossad. This top Egyptian spy had travelled to what is often described in Israeli literature as a 'European capital'; it was, in fact, London. How did he slip out of Egypt on the eve of the war? His boss Sadat must have known about it. Was it with the consent of Sadat who was using him to mislead the Israelis? We will probably never know for certain the answers to these questions, but at that late-night meeting between 5 and 6 October, in a flat in London, he told Zamir that war would break out at 6 p.m. on 6 October. This warning, he must have known, was too short a notice for the Israelis, whose main force was based on reserves which had to be called up. But even now he was clearly misleading the Israelis, for the war did not start at 6 p.m., as he told Zamir, but four hours before, at 2 p.m.

Mobilization of reserves started at around 10 a.m. on 6 October, but this only got under way after an acrimonious argument between Defence Minister Dayan and Chief of Staff Elazar. Dayan favoured a limited mobilization of the air force and two divisions, one to the north and the other to the south, which could, he mistakenly believed, together with the IAF hold up the attackers. Elazar, on the other hand, insisted on full mobilization so he could undertake an immediate counter-attack; Elazar was attack-minded but for this he urgently needed considerable force.[80] As the two failed to agree, the matter was brought to the Prime Minister to decide. 'My god', she later confided to her memoirs '*I* had to decide which of them is right?'[81] In the end, Meir opted for Elazar's proposal and full mobilization was ordered. But much time was lost; from the final confirmation given to the head of Mossad by Sadat's henchmen in London that war would break out – it was passed by Zamir to Israel at 4 a.m. on 6 October – to the actual start of war at 2 p.m. there remained ten hours, of which about five had been spent on endless arguments between Dayan and Elazar regarding how many troops to mobilize. In the meantime none were mobilized until Prime Minister Meir took the final decision. It is ironic that in the Six Day War of June 1967, stunning Israeli success was partly due to the recklessness of the Egyptian High Command, whereas now it was the other way round and the initial success of Egypt and Syria was partly due to the foolishness and ineptitude of Israel's leadership.

At 2.05 p.m., while the meeting at Meir's office was still under way, the aide-de-camp of the Defence Minister walked in and passed a note to Dayan. It said: 'The Syrians and Egyptians have opened fire, the Syrian air force dispatched aeroplanes, Egyptian dinghies cross the [Suez] Canal, Sherm [el-Sheike] and military bases in west Sinai are under bombardment'.[82] The Egyptian and Syrian offensive was now in full swing. The following is an extract from the diary of Egyptian Chief of Staff General Shazli describing the crossing of the Suez Canal:

> At 1420 hours, they [the Egyptian divisions] opened direct fire against the Bar Lev strongpoints. And the 4,000 men of Wave One poured over our ramparts and slithered in disciplined lines down to the water's edge. The dinghies were readied, 720 of them, and a few minutes after 1420 hours, as the canisters began to belch clouds of covering smoke, our first assault wave was paddling furiously across the canal, their strokes falling into the rhythm of their chants 'Allahu Akbar … Allahu Akbar … '.[83]

And head of operations Abdel Ghani Gamassy recalled: 'Our troops crossed the [Suez] Canal. They were shouting "God is great, God is great" and they planted the Egyptian flag on the Sinai itself'.[84] Each of the five Egyptian divisions crossed the Canal and built a bridgehead which connected with each other to create a continuity along the front. Every fifteen minutes a wave of troops crossed, and by 3.15 p.m. the Egyptian army had already put twenty infantry battalions – 800 officers and 13,500 men complete with portable and hand-dragged support weapons – into the desert. At 5.30 p.m the Egyptians began landing commando forces carrying portable anti-tank weapons deep in the Sinai in an attempt to prevent the Israeli reserve forces from reaching the front line at the Suez Canal. Forty-eight helicopters carrying commandos flew into the desert; twenty of them were shot down, but those which did get through did much damage to Israeli reserves arriving on the scene. In the meantime the crossing had continued in earnest. This is an extract from General Shazli's diary of war, dated Sunday, 7 October:

> By 0800 hours the battle of the crossing had been won. ... In 18 hours we had put across the canal 90,000 men, 850 tanks and 11,000 vehicles. ... Over the whole 24 hours, the total grew to 100,000 men, 1,000 tanks and 13,500 vehicles.[85]

The 505 Israeli troops in the Bar Lev line (when war broke out, fifty-five soldiers whose tanks had been hit joined the 450 in the strongholds) were mostly ill trained low-grade troops of the Jerusalemite brigade; they found themselves in desperate straits and could do little to stem the Egyptian troops who surged across the Canal like a tidal wave and had immense numerical superiority. The Bar Lev line crumbled quickly and the strongpoints fell. Worse still, because Shmuel Gonen – he was made OC Southern Command on 15 July 1973, succeeding Ariel Sharon – was told that war would start at 6 p.m., he had decided to deploy his forces at the last minute so that the Egyptians could not gain a clear picture of the layout of his forces, and could not alter their plans accordingly. But when the war started earlier than expected this proved to be a colossal error. General Gonen also made a further tactical error which proved very damaging; instead of deploying two thirds of his forces in advance positions and one third behind, he did it the other way round, and when the Egyptians opened fire the Israeli front line of defence was extremely weak.[86] Of the 290 Israeli tanks which were in the Sinai when war broke out, 153 were soon hit and put out of action.[87] The principal cause of the heavy loss of tanks was the way the Egyptian anti-tank guns, comparatively small and handy, were pushed out ahead of their own tanks to positions from where they could get close to the Israeli tanks and hit them.

The arrival of Israeli reserves at the front was crucial. Before the war it had been assumed that no more than 36 per cent of tanks and other vehicles would have to reach the front on treads, with the rest being carried on transporters. But so desperate was the situation and so urgent the need for more forces on the scene, that 82 per cent of the vehicles reached the front on treads. Worse still, the IAF was unable to provide support to these forces and check the enemy, having suffered horrific damage thanks to the efficiency of the Egyptian and Syrian missile system – thirty-five Israeli planes were shot down in the first twenty-four hours of the war. Given that 52 per cent of the defence budget in 1973 was devoted to the air force, this was a most disappointing performance, for whereas in the 1967 war the most decisive factor of the Israeli success was air power, now the IAF totally failed in its mission. In the first hours of war not only did the Bar Lev line crumble, but with it the entire Israeli theory – that the regular army supported by the IAF could hold up any Arab invasion – which proved to be wishful thinking.

Fighting back – the Golan Heights

Priority had to be given to the Golan Heights, where the Israelis could not afford to yield ground because settlements were close to the border and there were no physical obstacles to hinder the advancing Syrians. Following their successful air strike, Syrian armoured forces – a first wave of 500 tanks and a later addition of 300 – crashed through the Israeli lines along the entire front and penetrated into the Golan Heights. They had concentrated their main breakthrough at two points – one north and the other south of Kuneitra. So overwhelming and massive was the Syrian assault, that although Israeli forces on the Heights had been reinforced following the air battle of 13 September, they still failed in the opening phase to stem the Syrian southern thrust, where the attackers had managed to advance towards the descent of the Jordan river and at 1 p.m. on 7 October were only some 6km from it.

On the night of 6–7 October, the Israeli General Staff had decided to send a further division to reinforce the two now on the Golan Heights; but the situation was still critical and all the Israelis were interested in was to end the war on almost any terms. As Yisrael Tal, Deputy Chief of Staff later explained:

> The aim ... contrary to popular belief, was to put an end to the war ... to create a situation where the Syrians think that we are moving on Damascus and call for Russian support ... and we even decided [among ourselves] that [we will even accept that] the Egyptians remain in the [places they had already occupied in the] Sinai. [We] only [wanted] to put an end to the war ... this is the truth.[88]

To achieve this aim, Chief of Staff Elazar asked for political permission to strike at the morale of the Syrian civilian population by bombing its cities and thus pressurizing the Syrian leadership into stopping the war. According to Tal: '[Chief of Staff Elazar] had insisted on bombing the population in Damascus and Haled so that the Syrians would shout *gevalt* ["help"]'.[89] Indeed, upon receiving political permission, the IAF, on 9 October, struck at the Syrian Defence Ministry and the Air Force Headquarters in Damascus, as well as at targets in Homs. What provided an almost miraculous reprieve to the Israelis was the fact that on that day the Syrians ran out of ground-to-air missiles and the IAF made the most of this situation. This was a successful day on the Golan Heights; as Dayan later remarked in his memoirs:

> That night, 9 October, I found the mood had changed ... there was a feeling that on that day they had passed the rock-bottom point and

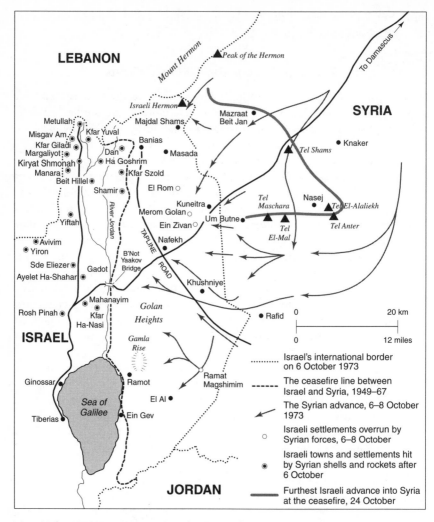

Map 4 The 1973 Yom Kippur War: the Syrian front

that the momentum of the Syrian attack had been broken. The enemy forces had begun to retreat.[90]

On 11 October the Israelis struck at the 40th Jordanian tank brigade – it lost twenty-seven killed and fifty wounded, and fourteen of its tanks were disabled beyond repair. The Israelis then turned on the Iraqis, hit them hard and drove back the entire Syrian–Jordanian–Iraqi assault and retook the Golan Heights.[91] 'At the end of the first week of war', noted Defence Minister Dayan in his memoirs, 'it was the Syrians who were on the defensive, and the campaign was being fought on their soil, east of the lines through which they had broken six days earlier'.[92]

The tide turns in the desert

In the Sinai, with the arrival of the reserves, the Israelis had on the scene a total of eight armoured brigades with 960 tanks (mainly Centurion M-48s and M-60s), compared with about 1,000 on the Egyptian side (200 T-62s, 500 T-54s and the rest T-55s). On 8 October, without waiting to concentrate, the Israelis opened a major offensive which was aimed at disrupting the Egyptian military machine and wiping out the forces that had crossed the Suez Canal before they could be properly established on its eastern bank. But the outcome was a disastrous failure and the Israelis paid a heavy price in men and material for the abortive effort. This stroke has often been criticized, after the event, as a rushed job, and so in a sense it was. But then the history of war shows that a stroke of this kind has very often been successful, especially because of its demoralizing effect on the opposing troops and their commanders.[93] But in the event, this failure turned 8 October into one of the darkest moments of the war for the Israelis, and correspondingly one of the brightest for the Egyptians. Defence Minister Dayan later wrote: 'The day [8 October] was a total failure',[94] while the Egyptian Chief of Staff el-Shazli noted with satisfaction in his war diary that

> The enemy persists in throwing away the lives of their tank crews. They assault in 'penny packet' groupings ... in the latest manifestation, two brigades have driven against the 16th [Egyptian] division. Once again, the attack had been stopped with heavy losses. ... Our strategy always has been to force the enemy to fight on our terms; but we never expected them to collaborate.[95]

But soon the scales tilted against the Egyptians. At the beginning of the war they had enjoyed the advantage of surprise and preponderant superiority of forces, but now the Israelis were nearly fully mobilized, they had recovered their balance, were regrouping, switching forces from the Golan Heights – where hostilities had more or less ceased on 11 October – and were ready to hit back. The coming Israeli success, however, was not so much a result of superior insight or strategy rather than the result of miscalculations and short-sightedness on the Egyptian side. We should recall that the original Egyptian plan was limited – to cross the Suez Canal, move only a few kilometres into the desert, obtain a lodgement and defend it while remaining under the safe cover of the SAM missile system. But aiming at following up their initial success, and under intense pressure from Damascus to keep on fighting in order to pin down the Israelis and relieve pressure on Syria, the Egyptians decided to alter their original war plans and push deeper into the Sinai in the direction of the passes.[96] Their Chief of Staff el-Shazli was vehemently against the sudden change of plan, since he knew that moving away from the missile umbrella would expose the troops as targets for the IAF, which still had over-whelming superiority in the air. El-Shazli pleaded as persuasively as he could with Sadat to adhere to the original limited plan, but he was overruled by Minister of War Ismail and the President himself.[97]

At first light on 14 October, four Egyptian armoured brigades and a mech-anized infantry brigade opened an offensive with four independent thrusts in the direction of the passes of Refidim, Giddi and Mitla. But as Mohamed Heikal rightly observed, 'What had been open for Egypt to accomplish on 7 October was no longer there to be achieved on 14 October'.[98] Indeed, as el-Shazli predicted, the move deeper into the desert made the Egyptian troops easy prey for the IAF which, away from the missile umbrella, had command of the sky and was able to harass the advancing troops and tanks with impunity. Additionally, the Egyptian T-62 and T-54 tanks were no match for the much more advanced Israeli Centurion M-48 and M-60. For the Israeli political-military leadership, the Egyptian offensive came just in time, for they were sharply divided and could not agree how to proceed. The practical ques-tion was one of timing and revolved around the question of *when* to move ahead and cross the Suez Canal. Chief of Staff Elazar wanted to wait, former Chief of Staff Bar Lev wanted to cross as soon as possible, and Deputy Chief of Staff Tal insisted that Israel should wait for the Egyptians to attack first, hit them from dug-in positions and only then move to the offensive and cross to the west bank of the Canal. And it was while this heated discussion was still under way that information came in that the Egyptians had opened their offensive; in practice this meant that Tal's view was accepted by default.[99]

In the desert, Ariel Sharon, a divisional commander, had witnessed the Egyptian offensive and its collapse, and recalling it later he wrote 'On Sunday October 14 at 06:20 massed Egyptian tank forces moved towards our lines. By early afternoon, 100–120 tanks of the Egyptian 21st armoured division were either flaming like torches or lying dead on the sand'. Indeed, the Egyptian offensive was a costly error and as disastrous as Israel's offensive on 8 October. By midday the attacking forces, which had managed to advance only a few kilometres into the desert, were brought to a complete halt and – suffering heavy losses of 250 tanks, which more than doubled their losses in the whole

Map 5 The 1973 Yom Kippur War: the Egyptian front

war to date – they began to fall back to the line from which they had started. Now the tables were turned and the Israelis took the offensive. Divisional commander Sharon recalls: 'That night approval came to cross the Canal. My division would break through the Egyptian lines, secure a corridor to the Canal and establish a crossing point at Deversoir on the east bank'.[100] Late on the night of 15 October, Sharon's forces approached the Suez Canal through the open seam between the Egyptian 2nd and 3rd armies and began crossing it just north of the Great Bitter Lake at Deversoir. By 18 October, Israel had on the west bank of the Canal a substantial force of three armoured brigades and an infantry brigade. By midday another armoured brigade had crossed, swelling the Israeli force to four armoured brigades and an infantry brigade. By 20 October the Israelis had secured three bridges across the Suez Canal, which enabled them to transfer more troops and tanks to the west bank.

On Monday 22 October, a ceasefire was announced, and it came into force at 6.52 p.m. But on 23 October, determined to improve their bargaining position, the Israelis breached the ceasefire and launched a concerted assault by four armoured brigades. They encircled the Egyptian 3rd army in the southern part of the Suez Canal and the town of Suez, and continued south to reach Adabiah, on the coast some ten miles below Suez. By 24 October, the 3rd army – two reinforced divisions, about 45,000 men and 250 tanks – was completely cut off, and that evening, after Soviet threats and growing American pressure, Israel agreed to a second ceasefire. It refused, however, to return to the lines of 22 October, and by now Israeli forces were within 101km of Cairo and 45km from Damascus.

In January 1974 Israel and Egypt signed disengagement agreements, and the terms of the disengagement between Israeli and Syrian troops were drafted on 31 May 1974. As Defence Minister Dayan noted in his memoirs: 'It marked the formal end to the Yom Kippur war. The fire at the front died down. The last of the prisoners came home. The Israel Defence Forces could release the reserves'.[101] It is estimated that the Arabs had lost some 15,600 men in the war, with 35,000 wounded and 8,700 captured. The IDF lost 2,687 men, with 7,251 wounded and 314 taken prisoner. The Arabs lost 440 aeroplanes; Israel lost 102. The Arabs lost 2,250 tanks compared with 400 Israeli tanks which were totally destroyed by enemy gunfire and 600 which were hit but were repaired and returned to full service. The Arabs lost 770 cannons; Israel lost twenty-five. Twelve Arab missile boats were sunk; the Israelis lost none.

War, peace and society

The 1967 Six Day War, the 1968–70 War of Attrition and the 1973 Yom Kippur War all took place within a short period of time – six years or so. But there was a huge difference in the way the Israeli public reacted to each of these wars, and in the way each of these confrontations affected Israeli society.

In 1967, the Israelis had a period of three weeks – the so-called 'waiting period' – in which they could assess the situation and express their views regarding the leadership and the way they were handling the crisis. When the people of Israel thought that their political leaders were not performing satisfactorily, they demanded a political change and the politicians were forced to accept it, as was the case when Dayan was nominated to the post of Defence Minister instead of Eshkol. Public reaction to the War of Attrition along the Suez Canal had its own characteristics. The war was relatively long and, as in 1967, the public had plenty of time to assess the situation and express its views regarding the way its political-military leadership was handling the crisis. Mounting public pressure caused the leadership to look for quick solutions to reduce the growing number of casualties, and this led to the construction of the Bar Lev line, and the attempt to de-escalate the war by initially intensifying it with bombing missions deep into Egypt. The Yom Kippur War of 1973 was different – it surprised the Israelis and caught them completely off their guard, and there was no time for the public to assess the situation and express its feelings. All Israelis could do was to join their units and be mobilized to the front to repel the attackers. The aftermath of the Yom Kippur War found Israeli society in a state of deep collective shock, but as soon as the guns fell silent there came a strong public reaction which put enormous pressure on the leadership to investigate the failures which had led to Israel being caught unprepared. The Agranat Commission, which investigated the events before and during the initial phases of the war, put much of the blame on the military commanders, and although it seemed at first that the politicians would emerge unscathed, this was not to be the case. The government had misjudged the Arab threat and this, in the postwar period, led to a general re-evaluation by society of the Labour government's ability to be trusted with the state's security. Indeed, about four years after the war the Israelis voted Labour out of office and elected a Likud government headed by Menachem Begin. This, after almost thirty years of Labour rule, was more than a change of government – it was a revolution Israeli-style, and it was mainly, though not exclusively, the result of the poor performance of the Labour leadership in the period leading up to the Yom Kippur War.

If we turn to Egypt we see that there, the general feeling after the war was that although in the end Egypt had lost the war, it had nevertheless won an important battle in the opening phase of hostilities, inflicting setbacks on the hitherto invincible Israelis, proving Egypt their match and regaining the nation's pride, self-respect and honour. This was good enough for President Sadat to embark on his next bold initiative and invite himself to Jerusalem to face the Israelis and offer to open a dialogue. Two years later, President Sadat and Prime Minister Begin signed the first-ever peace agreement between Israel and an Arab state. Although the price for this peace was the return of the Sinai Desert to Egypt, Israel accepted this without much protest. Ironically, however, the peace accord with Egypt, the implication of which was that the danger of Israel's being destroyed by a successful Arab invasion became remote, further removed the very cement – that is, an acute external threat – which had kept the turbulent Israeli society together for many years and made its people willing and determined fighters. Now, with the external danger diminished, Israelis, as we shall see in the following chapter, were less willing than before to take up arms.

CHAPTER FIVE

War in Lebanon

1982

The parties involved

Israel's invasion of Lebanon in the summer of 1982 was a traumatic experience for its armed forces and for its people as a whole. To understand fully how Israel plunged into the Lebanese quagmire and became involved in such a disastrous adventure, we should first identify the main players on the Lebanese scene.[1]

Since 1 January 1944, the day all remaining political power was transferred from the French to the Lebanese people, politics in this country had been a matter of a fragile and precarious balance between more than twelve officially recognized religious communities and sectarian groups, in particular Maronite Christians, Sunni Moslem and Shiia Moslem. Stability in Lebanon was dependent on a constitutional compromise by which a succession of Maronite Christians held the presidency, the prime minister was a Sunni Moslem and the speaker of Parliament was a deviationist Shiia Moslem. The arrival in Lebanon, from September 1970, of waves of Palestinians, mostly Moslems, had accentuated the traditional rivalry between left-leaning Moslems and rightist, mainly Maronite, Christians. These Palestinians, had, in fact, been pushed out of Jordan following failed attempts by some of its leftist groups to take over the country, which they wished to turn into a hinterland from which to attack Israel. A few of these Palestinian groups went even further by attempting to topple King Hussein, whom they considered to be a reactionary leader and the pawn of western powers in the region. In the process of trying to take over Jordan and bring down the King, the Palestinian guerrillas had turned Jordan, particularly its capital Amman, into a chaotic place; they manned road blocks, even levied taxes on thousands of Palestinian refugees, and provoked the King's loyal armed forces. 'It was a nightmarish scenario', the King later recalled, 'a breakdown of law and order; a situation where people were not able to go around without being stopped and searched by Palestinians, where vehicles were confiscated, people shot, people disappeared'.[2] The last straw came when Palestinians of George Habash's left-wing guerrilla group hijacked western aeroplanes, and after a stand-off in the

Jordan desert blew them up.[3] This humiliated the King, who, seeing power slipping out of his hands, turned on the Palestinian guerrillas, overcame them and expelled them from his kingdom. This is how they came to Lebanon.[4]

There, Yasser Arafat – by now Chairman of the Palestinian Liberation Organization (PLO) – and his guerrillas settled in the south of the country, close to the border with Israel, and established their headquarters in the capital, Beirut. They also formed an alliance with the Lebanese National Movement, the LNM, which was led by the Druze leader Kamal Jumblat, and was a loose confederation of various nationalist and progressive Moslem-dominated parties, including the Arab Ba'ath Socialist Party, the Progressive Socialist Party, the Syrian Social Nationalist Party, the Communist Party, the Communist Action Organization, the Popular Nasserist Organization and the Independent Nasserites. One of the demands of the LNM–PLO alliance was reform of the political system to make it equitable to Moslems, who now – largely because of the arrival of so many of them from Jordan – formed a majority in Lebanon.[5] The LNM–PLO alliance was in competition with the Lebanese Front. This was a confederation of Maronite Christian political parties, including the Phalange Party, the National Liberal Party, the Guardians of the Cedars and the Maronite League. It was officially headed by Camille Chamoun, but the Gemayel clan had considerable influence and, as we shall see, Bashir Gemayel later became the strongman of this group, and in the summer of 1982 was elected President of Lebanon. While the LNM–PLO alliance demanded reform of the political system so this would better reflect its numbers within the Lebanese population, the Lebanese Front insisted that the Maronites be entitled to a special position, irrespective of them being a minority in Lebanon. However divided against itself, the Front remained united in its enmity against the LNM–PLO group.[6]

Relationships between the two alliances were fragile, but had deteriorated dramatically following an Israeli raid on the heart of Beirut on 10 April 1973, where a commando squad led by Ehud Barak, a future prime minister of Israel, assassinated three Palestinian leaders – Kamal Nasser, Yusif Najar and Kamal Edwan – whom the Israelis held responsible for the killing of eleven of their athletes at the Olympic Games in Munich in September 1972. The Lebanese army – composed mostly of Maronite troops – which was located in the area where the Israelis were operating, did not intervene, and this reinforced mistaken Palestinian suspicions that the Maronite leadership had tacitly approved the Israeli raid in order to weaken the Palestinians in Lebanon.[7] With such tensions, only a spark was needed to ignite the Lebanese powder keg, and what eventually set it off was the killing, on 13 April 1975, of four Christians by a Palestinian gunman at a church in East Beirut, which was followed, on the next day, by the killing of twenty-seven Palestinians at the Tel Zatar refugee camp by the Maronites. This train of events, which heralded the so-called Lebanese civil war, soon sucked in two regional powers – Syria and Israel.

Syrian forces were invited into Lebanon by the Maronite President Suleiman Franjieh, in order to stop the raging civil war, keep the peace and save the Lebanese Front from total defeat at the hands of the LNM–PLO alliance, which by then controlled two thirds of the country. President Assad of Syria had welcomed the invitation, for he regarded Lebanon as Syria's own back yard; he also understood that, should a war with the traditional enemy, Israel, break out, control of Lebanon could enable him to prevent Israeli troops from approaching and threatening Damascus from the rear, namely from the direction of Lebanon. On 1 June 1976, Syrian troops marched into Lebanon, deployed along the road linking Beirut and Damascus, and took positions in Beirut itself and in the Beka'a valley in eastern Lebanon. Israel, which was then led by Prime Minister Yitzhak Rabin, did not object to Syrian intervention in Lebanon, but made it clear that Syrian troops must not move down beyond a line running south of Sidon to the east and 25km north of the Litani river.[8]

Israel's involvement in the Lebanese civil war can be traced back – grotesque as it may seen – to a crucial meeting on the steps of the Magdalene Church in Paris. There, back in the early 1970s, an Israeli agent of Mossad promised, albeit unofficially, to a Christian leader by the strange name Mugagbag, that, if asked, Israel would assist the Christians in Lebanon.[9] This led to a meeting in 1975 between Israel's Prime Minister Rabin and the Maronite Christian leader Camille Chamoun, on board an Israeli destroyer in the Mediterranean, to discuss Israeli aid to the Maronites in Lebanon. A year later, with the civil war in Lebanon raging and the Maronite Christian forces under growing pressure and in serious military straits, a Maronite Christian leader, Joseph Abu Khalil, approached Mugagbag, and on 12 March 1976 they set sail from Kaslik in Lebanon to the port of Haifa. Their ship was stopped at sea by an Israeli patrol boat, and after identifying themselves and explaining the purpose of their trip they were taken to Tel Aviv, where they met Israel's Defence Minister Shimon Peres. Peres asked Abu Khalil: 'Why have you come and what do you want?', to which Abu Khalil replied 'I have come to ask you for weapons. We need ammunition'.[10] Peres discussed the matter with Prime Minister Rabin, and they decided on a dramatic increase in material help to the Maronites in Lebanon.

It is often alleged that Israel's principal motive in offering support to the Maronites in Lebanon was sympathy and compassion. This, however, is utterly untrue; the truth of the matter is that in providing supplies and some other assistance to the Maronites Israel was perfectly serving her own national interests. First, the Maronites were fighting the PLO and other traditional enemies of Israel, and by assisting them Israel was using a proxy to do her 'dirty work' for her. Second, supporting the Maronites provided the Israelis, Mossad in particular, with a 'window' to the Arab world, which was crucial for the purposes of gathering intelligence.[11] We should also remember that the Maronite approach came *before* Israel had signed the Camp David accords with Egypt, and that to be approached for help by the people of an Arab state – albeit Maronite Christians – was a novel experience, and a request which the Israelis found difficult to decline. With political endorsement given, Israeli boats began sailing back and forth delivering arms to the Maronites. A boat would sail into Lebanese waters towing craft heaped with weapons and ammunition, and off the coast the craft would be released for the Maronites to tow away. Arming the Maronites was a major logistical operation and, although contacts with the Maronites in Lebanon were usually maintained by Mossad, in this case the huge supply operation was supervised by the Israeli defence ministry. It is estimated that between 1975 and 1977 the Rabin government spent $150 million on arming the Maronites.[12]

The Litani campaign: a rehearsal for the 1982 invasion

While supplying weapons to the Maronites was no more than an indirect involvement in Lebanese affairs, a major direct intervention, which has often been regarded as a rehearsal for Israel's invasion of 1982, came in March 1978. This followed a terrorist attack at the heart of Israel, when on 11 March 1978 nine Palestinians landed on a beach in Israel, walked to the Haifa–Tel Aviv coastal road, stopped two passing buses, crammed the passengers into one bus, and at gunpoint ordered the driver to go to Tel Aviv. In an exchange of fire between the kidnappers and Israeli security forces, just north of Tel Aviv, twenty-eight Israeli passengers were killed, seventy-eight wounded, and all nine terrorists killed.[13] The government – now headed by Menachem Begin of Likud – decided to hit back, and four days later dispatched the IDF into Lebanon to carry out what became known as 'Operation Litani'. It was launched on the night of 14 March 1978, went on for seven days, and was the biggest military operation the IDF had undertaken since the 1973 Yom Kippur War. Israeli troops, 7,000 in all, with armour and artillery and the close air support of the IAF, occupied the entire area north of the Israeli border up to the Litani river, destroying PLO infrastructure.[14] The operation was directed against the PLO, and the Israelis kept their distance from Syrian forces in order to avoid clashing with them.

What is so significant about this operation is its link with the 1982 invasion and the way it affected the thinking of Menachem Begin, who was Israel's Prime Minister in both operations. The link was as follows. The success of the limited 'Operation Litani', and in particular the fact that Israeli troops managed to operate without clashing with the Syrians, led Begin to believe, on the eve of the 1982 invasion, that it was possible to act in Lebanon against the PLO without having to fight the Syrians. As we shall see later, however, whereas in 1978 Defence Minister Ezer Weizman and his Chief of Staff Mordechai Gur took all possible measures to avoid a clash with the Syrians, the opposite happened in 1982, when Defence Minister Ariel Sharon, with the tacit agreement of his Chief of Staff Rafael Eitan, took direct action to provoke the Syrians and clash with them.

On 19 March, the UN Security Council adopted resolution 425 (by a vote of 12 to 0) calling on Israel to withdraw from Lebanon, and on 20 March the Council adopted resolution 426, entrusting a United Nations force, called UNFIL, to deploy in south Lebanon and monitor the activities of the Palestinian guerrillas; on 31 June 1978, Israel agreed to pull its forces out of Lebanon (except for her 'security zone').

In the years that followed, UNFIL failed to prevent the PLO from re-establishing itself in southern Lebanon, and there were many incidents in which the PLO and the Israelis exchanged fire. It seems, however, that in most cases it was Israel rather than the PLO which sparked the border clashes, for it was the policy of the Begin administration to keep the pressure on the PLO as a preventive measure. Begin clearly stated the aims of such an active policy, saying

> Our strategy [against the PLO in Lebanon] is not a retaliatory action [which comes] after [the other side has already] struck [at us], but the prevention of [the ability of the PLO] to hit [us] by inflicting blows on ... the murderers in their own bases.[15]

Or as he once put it in a speech in Tel Aviv: 'We go out to meet them [the PLO], we penetrate into their bases ... we no longer wait for them to come to [attack] us and spill our blood'.[16]

With the resignation of Ezer Weizman from the defence ministry on 26 May 1980, Israel's policy in Lebanon became even tougher, for it was now designed by Begin, who was not only Prime Minister but also Defence Minister, and had as his chief adviser the no-nonsense, hawkish Chief of Staff Eitan. In the summer of 1981 in particular, Israel put enormous pressure on the PLO in southern Lebanon. On 28 May, for instance, although unprovoked, the IAF began a massive bombing campaign against PLO bases in southern Lebanon; the PLO reaction was cautious and restrained. On 10 July 1981, the IAF struck again, this time in and around Beirut, killing 100 – thirty of them guerrillas – and wounding 600. Now the PLO lashed back, massively shelling Israeli settlements in Galilee, killing six Israelis and wounding thirty-eight. Israel then hit back in turn by launching a massive bombardment and causing Palestinians and Shiite civilians to flee northwards, and 70 per cent of the population of the Israeli town of Kiryat Shmona to flee southward. To stop the vicious circle, American President Ronald Reagan dispatched his special emissary Philip Habib, who with the help of the Saudi government, managed to broker a ceasefire between Israel and the PLO; this came into effect on 24 July 1981 and led to comparative peace along the border between Israel and Lebanon.[17]

Ariel Sharon and the 'Lebanese problem'

After Menachem Begin was re-elected Prime Minister for a second term, on 30 June 1981, he admitted Ariel ('Arik') Sharon, a man of great physical bulk and tremendous energy and toughness, into his cabinet as Defence Minister. It is often alleged that Begin's invitation to Sharon was due to the Prime Minister's admiration for generals – and Sharon was definitely one of the best soldiers Israel ever had.[18] But there is, perhaps, a more convincing reason why Begin wanted Sharon in his cabinet, and this relates to Israel's relations with Egypt.

We should remember that according to the Camp David accords, signed between Israel and Egypt back in 1978, Israel had to return the Sinai to Egypt – a final withdrawal was due by 25 April 1982. Begin, so it seems, could not bear the thought that he, of all people, would have to clash with Jewish settlers in Sinai over the dismantling of their villages and townships and the return of the land to Egypt. Instead, he preferred to leave this unpleasant task to Sharon who, he believed, could carry out the evacuation smoothly because he was regarded as the champion of the settlers' cause, and was also deeply involved in the building of many of the settlements in Sinai. But ironically, while Begin brought Sharon into his cabinet because of Egypt, Sharon – who lobbied hard for the job of Defence Minister – wished to join the cabinet mainly because of Lebanon, where he recognized two principal problems which he was determined to tackle and resolve. One was the presence of the Syrians and their ground-to-air missile system in the Beka'a valley; the other was the presence of the PLO in Lebanon.

In the entry of Syrian troops into Lebanon, which was approved by Prime Minister Rabin against the advice of Sharon, who at the time served as Rabin's adviser, Sharon saw 'the root of the [Lebanese problem]'.[19] He felt that Rabin's tacit agreement to the Syrian march into Lebanon of June 1976 was a grave error of judgement because it had allowed the Syrians to strengthen their grip – politically and militarily – on Lebanon. Sharon saw a great danger in the Syrian missile system in eastern Lebanon, which had been established – due to Israel's short-sighted policies – in the Beka'a valley in 1981. This is how it came about: on 28 April of that year, the Maronites attempted to take Zahle, mostly Christian, by force. But the Syrians would not allow this because they regarded the Maronites' attempt as an effort to extend their influence to eastern Lebanon. When the Syrians intervened to stop the Maronites, the latter called for help, and Israel dispatched aircraft which promptly shot down two Syrian helicopters, killing all the troops on board.[20] It is often alleged that the principal motive of the Maronites in their attempt to take Zahle, was to provoke the Syrians and thus draw Israel deeper into Lebanese affairs. This is hard to prove, although Prime Minister Begin did promise Camille Chamoun and Bashir Gemayel, when they visited him at his house in Jerusalem, that if the Syrians attacked from the air the IAF would come to their rescue.[21] In any case, if what the Maronites really wished to do was bring in the Israelis, then they succeeded, and indeed managed to complicate matters for Israel. For soon after the shooting-down of the Syrian helicopters, Damascus introduced SAM-6 batteries into the Beka'a valley to ensure that never again would the Israelis be able to intervene so aggressively in eastern Lebanon.[22] The Syrian move was regarded in Israel as a serious development, for it reduced the freedom of action of the IAF over Lebanese land. Acting on the advice of Chief of Staff Eitan, who was supported by the commander of the IAF, the Israeli cabinet authorized the IAF to destroy the Syrian missile system. But this did not take place, for a strike which was planned for 30 April was called off because of poor weather conditions, and later the operation was put off again because the IAF was preparing to strike at Iraq's Osirak nuclear reactor south of Baghdad.[23] Thus, when Sharon became Defence Minister, and on the eve of the 1982 war in Lebanon, the Syrian missile system was still in place.

Sharon believed that the PLO was attempting to turn the land of Lebanon – as it had tried to do in Jordan – into a base to strike at Israel.[24] He was not impressed with the ceasefire brokered by Habib – it was holding well – and he argued that the PLO was taking advantage of the ceasefire to rearm and organize itself. Furthermore, Sharon, like others in Likud, strongly believed that the destruction of the PLO in Lebanon would shatter Arafat's influence among the inhabitants of the West Bank. He said: 'Quiet on the West Bank requires the destruction of the PLO in Lebanon',[25] and one of his colleagues, the then Foreign Minister Yitzhak Shamir, said: 'The defence of the West Bank starts in West Beirut'.[26]

These two problems – the Syrian and the PLO presence in Lebanon – were so interconnected that it was impossible, in Sharon's view, to deal with each of them separately, and this led him to the conclusion that

> Even if [Israel] wanted only to remove the terrorists [namely the PLO, from Lebanon, it] had to take into consideration that the response of the Syrians would compel [it] to deal also with them – and this meant first of all [destroying] their missile [system].[27]

This is a most significant statement, for it shows that Sharon was well aware that if he were to order the IDF into Lebanon to root out the PLO – as thoroughly as he thought would be necessary – then the chances were high that Israeli troops would clash with Syrian troops stationed there. As we shall soon see, when he attempted to persuade the cabinet to endorse military action in Lebanon, Sharon would neglect to tell ministers that the implication of such an invasion was a high likelihood of a clash with the Syrians.

Sharon and the road to war

On 20 December 1981, about four months after being appointed Defence Minister, Sharon presented to ministers his plans for a military operation – it was not yet called a war – against the PLO. This was the first time ministers had been told of an intention to operate in Lebanon, and it took them completely by surprise.[28] The cabinet's overriding concern was that an attempt to destroy the PLO in Lebanon might lead to a clash with Syrian troops stationed there, which might, in turn, get out of hand and turn into a full-blown war between Israel and Syria on the Golan Heights. However, at this stage there was no vote on Sharon's proposal, and the cabinet did not have to commit itself to anything definitive; even if ministers were facing a dilemma they could delay any decision until the issue became imminent.

Sharon also began a campaign designed to prepare the American administration for the possibility of an Israeli invasion of Lebanon. Washington was, after all, Israel's most reliable ally, and it must not be faced with a *fait accompli*. In December, at more or less the same time as he presented the operational plans to the Israeli cabinet, Sharon also presented it, though in broad terms only, to the Americans. He invited US Special Ambassador Morris Draper, together with Philip Habib, President Reagan's envoy to the Middle East, to a meeting in Tel Aviv, and explained to them that Israel could not tolerate the shelling of its settlements from south Lebanon. He warned that 'If the terrorists continue to attack us we will wipe them out completely in Lebanon'.[29] Habib reacted furiously to this statement, telling Sharon: 'This is madness. ... The PLO isn't carrying out many raids. There is no need for such an Israeli reaction. We are living in the twentieth century ... you can't just invade a country like this'.[30] The evidence shows that Habib was right; the ceasefire he had brokered in Lebanon was more or less holding, and the PLO was keeping a low profile, perhaps because it knew that Sharon was looking for a pretext to strike at them. But to Sharon this seemed irrelevant and in a further meeting, this time in Washington on 25 May 1982, he repeated the same line of thought to the upper echelons of the State Department. In an eyeball-to-eyeball meeting at the State Department, US Secretary of Defence Alexander Haig warned Sharon: 'This is unsatisfactory ... nothing should be done in Lebanon without an internationally recognized provocation, and the Israeli reaction should be proportionate to that provocation'.[31] It is hard to say whether Haig meant to warn Sharon not to strike, or whether, in fact, he was hinting that under certain conditions Washington would accept an Israeli invasion of Lebanon. For how does one define an 'internationally recognized provocation'? And the same applies to Haig's warning that the Israeli response should be 'proportionate' – for how does one judge what 'proportionate' is? The possible interpretations are simply endless.[32] It seems that Haig did realize that his remark to Sharon was too open-ended, for after the meeting he found it necessary to send a personal letter to Prime Minister Begin (dated

28 May) where he said that he 'hoped there was no ambiguity on the extent of [Washington's] concern about possible future Israeli military actions in Lebanon ... [which] regardless of size, could have consequences none of us could foresee'.[33] To this Begin replied: 'Mr Secretary, my dear friend, the man has not yet been born who will ever obtain from me consent to let Jews be killed by a bloodthirsty enemy'.[34]

Searching for a pretext

With Washington effectively allowing Israel to act in Lebanon, given an 'internationally recognized provocation', the Israelis were now looking for one. On 3 April an agent of Mossad, Ya'akov Bar-Siman-Tov, was shot dead in Paris, and a proposal to invade Lebanon in order to strike at the PLO was made at a meeting of the cabinet on 11 April 1982; five ministers opposed such an operation and Prime Minister Begin decided to put it on hold.[35] Then, on 21 April, an artillery officer was killed in Lebanon and two others were injured when their vehicle hit a mine. In retaliation, the IAF struck at the PLO in Lebanon, killing twenty-three, and the PLO hit back (on 9 May) with rockets and projectiles. But what was so significant about the PLO response was that not one Israeli village, kibbutz or settlement was hit, which seems to indicate that the PLO was signalling: 'We're avoiding hitting Israeli civilian centres, but we are capable of doing so and if provoked sufficiently, we shall do so'.[36] Yet this signal was either misunderstood by the Israelis, or they preferred not to see it this way, and the next day (10 May) Begin asked his cabinet to authorize the invasion of Lebanon by the IDF. This time eleven out of Begin's eighteen ministers were in favour, and 17 May was fixed as the provisional date; but then, with seven of his minsters still resisting, Begin called the operation off just one day before it was due to start. It is interesting to note here that a day before his decision to call off the operation, Begin had received a message from Yasser Arafat via Brian Urquhart, Assistant Under-Secretary General of the UN, in which Arafat told Begin:

> I have learnt more from you as a resistance leader than from anyone else about how to combine politics and military tactics ... you of all people must understand that it is not necessary to face me on the battlefield. Do not send a military force against me. Do not try to break me in Lebanon. You will not succeed.[37]

Incongruously enough, the incident that eventually brought war took place neither in Lebanon nor in Israel, but in London. On 3 June 1982, Palestinian gunmen of the Abu Nidal group shot the Israeli Ambassador to London, Shlomo Argov, and seriously injured him. There was no reason intrinsically why such an incident should turn into a *casus belli* and necessitate a massive Israeli invasion to wipe out the PLO in Lebanon, especially given that

Abu Nidal was a sworn enemy of the PLO and its leader Arafat, whom he often dubbed 'the Jewess' son' and had even sent his people to assassinate him. But such was the mood in Israel following the attempt on the life of the Ambassador, that hardly any minister seemed to care that the assassins were from the Abu Nidal dissident group, and they were willing to accept the view expressed by the Chief of Staff and the Prime Minister that it did not matter which group had attempted to assassinate the Ambassador, and that Israel needed 'to strike at the PLO'.[38]

Thus, at its meeting on 4 June, which was a Friday, the cabinet instructed the IAF to strike at PLO targets in Lebanon. It is conceivable that those ministers and military advisers who favoured an all-out invasion assumed – rightly as we shall soon see – that the PLO would retaliate, and that this, in conjunction with the attempt on the life of the Ambassador, would provide Israel with the long-awaited pretext to invade.

That day at 3.15 p.m., Israeli aircraft took off from bases in Israel and a few minutes later struck at nine PLO targets – the sports centre in Beirut, which was a training camp and a military school, and another seven targets in south Beirut – this was a massive air bombardment on sensitive targets. When this happened Yasser Arafat was not in Lebanon, but in Jeddah, on a mediating mission to end the Iran–Iraq war, which demonstrates how much the Israeli invasion came as a total surprise to him in spite of evidence that the Israelis were planning a massive attack. In the absence of Arafat, his deputy Abu Jihad – the Israelis would later assassinate him – took the decision to hit back, and for twenty-four hours the PLO shelled Israeli settlements in Galilee. With the situation in Lebanon deteriorating by the hour, the Israeli cabinet convened on Saturday 5 June at Begin's residence in Jerusalem, and with almost universal support authorized a military invasion of Lebanon, to which it gave the innocent-sounding name 'Operation Peace for Galilee'; it would later be called 'The War of Lebanon'. The following is resolution no. 676 of the cabinet, authorizing the invasion:

> (a) The IDF is entrusted with the mission of freeing all the Galilee settlements from the range of fire of terrorists, their Headquarters and bases concentrated in Lebanon. (b) The operation is called 'Peace for Galilee'. (c) During the implementation of the decision the Syrian army should not be attacked unless it attacks our forces. (d) The State of Israel continues to strive to sign a peace treaty with independent Lebanon, while maintaining its territorial integrity.[39]

In this resolution the depth of penetration into Lebanon is not specified, but during the cabinet discussion, Defence Minister Sharon made it clear that 'The operation's objective [is] to remove the terrorists from firing range of the northern border, approximately 45 kilometres'.[40] Beirut, the Lebanese capital, also seemed not to be included in the invasion. Indeed, replying to a question raised by minister Simcha Erlich, Sharon said that Beirut was 'out of the picture'.[41] The evidence clearly shows that what the cabinet ministers had in mind was a Litani-type operation, namely a short and small-scale invasion directed against the PLO only. As Foreign Minister Shamir later wrote in his memoirs: 'Operation Peace for Galilee ... was intended to last no more than forty-eight hours, to penetrate Lebanon to a maximum depth of some forty kilometres and to destroy the PLO'.[42]

The Israeli military plan and the opposing forces on the eve of the invasion

The IDF

There is much confusion in the literature regarding Israel's military aims and operational plans in Lebanon. This is understandable, for it is a confusion which springs from the gap between the real operational plans as prepared and known to the military, and the false impression given by Defence Minister Sharon to the Israeli cabinet. There was, contrary to popular belief, only one operational plan for invasion, and this was called 'Big Pines Operation'. It envisaged a deep penetration of troops into Lebanon up to the Beirut–Damascus road – certainly beyond Sharon's '45 kilometres' – destroying the PLO infrastructure, linking up with Maronite Christian troops in the outskirts of Beirut and expelling the PLO from Lebanon, including Beirut. This plan had two versions, one which was known as 'Small Pines Operation' and the other 'Rolling Pines Operation', both of which envisaged a *temporary* limited penetration into Lebanon.[43] The reason why these operational plans were drawn up is that it was not clear to the military planners whether, when a decision to invade had been made by the cabinet, there would be sufficient forces at jump-off points to execute 'Big Pines Operation'. Therefore, it was planned that if and when political authorization to invade was given, the invasion would start immediately with the available forces implementing either 'Small Pines' or 'Rolling Pines' (the difference between the two was marginal) and then, with the arrival and accumulation of more forces, the operation would expand to complete the implementation of 'Big Pines Operation'.[44] In other words, the idea of the military planners was that even without all its forces in jump-off positions, a small invasion would start and then develop into a broader operation which would bring the Israelis to Beirut. Sharon confirmed, after the war, that this was indeed the case, explaining that 'the two versions of Pines [Small and Rolling]' were to lead up to the 'big operational plan in stages' and the 'intention of Pines in *all* the versions [was to bring about] the destruction of the terrorism infrastructure and the occupation of Beirut'.[45]

Unlike the Israeli ministers, who thought in terms of a limited Litani-style campaign in which troops would only penetrate to a depth of 40–45km into

Lebanon, the military planners always knew the way in which Sharon's mind was working and that he intended to get to Beirut. This they had learnt from Sharon himself, who told them, on a visit to Lebanon in February 1982, that there was no point in any action in Lebanon unless it was a thorough one, and no action against the PLO would be thorough unless it drove the PLO out of Beirut.[46] Later in this visit Sharon met Maronite leaders, to whom he said that when Israeli troops arrived in Beirut, 'we are asking you for two things. One to participate militarily in the Beirut battle, and second to sign a peace treaty with Israel'.[47] This suggestion was rejected out of hand by the older Maronite leaders attending, Pierre Gemayel and Camille Chamoun, but not by the young Bashir Gemayel. But, as we shall later see, when Bashir Gemayel was in a position to take part in operations in Beirut, he did sit around letting the Israelis do the job alone. That Sharon's hidden agenda was intended from the very start to go all the way to Beirut also became apparent in a crucial meeting with military commanders on 4 May 1982, when he explained that the solution to the problems caused by the PLO 'lies only in an action that will bring about the actual destruction [of the PLO], destruction of [its] military power, [its] military command posts, and [its] political command centres in Beirut'. At the end of the day, Sharon told his commanders, 'we will get there [to Beirut]'.[48]

So, ironically, the Israeli operational plan to penetrate deep into Lebanon and reach Beirut was known to the Israeli commanders and to the Maronite leadership, but not to the Israeli ministers, to whom Sharon said that 'Beirut is out of the picture' and that the intention was to penetrate no more than 45km north of the Israeli border. Furthermore, even the Syrians knew more about Israel's real intentions in Lebanon than most Israeli ministers did, for after the February meeting with Sharon, and through the mediation of Colonel Jonny Abdo, the Lebanese Chief of Military Intelligence, Bashir Gemayel, contacted the Syrian intelligence chief Mohammed Rahnim, telling him that the Israelis 'are preparing to invade Lebanon'.[49] He then gave Rahnim full details of his talks with Sharon. Furthermore, the PLO in Lebanon knew well before the Israeli ministers did that Sharon was planning a massive operation, penetrating well beyond 45km into Lebanon. For again, after the February meeting with Sharon, Gemayel, through the offices of Jonny Abdo, met Hani Hassan, a leading Palestinian and one of Arafat's closest colleagues, to whom he said 'I have information about a possible Israeli invasion that could reach as far as Beirut'. When Hassan said 'Our information is that the invasion will stop at Sidon', Gemayel replied, 'Don't bet on a limited invasion – expect a bigger one. The aim is to get you out of Lebanon'.[50]

The Israeli invasion was planned as a four-pronged attack of armour, mobile infantry and supporting units. Lebanon, because of its winding, undulating terrain and narrow mountain roads, is a very difficult country to invade because forces can hardly support each other. That is why Israeli planners envisaged an invasion in which forces operated in widely separated areas rather than in combination, namely a western theatre of war (along the coast and up to Beirut), an eastern sector (along the Beka'a and confronting the Syrians) and a central sector (forces 'sandwiched' between the western and eastern sectors).

The spearhead of the western force was to be the 211th armoured brigade, commanded by Colonel Eli Geva. Its task was to sweep along the coastal road, bypass the highly populated areas in the east and head on to Beirut.[51] It was to be followed by the 91st division under the command of Brigadier-General Yitzhak Mordechai, which was to mop up towns and camps and keep the narrow road to the north open; and by other forces coming from east and west, namely Brigadier-General Avigdor Kahalani's 36th division coming from the central sector, and Brigadier-General Amos Yaron's 96th division and elements of the 35th parachute brigade landing from sea. In the central sector, Brigadier-General Menachem Einan's 162nd division was to advance northwards through the Shouf mountains in the direction of the Beirut–Damascus road in an attempt to cut off Syrian forces in Beirut from those in the east.

In the eastern sector of Lebanon, two divisions under the overall command of Major-General Avigdor 'Yanoush' Ben Gal and his deputy Ehud Barak were charged with facing the main Syrian body in the Beka'a valley. It was envisaged that upon orders, forces in this sector would move northeast along the slopes of the Hermon Mountain in the direction of the Beka'a Valley and compel, as Sharon put it, 'a certain Syrian withdrawal'.[52] All Israeli forces in Lebanon were subordinated to the Northern Command, which was headed by Major-General Amir Drori. On the eve of the invasion, a substantial force of about 57,000 men and more than 1,000 tanks was assembled in jump-off positions ready to implement 'Big Pines Operation'; of these 22,000 men and 220 tanks were to carry out operations in the western sector (forces heading to Beirut), and about 35,000 men and 800 tanks to face the Syrians and fight them if attacked or if so ordered. Additionally, the entire IAF was ready to provide air cover and support to the forces operating in Lebanon.

The Syrians and the PLO

On the eve of the Israeli invasion, the Syrian force in Lebanon comprised some 30,000 men, 612 tanks, 150 armoured personnel carriers (APCs), and 300 pieces of artillery and anti-tank guns; additional forces were to join when the Israeli invasion began.[53] Syrian forces were deployed in the Beka'a valley under the protection of a missile system, along the Beirut–Damascus road, and in Beirut itself, where they were organized in the independent 85th brigade.[54] The Syrians had no offensive intentions in Lebanon, and did not wish to clash with the Israelis unless attacked.

PLO forces on the eve of the Israeli invasion comprised some 15,000 combatants and an additional militia which was recruited from among Palestinian refugees. These forces were organized in brigades and divisions, although they seldom operated in large units and preferred small guerrilla-style units.[55] Of these, the Kastel brigade comprised 6,000 combatants, deployed in the area of Sidon (Ein el-Hilwe camp), Tyre (Rachidya and el-Bass camps) and Nabatiya. The Yarmuk brigade comprised 6,000 combatants and was deployed in the area south of the Lebanon Mountain, and the Karameh brigade of 1,500 combatants or so was deployed within the Syrian positions in the area of Hasbaiya and Rachaiya. Most of the headquarters of the various Palestinian organizations were situated in Beirut, where there were also some 6,000 combatants.[56] The PLO forces were equipped with 100 tanks (T-34s, T-54s and T-55s), 350 pieces of artillery, 150 half tracks, more than 200 anti-tank guns and more than 200 anti-aircraft guns.[57]

The war

The race for Beirut

The Israeli cabinet's decision to authorize the IDF to invade Lebanon put an end to the long waiting, and on the morning of 6 June the race for Beirut was under way. The Israeli attack started promisingly. Armoured columns led by the 211th brigade crossed the Israeli–Lebanese border at Rosh Hanikra, bypassed Tyre (at 2 p.m.) and crossed the Litani river over the Kasmia bridge (at 4 p.m.). Early that day, an amphibious force of the 96th division sailed from the ports of Ashdod and Haifa northward to land and join forces on their way to Beirut. Since the landing location was not yet fixed, commanders were kept together on board the cruiser *Geula*, and when the order came (at 9 p.m.) to land at the mouth of the Aouali river, they were sent back by small boats to join their forces at sea.[58] The landing, which brought ashore a mixed force of tanks, APCs and four self-propelled 155mm guns, began at 11 p.m., with a marine commando unit taking positions and securing the beach against any hostile reception. After the landing, the force dug in, prepared to stay overnight, and continued to absorb reinforcements which arrived during the night; it then started moving towards Damour on the way to Beirut. On the morning of 7 June, the 36th division, coming cross-country from the central sector, linked up with the coastal column, encircled Sidon and besieged the Ein el-Hilwe camp outside the town. On 9 June the advance to Beirut continued, and on 10 June the 211th armoured brigade reached Kefar Sil, just south of the capital. There it was checked and met stiff resistance from a PLO force. This was overcome after an infantry force had been brought up to clear the way. After capturing Kefar Sil, the column resumed its advance until it reached the southern tip of Beirut's international airport.

While the advance along the coast continued, the 35th paratroop brigade, which had been landed at the Aouali river on the first night of the invasion, was advancing through the mountains in an attempt to link up, as planned, with the Maronites just outside Beirut in Baabda; the link-up was achieved on

Map 6 Lebanon, 'Operation Peace for Galilee' 6–11 June 1982

13 June. For the next two weeks Israeli forces continued to push north and encircle Beirut, and by 1 July the capital, which Sharon had told the cabinet was 'out of the picture', was very much in the picture and under siege. PLO guerrillas, 500,000 Palestinians, Moslem Lebanese civilians and the 85th Syrian brigade, were all encircled; the siege would last seventy days.

Fighting the Syrians

In the 1978 Litani campaign, as has been shown, Israeli troops operating in the Lebanon did not clash with Syrian forces. This was mainly because special precautions were taken by the Israelis not to provoke the Syrians in any way. Thus troop movements were always away from the Syrians, neither in their direction nor under their noses, and messages were transmitted to Damascus that the operation was limited and aimed only against the PLO. But now it was all different. Sharon, as we have already explained, considered the Syrian presence in Lebanon and its missile system in the Beka'a valley to be an immense problem for Israel, and although he understood that the cabinet was unlikely to approve an operation against the Syrians, he was nevertheless determined to make the most of the situation and provoke the Syrians to shoot first, in which case Israeli troops would be free to hit back – and hard.

General Avigdor ('Yanoush') Ben Gal, a veteran military commander who had distinguished himself in the Yom Kippur War and was now the overall commander of the eastern front, later explained to the author that it was clear to him and his colleagues that they were heading for a direct confrontation with the Syrians in Lebanon.[59] If one looks at 'the structure and composition of the force', Ben Gal explained, 'one realizes *a priori* that [Israel had intended] to fight against a regular Syrian army ... there was a force with a lot of artillery ... combat helicopters ... and hundreds of tanks'.[60] And as General Amir Drori, OC Northern Command, later testified: 'the big question was whether or not the Syrians would intervene ... *and it was clear to us that they would [intervene]*'.[61] A war game called *Shoshanim* ('Roses'), which took place on 8 March 1982 to test the operational plans, showed that, without any doubt, Israeli forces would clash with the Syrians in Lebanon.[62] Such high probability of a battle with the Syrians in Lebanon was frequently discussed in meetings between Defence Minister Sharon and the military. For instance, on 4 May 1982 at the HQ of Northern Command, military commanders warned Sharon – who was perhaps the ablest strategist among them and certainly understood what they meant – that the present composition of Israeli forces and their operational plans was sure to lead to a clash with the Syrians. The commanders' comments were professional in character, namely that the advance of substantial Israeli forces near the Syrian–Lebanese border in the direction of the Beirut–Damascus road and just under the noses of Syrian guns, as well as the concentration of a large number of Israeli troops close to the town of Jezzin, where Syrian forces were stationed, would certainly result in military contact with the Syrians.[63] Sharon, however, does not seem to have sought guidance from his generals – he had already decided his policy and thus rejected any alteration of the plans. For his overriding, though hidden, aim, as we have already explained, was to clash with the Syrians, and he was determined to provoke them. For Sharon, the war which cabinet ministers regarded as aimed at breaking the back of the PLO was also an opportunity to confront the Syrians in Lebanon.

As his military commanders had predicted – and as Sharon probably hoped – between 8 and 11 June Israeli and Syrian forces clashed in Lebanon. This confrontation had four crucial and significant turning points. First was the battle in Jezzin, which signalled the beginning of the Israeli–Syrian engagement; second was the battle in Ein Zhalata, which signalled the failure of the Israeli attempt to 'push' the Syrians – to use Sharon's jargon – out of the Beka'a without confronting them head-on; third was the head-on offensive against the Syrians; and fourth, finally, was the destruction of their missile system in the Beka'a.

After crossing into Lebanon on the first day of the war, the advancing Israeli forces in the eastern sector moved towards the Hasbaiya area where, at around noon, the Syrians opened fire.[64] When this happened Sharon issued instructions to Chief of Staff Eitan to prepare forces for the central sector to move north and outflank the Syrians; he gave this order without consulting the cabinet, but it seems he was confident that he could get its backing. At a late-night meeting of the cabinet in Jerusalem, Sharon reported: 'At noon the Syrians opened artillery fire without being fired at, from [their] heavy D-30 cannons from their emplacements, on our ... forces and we sustained several casualties'.[65] To overcome this resistance, Sharon – his mind always teemed with original ideas, and he could sustain these with technical arguments – proposed that ministers choose between two options: either a frontal assault against the Syrian forces, which he knew the cabinet would not want to approve and probably preferred them not to, or 'An advance [of Israeli forces] to the north in an attempt [to outflank] and confront the rear of the Syrians', which he rightly assumed would be seen as the lesser of two evils and as a result would be the ministers' preferred option.[66] A third option, which was simply not to take any action, for after all the cabinet did not wish any confrontation with the Syrians in Lebanon, was never put forward. As for the second option, namely the outflanking move, this was favoured by the Prime Minister, who swung his weight in support of it and praised it as 'Hannibal's manoeuvre', so leading his cabinet to endorse it (resolution 690).[67] The cabinet was not, however, aware of two crucial facts which Sharon had failed to mention; first, that in order to implement the proposed plan forces would have to pass through the emplacement of Jezzin, a critical strategic point which was held by a Syrian infantry battalion and an armoured force of T-55s and which, on the night of 6 June, was reinforced by another infantry battalion and commandos.[68] Second, that an outflanking manoeuvre would not necessarily induce the Syrians to withdraw, rather it might compel them to dig in and fight in an attempt to prevent the advancing Israelis from reaching the Beirut–Damascus road, thus cutting off the bulk of Syrian troops in Beirut from those in Damascus and the Beka'a valley. The decision of the cabinet was executed by the 162nd division, and led to a fierce clash with Syrian forces in Jezzin on 8 June. Calling up reinforcements, the Syrians fought back in fury and inflicted serious casualties on the Israelis. In the end, however, they gave way and the Israelis took Jezzin.[69]

But soon the battle took a turn for the worse, and the whole outlook in the eastern section of Lebanon changed dramatically when a force of the 162nd Israeli division ran into a Syrian trap and was checked at a place called Ein Zhalata. This was significant, because it meant that the force whose task was to outflank the Syrians could no longer proceed with its mission.[70] Sharon, with his 'Hannibal manoeuvre' bogged down, decided to recast his plan and ordered, at a meeting with commanders on the morning of 9 June, that Ben Gal's forces move northwards, as soon and as fast as possible, and destroy the Syrian 1st division which was just coming down from Syria as a reinforcement. This, in military terms, meant giving up the attempt to 'push' the Syrians by an outflanking manoeuvre, and instead confronting them head-on. The commanders who had attended the meeting with Sharon and understood that the implications of the Defence Minister's instruction were an all-out head-on offensive against the Syrians, resisted. Yekutiel Adam, a former deputy chief of staff – he would later be killed in a PLO ambush – stood up and bluntly asked Sharon whether his order did not 'contradict the objectives set by the cabinet [not to attack the Syrians]'.[71] Sharon disregarded this challenge, overruled Adam, who gave way in face of Sharon's force of personality and position, and went on to instruct General Ben Gal to go ahead with the mission.

With the 162nd division bogged down in Ein Zhalata and Ben Gal's forces moving straight towards the Syrians, a new problem emerged: the Syrian missile 'umbrella' which hindered the IAF from providing air support to the ground forces. It is often alleged that Sharon now saw an opportunity to strike at the missile system under the pretext of aiding the troops on the ground. Indeed, in a cabinet meeting on Wednesday 9 June, Sharon proposed destroying the missile system, marshalling all his arguments for taking this step. The Prime Minister was in favour – this Sharon already knew for he had discussed it with him previously – but other ministers had qualms about the proposed operation, fearing that it might escalate the war even further. When ministers expressed tentative reservations Sharon forced their hand by arguing that bombing the missile system was essential to 'minimize Israeli casualties', for devoid of air support they would be exposed to enemy fire. This argument had its effect, and when the old, wise and experienced Minister of the Interior Dr Yosef Burg agreed to support the operation, Sharon knew that he had won over the cabinet.[72]

This major operation against the Syrian missile system in the Beka'a was delivered that day at 2 p.m. by ninety-six F-15 and F-16 aircraft which, in a most efficient strike and within two and a half hours, knocked out seventeen of nineteen Syrian batteries and severely damaged the remaining two, which were also knocked out in a renewed attack on the next day. In the course of this assault, the Syrian air force intervened and lost ninety-six Migs without any cost to the Israelis.[73] This was a sensational triumph for the IAF, one which can be compared only with its successes on the morning of 5 June 1967, when it had destroyed almost the entire Egyptian air force on the ground, or its successful bombing of the Iraqi nuclear reactor on 7 June 1981. Following this massive air strike, Israeli forces on the ground embarked on an all-out assault against the 1st and 3rd Syrian armoured divisions, attacking them along the entire line, particularly east and west of Lake Karoun.

On 11 June, a ceasefire between Israel and Syria in the eastern sector of Lebanon came into effect; at this stage the Syrians still held the Beirut–Damascus road, but later, on Sharon's instructions, Israeli troops crept forwards and captured it. Thus, with the fight against the Syrians in Lebanon over, Sharon could congratulate himself on having achieved his hidden agenda. Although his colleagues had opposed any clash with the Syrians in Lebanon, he had managed to provoke the Syrians, and when they opened fire his forces had hit back and dislodged them from their positions. Moreover, by capturing the Beirut–Damascus road Sharon had effectively cut off the Syrians in Beirut from the bulk of their forces in the eastern part of Lebanon, a move which was crucial in order to tighten the noose on Beirut. And perhaps most important of all, he had managed to persuade the cabinet to approve a major air strike against the Syrian missile system and subsequently succeeded in destroying it.

Beirut under siege

The battle with the Syrians was short and decisive, but this was not to be the case in Beirut, where Arafat and his men dug in and became inextricably mingled with the civilian population, rather than leaving Beirut as the Israelis wished them to do. Bashir Gemayel – by now the undisputed Maronite Christian leader in Lebanon – was adamant in refusing to send his men into Beirut to clear it of the PLO. Even the daring Sharon would not send troops into an Arab capital to conduct bitter street-fighting with the PLO. With few options left, Sharon ordered his military command to tighten the siege on Beirut, to bomb areas where the PLO was hiding, and to take other measures such as cutting off water and electricity supplies and stopping food from reaching the population. The line of thought behind this brutal policy was that, if pressed hard enough, the people and government of Beirut would eventually demand Arafat's departure in order to save themselves from further hardships. So while the IAF bombed relentlessly, and guns poured salvo upon salvo into West Beirut, Israeli troops were tightening the noose around the Palestinian areas. On 3 July they seized the green line separating East and West Beirut, and took control of the Museum checkpoint in Gallery Samaan. This meant that West Beirut was totally sealed off from its eastern counterpart. On 4 July the Israelis cut off all food, water and fuel supplies and took over Beirut's international airport. At a meeting in Tel Aviv on 11 July, Sharon instructed the air force to hit 'terrorist camps' in the south of Beirut which, as Sharon put it, 'must be destroyed, razed to the ground'. More than 500 buildings were targeted, and destroyed from the air or by artillery, with naval vessels offshore joining the battle by launching missiles into West Beirut.

But not all went well, for as the war dragged on, the number of casualties mounted and plans to enter Beirut were being drawn up, opposition to Sharon began to grow within the ranks of the IDF. Around mid-July, the commander of the 211st armoured brigade, who had led the Israeli column along the coastal axis up to Beirut, told Sharon 'this is not our fight ... we must not let ourselves be dragged into Lebanon's internal affairs'.[74] He then took the unusual step of leaving his brigade while the war was still in progress, and was later relieved of his command. This was a significant event, for never before in Israel's military history had a commander of this rank abandoned his troops and, more than anything, it came to reflect a growing uneasiness among the rank and file. It was indeed bad news for Sharon (officially Defence Minister but effectively super-chief of staff of the IDF in all but name), who, like many great military commanders, had a clear picture of the battle and how he would win it, but failed to carry his subordinates with him.

But growing uneasiness within the IDF, and even among ministers, was still not strong enough to put an end to Israeli activities in Lebanon, and under Sharon's instructions pressure on the PLO and the Syrians in Beirut grew. On 4–5 August IDF troops entered the Hippodrome, thus increasing the pressure on the besieged forces, and on 9 August an intense artillery barrage on Beirut was accompanied by massive IAF attacks on the Palestinian refugee camps of Sabra, Shatilla and Bourj el Barajne. Three days later, on 12 August, the IAF conducted yet another massive air bombardment, which lasted for more than twelve hours; unofficial reports put the number of people killed in what became known as 'Black Thursday' at 300.

With Beirut in ruins and the Israelis intensifying the pressure, the siege became unendurable and the Lebanese government sent Chief of Intelligence Jonny Abdo to Arafat as a special emissary, with the demand that Arafat leave Beirut with his men in order to end Israeli harassment of the Lebanese.[75] Without the support of the government of Lebanon, and with the Israeli noose tightening about him, Arafat – with his shrewd sense of reality – came to realize that this was the end of the game. So he acquiesced to the Lebanese government's demand, and deposited a letter to this effect in the hands of Lebanese Prime Minister Shafiq al-Wazzan.[76] On 22 August the first PLO contingent of 379 men left Beirut, and over the course of the next twelve days 14,398 Palestinians were evacuated; Arafat left on 30 August 1982, and 5,200 Syrian troops also departed.[77]

On 23 August, Bashir Gemayel was elected President of Lebanon, and should have taken office on 23 September, but – as things go in Lebanon – he was assassinated on 14 September in Ashrafiya. This was a mortal blow to Sharon's plan in Lebanon, for he had invested enormously in Gemayel and hoped he would sign a peace treaty with Israel. The bomb that killed Gemayel destroyed every reasonable chance that Israel and Lebanon could sign a workable peace treaty. To 'restore order', Israeli troops, on 16 September at 5.00 p.m., marched into Beirut and took up positions there ('Operation Moach Ha'barzel'). This was the first time Israel had ever occupied an Arab capital. Yet there was still more to come. Between 16 and 18 September, with the approval of the Israelis, the Maronite Phalangist militia entered the refugee camps of Sabra and Shatilla to 'clean out' the 2,000 PLO guerillas who, according to reports, were still hiding there.[78] But, again, as things go in Lebanon, they massacred between 600 and 700 Palestinians – children, women and men. The Israelis did not take part in the killing, although they did provide artillery support and also – contrary to Israeli official statements – Israeli paratroopers of the 35th brigade were present in the camps while the killing was still under way or immediately after it.[79] The assassination of Gemayel and the massacre which followed it symbolizes, perhaps more than anything else, the total collapse of Israel's disastrous adventure in Lebanon in 1982. It had cost her more than 700 lives, and led to world condemnation.

The Lebanon War and Israeli society

The Lebanon invasion marked a new era in the attitude of the Israelis to war. If between 1948 and 1967 Israelis had shown an unconditional willingness to serve and to sacrifice and had hardly ever expressed criticism of their leadership, and if after 1967, in spite of growing criticism and dissent, Israelis were still willing to take up arms and rally behind their leadership in war, then in 1982, for the first time in Israel's history, Israelis criticized and also took a stand by refusing to cooperate and fight.

The Lebanon War was perhaps the most controversial of all of Israel's wars, and it broke the former national consensus on defence and encouraged the previously little known phenomenon of conscientious objection. While the war was still in progress, eighty-six reservists, including fifteen officers, had sent a letter to the government which became known as the 'Letter of the 100', stating their opposition to the war and requesting to do their reserve duty not in Lebanon but within Israeli territory.[80] A movement called 'Soldiers against Silence' was formed, calling for the removal from office of the Defence Minister and for an immediate end to the war. By September 1982, over 500 Israelis had enrolled as supporters of a new organization called

Yesh Gvul, which became the spearhead of opposition to the war. After the massacres in Sabra and Shatilla, opposition to the war grew dramatically, and the number of men expressing their unwillingness to serve in Lebanon soared.[81] In an attempt to keep the phenomenon of refusal to serve under the carpet, the authorities often came to 'private arrangements' with soldiers. According to a report in the *New York Times* citing an Israeli source, hundreds of refusers had been spared jail by the government to avoid publicity.[82] But there were still people who were sent to jail. By March 1983, twenty-eight people were known to have served time in prison rather than in Lebanon, and by September eighty-six jail sentences are known to have been given to reservists; by January 1985, thirty months after the invasion, 143 reservists had been jailed for refusal to serve in Lebanon.[83] These may be insignificant numbers for a state whose population at the time exceeded four million but, given that refusal to serve and fight was virtually unknown before this war, the figures are indeed significant and represent an important attack on what had been taboo in Israeli society.

The war also prompted some of the biggest demonstrations in the history of the state. On 26 July, while war was still raging in Lebanon, 10,000 civilians gathered in Tel Aviv to protest, and as one minister in Begin's cabinet put it: 'It was the first time in the history of Israel that such an event had taken place during the course of a war'.[84] Public agitation over the continuing war, its accompanying casualty list, and such horrors as were manifested at Sabra and Shatilla, brought to Tel Aviv in September more than 400,000 protesters, whose pressure led to the establishment of a Commission of Inquiry, whose findings when published led to the removal from office of the architect of the war, Ariel Sharon. The war in Lebanon was also Israel's first ever war in which a senior military commander, Colonel Eli Geva, resigned while war was still in progress, and it was the first time ever that a whole brigade let it be known that if called to serve in Lebanon it would refuse to obey orders.[85]

That Israelis were reluctant to take part in the war is often explained in terms of this being a 'war of choice', namely a fight which was not forced on Israel but rather one which it had forced on one of its neighbours. But this explanation is flawed, for the 1982 war was not the first 'war of choice' Israel had experienced. In 1956, for example, Israel forced a war on Egypt, and eleven years later, in June 1967, it repeated this exercise, forcing a war on Egypt and then on Syria. Yet the difference between then and now was that in 1956 and 1967 the Israelis had fully cooperated and supported the government in its war policy and were willing to take up arms, whereas now large segments of society, as we have shown, were strongly against the war, some even refusing to take part in it. The explanation for this change of attitude, so it seems, has to do more with a change of perception by the Israelis with regard to the level of the external danger to their state and existence. For both in 1956 and again in 1967, they had felt – rightly or wrongly – that a great external threat still existed and that they were being asked to take up arms in order to remove an acute danger. But in 1982 things looked different. For the peace with Egypt (which was holding well despite Israel's invading Lebanon) seemed to remove the danger to Israel's existence, while in the north and east the Golan Heights and the West Bank seemed to provide a buffer zone against any attempt to invade the country. With this in mind, Israelis felt less threatened than before and were thus more reluctant to take up arms and fight in wars.

CHAPTER SIX

Intifada

1987–93

The *Intifada* – the Palestinian uprising in the Gaza Strip, the West Bank and Jerusalem from 1987 to 1993 – imposed on the IDF and on Israeli society as a whole a new sort of warfare, one which Israel found difficult to cope with.[1] Very different from Israel's previous wars, the Palestinian uprising, nevertheless, had one common feature with the Six Day War of June 1967, and particularly with the Yom Kippur War of October 1973, and that is the way it surprised the Israelis, catching them off-guard and completely unprepared both mentally and physically for this new challenge. How did the *Intifada* come about? Who were the rebels and what were their motives? What effect did the uprising have on the Israelis?

The surprise

It is natural to cling to the last in a train of incidents as being the actual cause of great events. We often say such things as: 'The killing of four Christians by a Palestinian gunman at a church in East Beirut on 13 April 1975 caused the civil war in Lebanon', or 'The attempt on the life of Israel's Ambassador to London, Shlomo Argov, on 3 June 1982, caused the Israeli invasion of Lebanon'. But rather than being the causes, these incidents should be regarded as the triggers, the sparks, the last straw in an accumulation of incidents which leads to the big event. This is how we should regard the traffic accident, on Tuesday 8 December 1987, between an Israeli vehicle and a car carrying Palestinian labourers returning from a day's work in Israel, which touched off the *Intifada*; it was the spark rather than the real cause of the uprising. Indeed, there have been traffic accidents like this before, and there was nothing to suggest that this particular one, in which four Palestinians were killed and several others injured, should lead to an all-out revolt which would last almost six years and result in hundreds of casualties on both the Israeli and Palestinian sides. But such was the tension, and so charged the atmosphere in the occupied territories at that time, that even a traffic accident was sufficient to trigger a big explosion, particularly since rumours persisted that this was not a straightforward accident but an act of vengeance by the Israeli driver, whose relative, Shlomo Sekle, had been stabbed to death in the *Souk* of Gaza two days earlier.[2] The view that this was not an innocent accident was reinforced by a statement issued by PLO leader Yasser Arafat in Tunis on 13 December 1987, saying that the killing of the four was a 'premeditated Israeli attack'.[3]

Big gatherings are notorious for having the potential to turn into ugly demonstrations, and this is precisely what happened when hundreds of mourners in Jabalya, Gaza's largest and poorest camp where more than 60,000 refugees dwell, returned from the funerals of the four victims of the accident and turned on Israeli troops stationed in the area, hurling stones and bottles at them. These, we now know, were the first events of what soon became known as the *Intifada*.

At first, the Israeli military and political establishment failed to acknowledge the real nature of the disturbances which were still confined to the Gaza Strip. They thought – and on the face of it there was no reason for them to think otherwise – that this was no more than a flare-up of unrest not radically different from previous periods of disorder.[4] So much so that even Yitzhak Rabin, an experienced soldier and by then Defence Minister in Yitzhak Shamir's Likud–Labour government, did not even cancel his previously scheduled trip to Washington (10 December), where he was due, among other things, to agree the final price for seventy F-16 fighter planes that Israel was intending to purchase from the US. With hindsight, it is ironic that Israel was about to buy perhaps the most sophisticated weapons on the market, without realizing that in the war which had already started in the territories these weapons would be totally useless. What is more puzzling is that, even after ten days of intense disturbances in the territories, the Israeli government was still unaware of the real nature of the events. Rabin demonstrated this when, upon his return to the country on 21 December, he convened an airport press conference where he stated that 'Iran and Syria were behind the unrest in the territories'.[5] And Prime Minister Shamir, who in the absence of Rabin was also the acting Defence Minister, put the blame for inflaming the situation on the leadership of the PLO. These, we now know, were totally unfounded statements, for the reality is that neither Iran nor Syria was involved in inciting the Palestinians, and they were as surprised as both the PLO and indeed the Israelis by the outburst of violence.[6]

With the benefit of hindsight, which should not, however, be seen as wisdom after the event, we can categorically state that the *Intifada* was not, as is sometimes alleged, a wholly unexpected phenomenon. Indeed, there had been plenty of indications that a major transformation was underway in the occupied territories, that forces were bubbling under the surface and that there was considerable unrest in the Gaza Strip and the West Bank. Figures for the West Bank, which were available to the Israelis on the eve of the uprising, show that between April 1986 and May 1987 there was a weekly average of fifty-six violent demonstrations, involving stone throwing, blocking of roads, raising of the banned Palestinian flag, distributing of leaflets, burning tyres and daubing walls with nationalist graffiti. There was also an average of four incidents a week involving the use of firearms, knives, explosives and petrol bombs, in addition to a weekly arrest of an average of eighty-one West Bankers accused of taking part in demonstrations or engaging in what the Israelis had defined as 'acts of terrorism'.[7] Compared with the previous year these figures indicate a stunning rise of 133 per cent in the number of demonstrations, 183 per cent in the burning of tyres (487 incidents up from 172), 140 per cent in the throwing of stones, and 68 per cent in the blocking of roads.[8] In October 1987, just before the *Intifada* broke out, one correspondent had reported:

> You can feel the tension. Worshippers – Jew and Moslem alike – scurry rather than walk. Tourists cluster together and are protected by armed soldiers. ... In Gaza, you drive a car with Israeli plates at peril. ... The marketplaces are empty of Israeli shoppers and thousands of Gazans have stayed away from jobs in Israel – some in protest, others out of fear. ... Fear, suspicion and growing hatred have replaced any hope of dialogue.[9]

There was also a remarkable change in the quality of Palestinian operations directed against the Israelis, which had become bolder and more daring than in the past, as was manifested in the killing of an Israeli soldier who was shot in broad daylight in the main street of Gaza, in August 1987.

Israeli troops on the ground realized that methods which had been used in the past to dispel demonstrations (which as we have already shown were rife in the pre-uprising period) were not, on the eve of the *Intifada*, as effective as they had previously been. Firing into the air, for instance, which had in the past caused Palestinian demonstrators to scatter, was no longer effective; neither was the method commonly used to disperse college girls, which was for an Israeli soldier to open his fly and begin tugging down his pants. But then, as the saying goes, 'Eyes have they but they see not', and the Israeli political-military leadership had failed, in spite of available information (as in October 1973), to read the writing on the wall and see that what they were facing was a much more serious event than a bout of violence.

A social uprising

The rebels: their motives and aims

Who were the rebels? Schiff and Ya'ari say they were first and foremost 'the poor ... the forsaken and forgotten at the bottom of the social heap'.[10] These were desperate people, mostly refugees from previous wars between Israel and the Arabs, who had been living in appalling, disgraceful, harsh and insanitary conditions in the occupied territories, mainly in Gaza's eight refugee camps, where unemployment was running at 50–60 per cent and where large families, often two or three generations, were crammed into small tumbledown dwellings. Their conditions and standards of living were better than they had been when Israel had occupied the territories twenty years before – telephone subscribers multiplied sixfold, and the number of private cars grew tenfold – but standards were still appalling. In 1973 the Israelis embarked on a programme aimed at rehabilitating the refugees by constructing apartments and providing money to inhabitants to build their own houses. But this was done at a snail's pace and fell short of Palestinians' expectations. On the eve of the *Intifada* only 8,600 families had been moved to new housing, and at this rate it was apparent that the camps would never be dismantled, for it would take about fifty years to build new homes for the other 33,000 families, while natural increase proceeded at more than double the pace of construction.[11] This was frustrating, especially for the younger generation of Palestinians, many of whom were working in Israel, where high standards of living demonstrated to them how appalling was their own situation.[12]

Indeed, most of the demonstrators, at least on the eve of the uprising, were labourers who worked from dawn to dusk in 'dirty jobs' of the sort Israelis shunned; they knew the Israelis well and spoke their language. But when questioned, after being arrested by the Israelis, regarding their motives in joining the *Intifada*, they often complained of injustice done to them by Israeli employers. They talked of the harsh way they were treated by a country which demanded they pay social security – which they knew would never be repaid to them – but also banned them from joining labour unions and establishing workers' committees. They were humiliated and often delayed for hours with no explanation at the Erez Checkpoint, which is the main gate from the Gaza Strip to Israel, and they were occasionally forced to imitate barking, bleating, or other animal sounds before being allowed to cross into Israel. They were not allowed to stay overnight in Israel and, while many of them did make the long daily journey back home, some preferred to break the law and hide overnight in Israel to spare themselves the humiliation at the Erez crossing just to emerge the next morning at their working place. These people, who became the spearhead of the *Intifada*, had no wish to cultivate Palestinian national consciousness, and in fact many of them knew little about the Palestinian National Covenant or about such concepts as 'the right to self-determination'. What they were looking for when joining the demonstrations was simply a better life.

Another group to join the *Intifada* were graduates. In the 1970s graduates could easily find jobs, especially in the Gulf, but the crisis in the oil economies and fewer opportunities in Jordan meant that some 15,000 Palestinian college graduates were unemployed on the eve of the *Intifada*; they were desperate and bored and they directed their anger and frustration at the Israelis. The Israelis, in turn, were aghast, for after all it was during the twenty years of occupation that they had allowed the building of seven new universities on the West Bank, and when graduates of these institutions now joined the uprising, the Israelis felt betrayed; they felt that the graduates were biting the hand which had fed them.

Islamic militants, such as a group calling itself 'Islamic Jihad', also involved themselves the moment the first attacks on the Israelis started. Established in 1981, after splitting from the Moslem Brotherhood in the occupied territories, Islamic Jihad first became widely known in February 1986, when some of its members tossed a grenade at a group of Israeli soldiers and Jewish settlers. This was followed by more attacks, notably in October 1986, when Islamic Jihad activists threw hand grenades at an Israeli military graduation ceremony at the Western Wall. At a later stage of the *Intifada* another fundamentalist group, Hamas, would join and play a leading part in the revolt.

The rebels of all groups represented a new generation of Palestinians, who after twenty years of Israeli occupation were far more militant and radical than previous generations, and whose role models were not Yasser Arafat, George Habash and others of the PLO old guard, but rather such young daring activists as the six Palestinians who escaped from the Gaza Central Prison in May 1987 and later in October were shot dead in a shoot-out with *Shin Bet*, Israel's internal security police. Another role model to catch the imagination of these young Palestinians was the young member of Ahmed Jibril's Syrian-backed PFLP, who on 25 November 1987 – just before the outbreak of the *Intifada* – flew across the Lebanese border in an ultra-light hang-glider, landed in a field, entered a nearby Israeli army camp and mowed down six soldiers and wounded thirteen before being shot.[13] In the occupied territories the attack caused 'widespread satisfaction', and it was seen as a 'heroic operation … which destroyed the myth of Israeli defences'.[14] Indeed, what these daring operations did was to help puncture Israel's image of invincibility among young Palestinians in the occupied territories, and prepare them, above all mentally, for the *Intifada*.

The explosion

Palestinian action – Israeli reaction

The day after the funerals at Jabalia, Palestinians in the Gaza Strip blocked roads with rocks, tyres, broken furniture and steel sewage pipes; they also stoned Israeli soldiers. Unlike the events of the previous day, which had been spontaneous, these were preplanned by local leaders. When met by a hail of stones, Israeli troops resorted to live ammunition, and this resulted in the killing of seventeen-year-old Hatem Abu Sisi, who was shot by a bullet through the heart and became the first 'martyr' of the *Intifada*. From Jabalya the demonstrations and riots spread like a wildfire to other refugee camps – to Khan Yunis, al Bourej, Nuseirat and Ma'azi, and then to Rafah. They then spread to the more secular and affluent West Bank – to Balata, Kalandia and other villages and towns. This opening wave of riots lasted twelve consecutive days and was particularly intense in the Gaza Strip, where it seemed as if all ages and classes were out on the streets confronting the Israelis.

It was clear from the start that the IDF was ill prepared and had no ready made answer to the problem of civil resistance on this scale, in which the weapons used by the rebels were so primitive that Israel's tanks, aeroplanes, rockets and artillery lost all significance. It was an odd situation, in which the Israelis were so powerful that they could not apply their might and, ironically, if they were to be able to deal effectively with the problem without shooting the demonstrators – for Israel could not afford this due to public opinion at home and abroad – they had to downgrade their weapons. It is important to note here that the Palestinians' policy was not to resort to arms, for they knew that if they did use guns the Israelis would then have a pretext to use their might and crush the uprising by using their more sophisticated arms. What the Israeli troops needed was the most basic and elementary riot gear such as shields, helmets, clubs and tear gas, but these were all in short supply, and as Deputy Chief of Staff Ehud Barak later admitted, 'We were not technically prepared to deal with a violent popular riot on this scale'.[15]

Why the Israelis were not 'technically' prepared for the outbreak of an uprising is hard to explain, but the fact remains that although officials at the defence ministry did contemplate, in the years before the *Intifada*, the idea of purchasing vehicles equipped with water cannon for dispersing demonstrations, as well as other anti-riot devices such as electric arrows, slippery dust to coat the streets, nets for trapping demonstrators, and sneeze bombs, no action had followed. Special dogs were trained to disperse demonstrators, but were never throughout the twenty years of occupation put on the streets lest Israel be accused of resorting to methods used in South Africa or Nazi Germany. What was also evident from the start was that the Israelis lacked any experience in dealing with large-scale riots. In the past it had been suggested that special units be trained to deal with potential riots, but the army High Command objected to this, preferring to have army units serve occasionally in the territories so they could gain some experience in dealing with civil unrest and get to know the terrain.

During the opening days and weeks of the *Intifada* the Israeli High Command was in a state of disarray; it was simply at a loss and did not know how to deal with the new warfare which had been imposed on it. Its first move, however, was to react to calls for reinforcement, and within three days the number of troops patrolling the occupied territories had increased three-fold in comparison to normal times.[16] Although renowned for its flexibility and ability to alter and adapt itself to changing situations, the Israeli High Command was, in the opening phases of the uprising, no match for the Palestinians, whose ability to devise quick new methods to adapt to changes in the IDF's tactics had made the latter obsolete even before they were fully implemented. Thus, when the Israelis decided that foot patrols were ineffective in dealing with the riots, and that they should turn to motorized patrols in jeeps and command cars, the Palestinians immediately reacted by sprinkling the roads with nails to puncture the tyres of the Israeli vehicles.

Israel's worst fear was that the riots might spread to Jerusalem, where the international media had a strong presence and could broadcast the disturbances and Israeli reaction to the world. This nightmare came true when, on 19 December 1987, riots started simultaneously in a number of locations in the capital, with no fewer than 5,000 Palestinians taking part in them. East Jerusalem now experienced the worst violence since the Six Day War of June 1967, and the scenes previously seen on the streets of the Gaza Strip and West Bank of barricades, burning tyres, Palestinian flags and stone-throwing were evident in Jerusalem. Demonstrators set fire to municipal vehicles and stoned Israeli-owned restaurants in East Jerusalem, and cars carrying Israeli plates passing through the Arab districts of Jerusalem – Abu Dis, Shuafat, Jebel Mukaber and Azariah.

Israeli strategy in Jerusalem was a systematic campaign of harassment aimed at putting indirect but intense pressure on the Palestinians: they stopped and searched Arab cars, checked the condition of windscreen wipers and seat belts or made sure that the driver and passengers had paid their taxes. Furthermore, a new rule forbade Moslems from outside the city to pray at the al-Haram al-Sharif, the noble sanctuary, where the Mosque of Omar and the al-Aqsa Mosque had stood for almost 1,500 years; everyone entering a mosque in Jerusalem was checked for this purpose. In addition, neighbourhoods where violence recurred were placed under curfew. But still the disturbances continued.

The local Palestinian leadership in the Gaza Strip and West Bank was quick to organize itself and give a clear direction to what seemed to be, at first sight, utter chaos. Representatives of Fatah (Yasser Arafat), the Popular Front (George Habash), the Democratic Front (Naif Hawatmeh), the Palestine Communist Party and Islamic Jihad all joined forces against the common enemy, Israel, and established the 'Unified National Leadership of the Uprising' (UNLU) which became the coordinating body of the *Intifada* on the West Bank. The names of UNLU's leaders remained anonymous, partly because of the fear that revealing their identity might lead to a situation where fellow Palestinians refused to obey their instructions, for after all they were petty, often unknown, local leaders. There was also the fear that coming out into the open might invite pressure from the PLO, which was alarmed from the start in case the local leadership took over and marginalized it. And obviously, if UNLU leaders were to identify themselves it would become much easier for Israeli security services to arrest them.

The UNLU leaders communicated to and led the Palestinians by issuing leaflets and communiqués in which they encouraged their followers to take direct action against the Israelis. The 60,000 copies of the first communiqué were issued on 10 January 1988.[17] It called on 'the heroes of the stone and firebomb war to redouble the revolutionary content ... shake the oppressive regime down to its foundations [and create] ... inviolable unity'. More practically it called on the Palestinians to take the following measures:

> All roads must be closed to the occupation forces ... its cowardly soldiers must be prevented from entering refugee camps and large population centres by barricades and burning tyres. ... Stones must land on the heads of the occupying soldiers and those who collaborate with them. Palestinian flags are to be flown from minarets, churches, rooftops, and electricity poles everywhere. ... We must set the ground burning under the feet of the occupiers. Let the whole world know that the volcanic uprising that has ignited the Palestinian people will not cease until the achievement of independence in a Palestinian state whose capital is Jerusalem.[18]

In this and other communiqués the aims of the uprising were further crystallized, and included among others: forcing the withdrawal of the IDF from cities, towns and refugee camps; evacuating Ariel Sharon from his house in the Old City of Jerusalem;[19] repealing the Emergency Regulations (such as administrative detention, deportation, the demolition of houses and other collective punishments implemented by the Israelis); releasing detainees; halting the expropriation of land and the establishment of new Jewish settlements on Arab land; abolishing value-added tax; dispersing all the municipal, village and refugee camp councils, and the holding of democratic elections in the West Bank and Gaza Strip.

Most communiqués were drafted by Mohamad Labadi, who became a leading figure during the period of the *Intifada*, and were then sent to his colleagues, who represented all factions of the PLO, for final approval. Occasionally, however, the entire command would meet, each time in a different location in East Jerusalem to escape Israeli interference, to decide its policy and work on its leaflets, which were then distributed by young boys and girls who placed them in the entrance of mosques, or plastered them on telephone poles alongside Palestinian flags. Later, the texts of the communiqués would be also broadcast by the Voice of the PLO radio station in Bagdhad and the Al Quds Palestinian Arab Radio based in Damascus.

It is notable that the PLO leadership in Tunis was not at all involved in organizing the *Intifada* during its initial stages, but was indeed very worried that local leaders would gain influence at its expense. This is why it put strong pressure on the local leadership and, beginning with communiqué no. 3 of 18 January 1988, all leaflets were signed also by the PLO and read 'Palestine Liberation Organization – Unified National Leadership of the Palestinian Uprising in the Occupied Territories'. This, so PLO-Tunis believed, would make it clear that the UNLU leadership was no more that an 'arm' of the

PLO acting on its behalf in the occupied territories. While the UNLU was functioning on the West Bank, a similar body was established in the Gaza Strip. It was, however, not as influential as its West Bank counterpart, mainly because the Islamic fundamentalists held themselves aloof and refused to take part in this committee of leaders.

The first few weeks of the *Intifada*, that is from 9 to 31 December 1987, were chaotic and violent. Figures show that in this short period twenty-two Palestinians were killed by Israeli gunfire; five of them were children aged between thirteen and sixteen. In addition, some 320 were injured, two thirds of them aged between seventeen and twenty-one.[20] The high toll amongst children was the direct result of them taking an active part in the revolt, but it was also because the practice of Israeli troops was to shoot at the legs of the demonstrators in order not to kill them – which for small children was lethal. On the Israeli side, fifty-six soldiers and thirty civilians were injured by stones and bottles. In this single month there were 1,412 separate incidents of demonstrations, stoning, tyre-burning, blocking roads and raising barricades. At least 109 firebombs were thrown, in addition to twelve instances of arson and three grenade attacks; some 270 Palestinians were arrested.[21]

In the meantime, after recovering from its initial shock, Israel, in mid-January 1988, deployed two divisional commands on the West Bank and a third in the Gaza Strip; the number of men patrolling Palestinian areas rose to the point where there was a shortage of equipment, and it was necessary to open up emergency stores and distribute equipment usually reserved for all-out wars with Arab regular armies.

In spite of growing pressure, the riots continued: the UNLU continued to function, and its prestige among the Palestinians steadily grew. In fact, it became so influential that under its pressure four municipal council members appointed by the Israelis resigned in February 1988, and on 11 March there was a mass resignation of Palestinian policemen. The Palestinians also organized communal support, with 'Popular Committees' springing up in almost every city and village of the Gaza Strip and the West Bank, and covering every sphere of life from education and security to business activity and sanitation, as well as youth, student, women's and workers' affairs. It is estimated that during the years of the *Intifada* there were around 45,000 local committees of various kinds in the territories.

Enter Hamas

A nasty surprise awaited Israelis in February 1988 when a new militant fundamentalist group which was an offshoot of the Moslem Brotherhood joined the *Intifada*. It was called the 'Islamic Resistance Movement' (*Harakat al Muqawama al Islami*), that is 'Hamas' from the Arabic acronym whose literal meaning is 'courage' or 'zeal'. Hamas was set up by Sheikh Ahmad Yassin and six other leaders of the Moslem Brotherhood in the occupied territories, and it was financed mainly by its supporters worldwide, who made contributions as part of the *zakat* – the Islamic tax. It was well organized, especially in the Gaza Strip. Three of its Islamic activists were appointed to serve as commanders: one was put in charge of political affairs, the second in charge of propaganda and the printing and distributing of handbills, and the third, Salah Shehadeh, whose code name was '101', was put in charge of military matters and led the armed wing of Hamas, which was named after Izz al Din Qassam, leader of the Arab *Intifada* against the British from 1936 to 1939. It had about 200 volunteers, who received the title *Mujahedu Falastin* ('holy fighters of Palestine'). Hamas divided the Gaza Strip into five districts, each headed by an operations officer and a liaison officer whose job was to maintain regular contact with Islamic activists on the West Bank. Hamas swiftly rose to prominence, and by the second month of the *Intifada* it was playing a leading role.

It should be mentioned that the emergence of the fundamentalists, both Islamic Jihad and Hamas, to power and influence on the West Bank and particularly in the Gaza Strip, was partly the result of Israel's folly and short-sighted policy which attempted, in the years before the uprising, to play the fundamentalists off against the PLO in order to counterbalance and weaken the latter.[22] Ironically, however, while the PLO had avoided any hint of anti-Semitism, the fundamentalists gloried in it, and Jew hatred was a common feature of their publications, as shown in the following extracts from *The Covenant of the Islamic Resistance Movement*:

There is no solution to the Palestinian problem except by Jihad. ... The Nazism of the Jews does not skip women and children, it scares everyone. ... This wealth [of the Jews] permitted them to take over control of the world media such as news agencies, the press, publication houses, broadcasting and the like. [They also have used this] wealth to stir revolutions in various parts of the globe. ... They stood behind the French and the Communist Revolutions. ... They also used the money to establish clandestine organizations which are spreading around the world in order to destroy societies and carry out Zionist interests. Such organizations are: the Free Masons, Rotary Clubs, Lions Clubs, B'nai B'rith and the like. All of them are destructive spying organizations. They also used the money to take over control of the Imperialist states and made them colonize many countries in order to exploit the wealth of those countries. ... [the Jews] stood behind World War I, so as to wipe out the Islamic Caliphate. ... [The Jews] ... established the League of Nations in order to rule the world by means of that organization. They also stood behind World War II, where they collected immense benefits from trading with war materials. ... They inspired the establishment of the United Nations and the Security Council ... in order to rule the world. ... There was no war that broke out anywhere without their fingerprints on it. ...

The Zionist invasion is a mischievous one. ... [The Jews] stand behind the diffusion of drugs and toxic of all kinds in order to facilitate its control and expansion. ... After Palestine [the Jews] will covet expansion from the Nile to the Euphrates. Only when they have completed digesting the area on which they will have laid their hand, they will look forward to more expansion. ... Their scheme has been laid out in the Protocols of the Elders of Zion. ... We have no escape from pooling together all the forces and energies to face this despicable Nazi-Tatar invasion.[23]

Given this approach, it is indeed puzzling that the Israelis came to regard Hamas as less wicked than the PLO and opted for the fundamentalists, allowing them to blossom. Indeed, for a time before the *Intifada*, fundamentalist, Moslems could move, with tacit Israeli agreement, into positions of power in the Gaza Strip and the West Bank; some were even allowed to take jobs in the Israeli Civil Administration, the body in daily contact with the Palestinian population at all levels of life. The strengthening position and growing influence of the fundamentalists in Gaza is manifested in figures showing that in the mid-1980s there was a rise in prayer attendance and a return to the traditional Moslem way of life, with Gaza's seventy-seven mosques at the end of the 1967 war multiplying to 160 in the following two decades. On the West Bank new mosques were being built at a rate of forty per year.[24] Although less influential on the West Bank, the Islamic fundamentalists nevertheless held key positions in the small Islamic College in Hebron, and in Nablus it controlled the allocation of welfare to 10,000 needy families, granting loans and scholarships, and running orphanages, homes for the aged and even an independent high school.

It was only in the second year of the uprising that the Israelis came to realize that activists of Hamas were at the forefront of the *Intifada* and, unlike other Palestinian groups which made it their policy to refrain from the use of arms, were preparing caches of arms and explosives. In July and September 1988 the Israelis struck at Hamas, arresting 120 activists and liquidating its command. But this did not spell the end for this group, since it took the movement's middle echelon only a few weeks to recover from the blow and re-embark on anti-Israeli activities as part of the *Intifada*.

Recovering the initiative but failing to suppress the uprising

To quell the growing resistance and put an end to the uprising, the Israelis resorted to various methods ranging from cutting off telephone lines and electricity to placing extended curfews on villages, towns and whole cities. On the West Bank localized curfews were imposed, while in Gaza more broader curfews were used. During 1988, no fewer than 1,600 curfew orders were issued in the territories, 118 of them for five days or more; all in all some 60 per cent of the Palestinian population experienced life under curfew. The Israelis also uprooted trees and occasionally entire orchards to deny the Palestinians the hiding places from where they could strike at Israeli troops; according to Palestinian figures, during 1988 the Israelis uprooted more than 25,000 olive and fruit trees. Furthermore, the demolishing of houses, which before the outbreak of the *Intifada* was considered an extraordinary measure used only against Palestinians who had committed serious offences, became, as from December 1987, a common means of administrative punishment. Thus, whereas before the outbreak of the *Intifada* demolishing a house had required the special approval of the Defence Minister, now with the *Intifada* underway, it was left to the discretion of an area commander. And figures show that it was used frequently: in 1987 the number of houses demolished was 103, and in 1988 it rose to a staggering 423.[25] Deportations, another draconian measure, were also used to quell the disturbances, as well as the closure of schools and universities which had been shut down for most of the first eighteen months of the *Intifada*.

The use of live ammunition against stone-throwers who were mostly young children was disastrous for the Israelis from a public relations point of view. Yet it was necessary to provide troops with ammunition which would enable them to hit Palestinians from a distance but not kill them. In 1989 rubber bullets were introduced. But these proved to be ineffective and so were replaced by plastic bullets, which proved to be more lethal than expected and so were replaced by rubber bullets with steel centres.[26] Troops were also provided with light, easy-to-handle clubs, strong enough not to break even when inflicting the heaviest of blows (ironically, the firms that manufactured these clubs employed mostly Arab workers from the Gaza Strip). At a meeting with troops in Ramallah, Defence Minister Rabin told them: 'Gentlemen, start using your hands, or clubs and simply beat the demonstrators in order to restore order'.[27] This became known as Rabin's 'break their bones' policy, and it is a testimony to the troops' frustration that they took Rabin's advice literally: the blows they inflicted on Palestinians left many of these people handicapped. So, ironically, as Schiff and Ya'ari have observed:

> Rather than being hailed as a symbol of sanity, or at least the lesser of two evils, and rather than being used with discretion to subdue rioters resisting arrest, the club reverted to being an emblem of barbarity and was employed with abandon by men who had simply let the uprising get their goat.[28]

In the face of worldwide condemnation, the Israeli authorities were forced to modify Rabin's instructions, which subsequently stated: 'Force is not to be used against sensitive parts of the body', and later,

Force may be used against violence and those resisting arrest while the violence is being committed, up to the point of capture. [But] the exercise of force against anyone who has been stopped, is under arrest, or is already in custody and is not behaving violently is absolutely forbidden.[29]

The Israelis also revised and amended legal procedures to facilitate mass arrests of rioters, and the establishment of new detention facilities in March 1988 in Ketziot, which had a capacity of 7,000 prisoners, and at Daharieh, near Hebron, made it possible to hold thousands of detainees for extended periods. About 50,000 Palestinians were arrested during the first eighteen months of the *Intifada*, with more than 12,000 of them held in administrative detention for periods of varying length. One in every eighty Palestinian adults in the territories was imprisoned by administrative order, while one in forty had spent more than twenty-four hours in detention for taking part in the uprising.[30] But jails, as the Israelis later learnt, only produced more militants; for while the Israelis could ensure that their prisoners did not run away, they could not really control lives inside the jails. Thus the jails had effectively turned into political schools, where a new generation of Palestinian leaders was formed and a strong bond created among the Palestinians.

Economic measures were also used by the Israelis to put down the rebellion. For example, a systematic campaign was launched to break the Palestinian tax strike, which had been introduced by the Palestinian population following UNLU's instructions. The campaign was carried out during curfews, with the security forces' full cooperation, and proved to be highly effective from the Israeli point of view; in the Gaza Strip, for example, the income from taxes actually rose at the end of 1988. Furthermore, individualized types of economic punishment were imposed, such as the banning of Palestinian villages in the Jordan Valley from bringing their harvest to market in Jericho, which was a devastating blow for them for they relied heavily on selling their crops in Jericho. Economic measures hit the Palestinians hard. In 1988 their standard of living, which was already low, fell by as much as 30–40 per cent, and by the beginning of 1989 the unemployment figure had risen sharply, with the number of people working in Israel, a critical source of income for the Palestinian economy, declining by more than 25 per cent.[31] But even these measures failed to stop the rioting – the Palestinians continued to throw stones, to raise the Palestinian flag, and to spray walls with political graffiti, often in one of the four colours of the Palestinian standard.[32] A revolt, which at its opening stage was carried out by the impoverished classes who only wished to improve their standards of living, now turned into a statement of political import.

A year of uprising, from December 1987 to December 1988, proved to be very violent and produced a high death toll. Three hundred and eleven Palestinians were killed, forty-four of them children aged 13–16, and nine children under the age of nine lost their lives. In addition, fifteen Palestinian civilians were killed by Israeli civilians, six Israeli civilians were killed by Palestinian civilians, and four Israeli security force personnel were killed by Palestinian civilians. The number of houses demolished during this period had reached a staggering 526.[33]

There were times when it seemed as if the revolt was spreading from the occupied territories to Israel itself. In July 1989, for instance, a Palestinian refugee from Gaza wrested the steering wheel of a passenger bus from its driver and sent it over a cliff, killing fifteen people. In May 1990, a former Israeli soldier opened fire on unarmed Arab workers south of Tel Aviv, killing seven. Hamas was also causing Israel great problems, and in May 1989 the Israelis inflicted a second blow on the organization, arresting the organization's spiritual leader Sheikh Yassin along with his aides and some 260 activists. But fundamentalism remained, especially in the Gaza Strip, a mass movement resolved to destroy Israel and change the face of Palestinian society. When in the early 1990s Israelis and Palestinians embarked on the road to peace, Hamas was to inflict apalling acts of terrorism which would often halt and reverse the entire peace process.

Assessing the balance sheet

Officially, the *Intifada* continued until Israel and the Palestinians had signed the Oslo Agreement on 13 September 1993.[34] In the period between 9 December 1987 and 13 September 1993, some 1,070 Palestinian civilians were killed by Israeli security forces in the occupied territories and seventeen more in Israel. Of those killed, sixty-four were children under the age of twelve, and 173 were aged 13–16. In addition, fifty-four Palestinian civilians were killed by Israeli civilians (mostly settlers) in the territories, and a further twenty-one in Israel. In the same period, forty-eight Israeli civilians were killed by Palestinians in the occupied territories, and fifty-three within Israel itself. Forty-two Israelis of the security forces were killed by Palestinians in the occupied territories, and seventeen were killed in Israel. Thousands of Palestinians and hundreds of Israelis were injured, and 1,473 Palestinian houses were demolished.[35] Deportation of activists was also rife; 413 Hamas and Islamic Jihad activists were deported to southern Lebanon in December 1992.

Intifada and Israeli society

The Israelis were shocked to the core by the magnitude and ferocity of the Palestinian uprising, for as Schiff and Ya'ari correctly observed:

> There seemed to be a collective mental block in Israel [with regard to the Palestinians and territories]. ... The Jewish public tended to repress the Palestinian issue entirely, relating to the territories as

though they were a distant land. In a sense the Israelis discovered the territories twice: at the end of the Six Day War, when attention was riveted on their historical landscape with all its biblical landmarks, and again some twenty years later, in December 1987, when the Palestinian population made it impossible for them to cling to the blinders that had made the million and a half Arabs under Israeli military rule so conveniently invisible.[36]

And as the Israeli novelist David Grossman observed in *The Yellow Wind*, just before the *Intifada* erupted: 'We [Israelis] have lived for 20 years in a false and artificial situation based on illusions, on a teetering centre of gravity between hate and fear, in a desert void of emotion and consciousness'. Someday, Grossman warned, 'it will exact a deadly price'.[37] Indeed, Israelis by no means ignored the territories, and when the *Intifada* came it sent a sharp jolt through the whole of society, forcing it to re-examine propositions that had long been taken for granted. As the uprising dragged on from week to week, month to month and year to year, and with a high death toll on both sides, Israelis came increasingly to realize that their country was slipping back to the starting line in its conflict with the Palestinians. Through this shocking experience, the Israelis came to realize that their leaders had deceived them in pronouncing that the Palestinian people did not exist, or, as Prime Minister Golda Meir used to put it, 'there is no Palestinian nation'. Israelis now saw how they had all been dragged down to the level of brute violence, and they ceased to believe that 'benevolent occupation' was possible.

What the *Intifada* did to Israeli society was to divide it and sharpen its polarization, with the first division drawn between Israelis and the 700,000 Arab Israelis living within the Green Line.[38] We should remember that although most Arabs left Palestine during the years 1947–8 and also during the 1967 war, there was still in Israel, on the eve of the *Intifada*, a community of Arabs making up about 17 per cent of Israel's total population. Throughout the years these Arab Israelis had become an integral part of Israeli society; they held Israeli identity cards, spoke Hebrew, studied and worked in Israel. But with their fellow Palestinians revolting in the occupied territories, the Arabs of Israel found it increasingly difficult to stand aside. On 17 December, just a week after the outbreak of the *Intifada*, they held a general strike and rallies in support of the Palestinians in the territories, and on 21 December embarked on a general strike. They also sent food and drugs to the territories, and donated blood; a few even made their bank accounts available to the PLO for transferring funds to the territories.[39] In taking these actions, the Arabs of Israel showed themselves to be more Palestinian than Israeli, and for the Jewish Israelis this was a shocking realization.

But the *Intifada* also sharply divided the Jewish population itself, and although there was a general move to the political right and a wave of extremism in Israel, there was also a sharp move to the left, where a growing number of Israelis emerged to declare themselves unwilling to serve in the territories and put down the uprising.[40] From this point of view, the trend which had begun in the Lebanon war, of Israelis refusing to take up arms, was continuing. In fact, as far back as October 1987, that is just before the outbreak of the *Intifada*, a group of fifty high school students about to become eligible for military service had signed a letter to Defence Minister Rabin expressing their intention to refuse to serve beyond the Green line; at the time they claimed they had 'hundreds of supporters'.[41] With the *Intifada* rearing its ugly head, the number of Israelis refusing to serve in the territories increased rapidly, with the protest movement *Yesh Gvul* (which had played a leading role during the Lebanon war) encouraging this stand. At the end of December 1987, sixteen more students joined the group which had sent the October letter to the Defence Minister.[42] Also that December, 160 reservists, including one woman, one Jerusalem city councillor and several officers, followed suit by declaring that they refused to participate in putting down the *Intifada*.[43] In mid-February 1988, *Yesh Gvul* announced that 260 reservists had proclaimed that they would not carry out any orders to beat Palestinians.[44] With the number of Israelis refusing to serve in the territories growing by the day, the military authorities attempted to keep the phenomenon under the carpet, as it had done during the Lebanon war, and it came to arrangements with many of those refusing to serve, promising not to send them to fulfil missions in the occupied territories. Nevertheless, as was the case during the Lebanon war, there were those who were sent to jail: on 18 July 1989, it was reported in the *Jerusalem Post* that seventy-seven Israeli soldiers had been imprisoned for refusing to serve in the occupied territories. Although these numbers are small, they are not insignificant, especially if we remember that from the immediate pre-state period until 1970, only a little over 100 Jewish Israelis publicly refused to serve. Also, as was the case during the 1982 war in Lebanon, huge demonstrations took place in Israel while troops in the territories were still grappling with the uprising. Thus, on 23 January 1988, between 80,000 and 100,000 Israelis took part in a demonstration in Tel Aviv to denounce Israeli policies in the occupied territories, and in Nazareth Jews and Arabs held a rally, carrying banners with names of Palestinians killed by Israelis.

CHAPTER SEVEN

Conclusions

Wars between Arabs and Israelis have taken place from the day the state of Israel was established on the land of Palestine in May 1948, dominating the headlines and featuring prominently in books about Israel. Separate and short, the Israeli–Arab wars can be seen, in a historical perspective, as a single war with a single continuity, where land – first the land of Palestine and then lands occupied by Israel in subsequent wars – is identified as the main – though not exclusive – trigger to the repeating conflagrations. The balance sheet, after more than fifty years of Israeli–Arab conflict, indicates that on the battlefield there has been no clear victor – neither Arab nor Israeli.

In the war of 1948, the first contest between the parties, Israel held its ground and even defeated Egypt and Lebanon. But the Jordanians and Syrians did well; the former managed to occupy the West Bank and the latter to cross the international border and occupy lands which had been allotted to the Jews by the UN in the 29 November 1947 Partition Plan (Chapter 1). Then in 1956, Israel struck hard at Egypt (Chapter 2), and eleven years later in the war of June 1967 she defeated Egypt, Jordan and Syria (Chapter 3). However, in the 1968–70 War of Attrition along the Suez Canal, there was no clear winner (Chapter 3), as was also the case in 1973's Yom Kippur War, where Egypt and Syria managed to win an important battle in the initial phase of the conflict but were later forced to yield their gains to the victorious Israelis (Chapter 4). In the war of 1982 in Lebanon, Israel struck hard at the Syrians and the PLO, forcing the latter out of the country and into exile; but this war was still considered a disastrous failure, especially after the assassination of Israel's protégé Bashir Gemayel, and the subsequent massacre of Palestinians in the refugee camps of Sabra and Shatilla (Chapter 5). Then, during the years of the *Intifada*, Israel failed to contain the disturbances, and the Palestinian revolt which began in 1987 was only ended after the signing of the Oslo Agreement in 1993 (Chapter 6).

Wars, however, are a clash not only of arms but of words, and if, as we have just stated, there was no victor on the battlefield, there was indeed a clear victor in the war of words – Israel. For throughout the first decades of the conflict Israel's leaders had managed – most successfully – to portray Israel as the injured party and to instil in the minds of their fellow Israelis, and of the world in general, the idea that Israel was always the victim of Arab aggression. But this was only partially true, for while in 1948 the newborn state of Israel was indeed the victim of Arab aggression and attempts to destroy her (Chapter 1), eight years later it was Israel who, together with France and Britain, initiated and launched a war against Egypt (Chapter 2). Then in 1967, it was again Israel who forced war upon Egypt and Syria – Jordan was the only country to attack Israel in this war (Chapter 3). However, immediately after this conflict, it was President Nasser of Egypt who imposed a War of Attrition on Israel, and later, on Yom Kippur 1973, Egypt – now led by Nasser's successor Sadat – and Syria opened fire, attacking Israel on two fronts (Chapters 3 and 4). In the summer of 1982 it was again Israel who started a war, this time in Lebanon (Chapter 5); but five years later it was the Palestinians in the West Bank and the Gaza Strip who forced a stone-throwing war upon the Israeli occupying forces (Chapter 6).

These wars (and we must include preparations for war, even when there was no resulting conflict) cost a fortune and caused great damage, suffering and sorrow to the Israeli people (as it did to the Arabs); but they also proved to be the bond – the very cement – which kept the Israelis together. For, especially during the first decades of the state, Israel was the gathering place of Jewish immigrants from the four corners of the earth, and rather than a homogeneous society it was an assembly of communities and diverse people, some of whom were still 'adding up the grocery bill in Arabic; others dream[ing] in Yiddish and singing to their children lullabies in English or Russian'.[1] And, as shown in Chapter 2, it was the transformation of these people into a nation-in-arms, and the establishment of a military system where almost every citizen – male and female – was a trained soldier and a reservist, that transformed the Israeli-born *Sabra*, the orthodox Jew from New York, the scientist from London, the silversmith from Yemen, the lawyer from Egypt and the small shopkeeper from Morocco – from individuals into a society and a nation. And above all, what kept this Israeli organism together and helped rally Israelis round the flag and its leadership, was a deep sense of external danger and the fear that the Arabs intended and *would* try to destroy Israel, and that to cope with this problem Israelis must stick together and take up arms whenever its leadership requested them to do so. As Abba Eban, an intelligent and well informed eyewitness, wrote in his book *My Country*: 'The Israeli scene is often turbulent, contentious and effervescent but when *danger threatens* ... the ranks tighten'.[2]

Indeed, throughout the formative years of the state of Israel, threatening declarations by Arab leaders reinforced the tendency of the Israeli leadership to exaggerate the external threat in order to engender a sense of insecurity among Israelis, which in turn made them very willing to fight in wars and to finance them. But, as we have shown, during the mid- and late 1970s there were many changes in Israel, most notably the growing sense that her place in the Middle East was now more secure, and that the external threat was diminishing. This change of mood came about not only because the IDF had managed to prove its efficiency and ability to defend the country; it was also the result of the beginning of a process of reconciliation between Israeli and Arab, evidenced by the signing of a peace accord between Israel and Egypt in 1979, which meant that Egypt – the strongest of Israel's foes – was removed from the circle of war; with this, the danger to Israel's existence declined dramatically (Chapter 4). In a 1986 survey, 89 per cent of Israelis expressed confidence in Israel's long-term existence, and in 1987 this figure rose to 96 per cent.[3]

The experience of the Holocaust, which had taken place just a few years before Israel was established, had a strong impact on Israeli attitudes during the first decades of the state. Indeed, within Israeli society the Holocaust survivors became living testimony to what could be the fate of Israelis if they failed to defend themselves. Just how strongly this trauma affected Israelis is shown by *The Seventh Day: Soldiers Talk about the Six Day War*, which became a bestseller in Israel after the 1967 war, and was a book in which returning soldiers talked about their experiences and thoughts. One of these soldiers, Yariv Ben-Aharon, said, in what seems to represent the general opinion in Israel at the time:

> people believed [before the outbreak of the June 1967 war] that we would be exterminated if we lost the war. ... We got this idea – or inherited it – from the concentration camps. ... Genocide – it's a feasible notion. ... This is the lesson of the gas chambers.[4]

But it was after, and as a result of, the Six Day War that attitudes in Israel began to change, and with the gradual disappearance of the Holocaust generation the over-sensitivity of Israelis to the danger of total extermination was also somehow diminished. For many of the older generation of Israelis, the Holocaust was the central experience of their lives, and their thoughts and actions were dominated by the knowledge that what had happened once could happen again, an idea which was much used by Israeli politicians throughout the years in order to rally the people. But the younger generation of Israelis, those born in the 1970s and in later years, saw the world in less threatening colours than did their parents. They may have heard anecdotes of the Holocaust from their elders, but they were more likely to learn of it from books, and it did not dominate their actions and worldview as it did their parents'. For the sons and daughters of non-European Israelis, the Holocaust seemed an even more remote event. In a survey carried out in 1986, 82 per cent of Israelis thought there was absolutely no chance (42 per cent) or only little chance (40 per cent) that the Jewish people would face another Holocaust.[5]

Throughout the years another important change took place within Israel, namely a shift from collective ideals and priorities to individual ones. Indeed, while the early generation of Israelis – the builders and founders of the state – possessed an ideological sense of mission and took it for granted that the state came before the welfare of the individual, the younger generation of Israelis saw things differently. For them, individual priorities often seemed more important than collective ones, and in contrast with their parents they were motivated by their individual achievements rather than by patriotic values.[6] Thus while the older generation was willing to pay a heavy price in terms of taxation and sacrifice of social services in order to subsidize expensive wars, the younger generation was much more reluctant to do so. In 1987, two thirds of Israelis stated that they would not support social services cuts in order to increase the defence budget, and in 1992 only 24 per cent of Israelis said they would be willing to finance increased defence spending.[7]

These changes in the environment and within Israeli society were significant in that they had a strong effect on the attitudes and behaviour of Israelis and their willingness to fight in wars and pay for them. Indeed, as has been shown in previous chapters, the perception of a decreasing external threat, the disappearance of the Holocaust generation and a shift from collective ideals and priorities to individual ones, meant that a more confident Israeli nation, less fearful for its very existence and less traumatized and haunted by its past, was also showing itself to be less single-minded and more reluctant to take up arms and sacrifice, as was clearly demonstrated in Lebanon in 1982 and during the years of the Arab revolt in the territories between 1987 and 1993.

Notes

CHAPTER ONE

1. J. K. Galbraith, *The Great Crash 1929* (London, 1961) 25.
2. On the dispute between Jews and Arabs being focused on land, see A. Horani, 'Palestine and Israel', *Observer*, 3 September 1967; see also J. L. Talmon, 'Israel and the Arabs', *Observer*, 10 September 1967; also R. Ovendale, *The Origins of the Arab-Israeli Wars* (London, 1984) 11.
3. On the defeat of the Turks at the hands of the British, see B. H. Liddell Hart, *History of the First World War* (London, 1970) 211–13.
4. I say 'Arab' Palestinians, but in fact there were among them Christians and people of other ethnic and religious groups.
5. Genesis XV:18.
6. *Pogrom* is a Russian word meaning massacre. It passed from Russian into the English language with the specialized meaning of a massacre of Jews. Pogroms became part of the life of the Jews in Europe. In Poland, for example, in 1648–58, at least 100,000 Jews were massacred. In the Ukraine, between 1917 and 1920, at least 75,000 Jews were slaughtered, as well as smaller numbers in some of the newly independent nations of Eastern Europe; on this, see B. Lewis, *Semites and Anti-Semites* (London, 1986) 60, 77.
7. C. Weizmann, *Excerpts from His Historic Statements: Writings and Addresses* (The Jewish Agency for Palestine, New York, 1952) 48.
8. This statement was coined by the Anglo-Jewish writer Yisrael Zwangwill, a leading Zionist; see 'The return to Palestine', *New Liberal Review II*, December 1901, 627.
9. A. Elon, 'Israel and the end of Zionism', *The New York Review*, 19 December 1996, 22.
10. A. Elon, *The Israelis: Founders and Sons* (London, 1983) 172.
11. *The Complete Diaries of Theodore Herzl, Vol. I* (New York, 1960) 343 (entry for 12 June 1895). On the possibility of transfer of the Arabs of Palestine, see M. Laqueur, *A History of Zionism* (New York, 1989) 231–2. Theodore Herzl was, in fact, willing to give up Palestine altogether and accept the proposal put to him in 1903 by the British Minister for the Colonies, Joseph Chamberlain, to have Uganda as an alternative to Palestine. But Herzl was vigorously opposed by Russian Zionists, and in the end gave up the idea of acquiring any place but Palestine.
12. Estimates of the number of Jews in Palestine are unreliable and vary. The figure of 85,000 Jews is also quoted in D. McDowall, *The Palestinians: Minority Rights Group Report no. 24* (London, 1975) 7. A British census of 1918 gives an estimate of 700,000 Arabs and 56,000 Jews in Palestine; see P. Mansfield, *The Arabs* (London, 1992) 173.

13. H. Draper, 'The origins of the Middle East crisis', in *The Israel-Arab Reader* (London, 1994) 292. According to one source only 5,000 Jewish refugees from Europe had been admitted into the United States in the first two years after the war; see C. Sykes, *Cross Roads to Israel* (London, 1967) 341; also B. Lewis, *The Middle East: 2000 Years of History from the Rise of Christianity to the Present Day* (London, 1995) 361–2; also A. Koestler, *Promise and Fulfilment: Palestine 1917–1949* (London, 1983) 103.

14. The Arab population in Palestine also increased between the late 1880s and 1947. This was due to high rate of natural increase, but also because the development of Palestine turned it into a place attracting Arab immigration from adjacent Arab countries.

15. One quarter of all Jewish land in Palestine was acquired from a single Arab Christian family called Sursock, which lived outside of the country but owned large tracts of Palestinian land. In 1910 the entire region of Foule was bought from the Sursocks, and ten years later the rest of their holdings in Palestine was purchased. Eight thousand Arab peasants had lived on this land in twenty-two villages; see A. Grannott, *The Land System in Palestine* (London, 1952) 80; also D. Hirst, *The Gun and the Olive Branch*, 29; also W. Laqueur, *Zionism*, 227.

16. U. Milstein, *The War of Independence: The Roots of the Struggle*, vol. I (Tel Aviv, 1989) 14 (Hebrew).

17. The Zionists put in a claim for Palestine as '*the* national home' or 'a national *state*', but the British would not accept this; they thus compromised on 'a national home'. On the Balfour Declaration, see W. Laqueur and B. Rubin (eds) *The Israel-Arab Reader*, 16. The principal motive of the British government in promising the Jews Palestine as their 'national home' was to secure American support in the war by placating the influential American Jewry; on this see the testimony of Lloyd George in *Palestine Royal Commission Report* (London, HMSO, 1937, reprint 1946) 17. According to A. J. P. Taylor, another motive of the British was to block French influence in the Middle East: 'The British government did not at all welcome the prospect of the French as neighbours next door to the Suez Canal. Zionism was a way of keeping them out' – A. J. P. Taylor, *English History 1914–1945* (London, 1965) 107, 138; also V. Mayir, 'The Balfour Declaration and its makers', in E. Kadourie and S. Haim (eds) *Palestine and Israel in the 19th and 20th Centuries* (London, 1982); also A. Koestler, *Promise and Fulfilment*, 5.

18. D. Thomson, *Europe since Napoleon* (London, 1966) 629. In a letter sent by Sir Henry McMahon, British High Commissioner in Cairo, to Husain Ibn Ali, the Sherif of Mecca, the British government promised to support his bid for the restoration of the Caliphate (the leadership in the Arab world) if Husain supported the British war effort against Turkey. Palestine was not mentioned by name in this exchange. The Arabs subsequently claimed that it had been included in the promise of an independent Arab state. For this letter, see W. Laqueur and B. Rubin (eds) 'The McMahon letter', in *The Israel-Arab Reader*, 14–16.

19. Britain's mandate for Palestine was assured by the peace conference decision at San Remo in April 1920, and was ratified by the League of Nations on 24 July 1922. For the document known as the 'British Mandate', see W. Laqueur and B. Rubin (eds) *The Israel-Arab Reader*, 30–6.

20. A. Koestler, *Promise and Fulfilment*, 5.

21. H. Z. Nuseibeh, *Palestine and the United Nations* (London, 1981) 20.

22. These were called the Nebi Mussa disturbances. Nebi Mussa is a place east of Jerusalem where according to Arab belief Moses – Mussa in Arabic – is buried. Palestinian Arabs made a pilgrimage there each spring, and when they came this spring they attacked Jews in Jerusalem.

23. A. J. P. Taylor, *English History*, 500.
24. This was said by Winston Churchill; see *The Times*, 1 August 1946.
25. The United Nations Special Committee on Palestine (UNSCOP) was composed of eleven members: Sweden, the Netherlands, Czechoslovakia, Yugoslavia, Australia, Canada, India, Iran, Guatemala, Mexico and Peru. The Chairman was a justice of the Supreme Court in Sweden, the Canadian a high court judge, the Australian a professional diplomat, the Dutchman a former colonial governor in the Dutch East Indies. It was decided that the major states should not be members.
26. Letter of Ben Gurion to his wife Paula, as quoted in A. Shlaim, *Collusion across the Jordan* (Oxford, 1988) 17; see also Ben Gurion as cited in U. Ben-Eliezer, *The Emergence of Israeli Militarism 1936–1956* (Tel Aviv, 1995) 228–9 (Hebrew); also D. Ben Gurion, *Diary of War* (Tel Aviv, 1983), entry for 3 December 1947 (Hebrew).
27. R. Fisk, 'Flirting with the enemy', *Independent*, 20 February 1999.
28. On the report and comments see H. Wilson, *The Chariot of Israel: Britain, America and the State of Israel* (London, 1981) 203–9.
29. Interview with Hazem Zaki Nuseibeh, 28 February 1997, Amman, BLA.
30. The Nashashibis wanted partition because they were close to Jordan's King Abdullah, whom they believed would annex the West Bank to his kingdom. The communists argued that if some form of agreement was not reached the problem would never be resolved.
31. J. Vatikiotis, *Among Arabs and Jews*, 59.
32. R. Fisk, 'Flirting with the enemy', *Independent*, 20 February 1999.
33. M. Pail, *Independence 1948–1949* (Tel Aviv, 1990) 13 (Hebrew); also U. Milstein, *The War of Independence: The First Month*, vol. II (Tel Aviv, 1989) 25 (Hebrew).
34. Z. Ostfeld, *An Army is Born* (Tel Aviv, 1994) 54 (Hebrew).
35. Y. Beer, *Essays* (The College for Command and Staff, Herzeliya, n.d.) 7 (Hebrew).
36. On the lack of cooperation and the division among Arab forces, see telephone conversation between Sheikh Hassan Abu Saud and the Mufti of Jerusalem as taped by the Jews and published in D. Ben Gurion, *Diary of War,* entry for 21 January 1948, 169 (Hebrew).
37. 'Plan Dalet' was distributed to field commanders on 29 February 1948, and on 10 March it became a directive to all units. Y. Wallach, 'Kavim Be'hitpatchut Torat Ha'bitachon shel Ha'Yishuv Be'term Medina', *Skira Hodshit*, vol. 29, no. 2 (Tel Aviv, February 1982) 47 (Hebrew).
38. The Soviet Union had always opposed Zionism, fearing that it would inflame its Jewish citizens. One can only conjecture about the reasons for Russia's *volte-face*. Possibly Moscow calculated that the creation of a Jewish state would undermine Western relations with the Arab states and thus provide for the Soviet Union a means of extending its influence in the Middle East, or even that a socialist Israel would become an ally.
39. B. Morris, 'Haifa's Arabs' displacement and concentration, July 1948', in *1948 and After: Israel and the Palestinians* (Oxford, 1994) 215–37.
40. Most of them fled to Gaza by sea. For a vivid first-hand description, see A. Iyad, *Without Homeland* (Jerusalem 1978)(translated from the French into Hebrew).
41. U. Milstein, *The War of Independence: The First Month* 77–8 (Hebrew).
42. U. Milstein, *The War of Independence: The First Invasion*, vol. III (Tel Aviv, 1989) 89–91 (Hebrew). Following a visit to the scene where the bomb had exploded on 23 February 1948, Ben Gurion recorded in his war diary: 'Such a destruction. ... I could not recognize the streets ... but I could not forget that our thugs and murderers [meaning the dissidents] had opened the way', that is, brought about

this Arab reaction by their own terrorist actions, see D. Ben Gurion, *Diary of War*, entry for 23 February 1948 (Hebrew).

43. U. Milstein, *The War of Independence: The First Invasion*, 95–6 (Hebrew).

44. On expulsion by force, see for example Letter from members of the settlements Dorot, Nir Am and Ruama to Ben Gurion, IDFA, 1557000, 4 August 1948; see also Summary of occupations in the southern district, 11 June 1948, HA, 105/92.3.

45. Interview with Hazem Zaki Nuseibeh, 28 February 1997, Amman, BLA; see also B. Morris, 'The causes and character of the Arab exodus from Palestine: the Israel Defence Force intelligence service analysis of June 1948', in *1948 and After*, 83–102.

46. See for example, Discussion in the Histadrut's executive committee, 14 July 1948, LILR; Summary of the meeting of the advisers of Arab affairs in Netanya, 25 April 1948, LILR, file V-115–1.

47. D. Ben Gurion, *Diary of War*, entry for 19 December 1948 (Hebrew).

48. D. Ben Gurion, *Diary of War*, entry for 10 November 1948 (Hebrew); also T. Segev, *1949: The New Israelis* (Tel Aviv, n.d.) 90.

49. D. Ben Gurion, *Diaries*, entry for 27 April 1953, in BGA, Sde Boker. Full details of casualties can be found in A. Bregman, 'Civil–military relations in Israel: military influence on war policy', Ph.D. dissertation (Department of War Studies, King's College London, 1993) 113, n15.

50. D. Ben Gurion, *Diary of War*, entry for 14 May 1948 (Hebrew); see also G. Meir, *My Life: The Autobiography of Golda Meir* (London, 1975) 187.

51. Interview with Gideon Rafael, Jerusalem, 19 January 1997, BLA.

52. The State of Israel was proclaimed before the official termination of the Mandate. The reason is that the Mandate was due to expire on Friday at midnight, and because this was during the Jewish sabbath, it was decided to bring forward the proclamation ceremony. Thus the British High Commissioner of Palestine remained at his post in Israel; see D. Ben Gurion, *Diary of War*, entry for 14 May 1948 (Hebrew). The British evacuation had lasted for weeks, starting from the south and rolling north. The last British soldier left the land of Israel on 30 June 1948 at 12:30 a.m.

53. A. Eban, *My Country: The Story of Modern Israel* (New York, 1972) 74. On 11 May 1949, Israel would take its seat as the 59th member of the United Nations, thus securing its place in the international community as a partner equal in right to the Arab states and all others.

54. D. Ben Gurion, *Diary of War*, entry for 15 May 1948 (Hebrew). About the debate within the American administration on whether or not to recognize Israel, see A. Bregman and J. el-Tahri, *The Fifty Years War: Israel and the Arabs* (London, 1998) 34–6; also C. Clifford, *Counsel to the President: Memoirs* (New York, 1996) ch. 1.

55. A few minutes before midnight, King Abdullah of Transjordan arrived at the eastern side of the Allenby bridge to wait for the British mandate in Palestine to expire officially. At midnight he took out his pistol, fired a shot into the air, and shouting 'forward' he dispatched his forces across the Jordanian river to the West Bank; see A. Shlaim, *The Politics of Partition: King Abdullah, the Zionists and Palestine, 1921–1951* (Oxford, 1990) 175.

56. A. Eban, 'The refugee problem', in W. Laqueur and B. Rubin (eds) *The Israel-Arab Reader*, 131.

57. B. H. Liddell Hart, *History of the Second World War* (London, 1970) 165.

58. Gunther Rothenberg puts the number of Arab troops committed to the battle at less than 30,000 men, of them 10,000 Egyptians, 6,000 Jordanians, 4,000 Iraqis,

4,000 Syrians, 1,500 Lebanese, and small contingents from Saudi Arabia, Yemen and Morocco; see G. Rothenberg, *The Anatomy of the Israeli Army* (London, 1979) 51. Glubb Pasha, the commander of the Arab Legion, gives the following numbers: Egypt: 10,000, Arab Legion: 4,500, Syria: 3,000, Lebanon: 1,000, Iraq: 3,000. This makes a total of 21,500; see G. J. Glubb, *A Soldier with the Arabs* (London, 1958) 94. According to Benny Morris the invading armies had a total of between 25,000 and 30,000 troops; see B. Morris, *1948 and After*, 34.

59. According to Ben Gurion, on the eve of the Arab invasion Hagana had a total of 29,677 men distributed as follows – Palmach: three brigades a total of 6,000 men; Golani brigade: 4,095; Carmeli brigade: 2,238; Alexandroni brigade: 3,588; Kiryati brigade: 2,504; Givati brigade: 3,229; Etzioni brigade: 3,166; training forces: 398; air force: 675; artillery force: 650; engineers: 150; military police: 168; transport units: 1,097 – a total of 1,719 new conscripts in training; see D. Ben Gurion, *Diary of War*, entry for 15 May 1948 (Hebrew).

60. Total arrival of new immigrants in 1948 was 123,999, which averages at 10,300 per month. D. Ben Gurion, *Diary of War*, entry for 1 January 1949 (Hebrew).

61. D. Ben Gurion, *Diary of War*, entry for 10 November 1948 (Hebrew).

62. D. Ben Gurion, *Diary of War*, 874 (Hebrew).

63. D. Ben Gurion, *Diary of War*, 930 (Hebrew).

64. J. B. Glubb, *A Soldier with the Arabs*, 195.

65. J. Kimche, *Both Sides of the Hill* (London, 1960) 161.

66. Y. Beer, *Be Ma'agal Beaiot Bitachon* (Tel Aviv, 1957) 166–7 (Hebrew).

67. G. Meir, *My Life*, 192; also E. Avriel, *Open the Gates* (Tel Aviv, 1976) (Hebrew).

68. T. Kollek, *For Jerusalem: A Life of Teddy Kollek* (London, 1978) 67–89.

69. Y. Meridor, *Shlichout Aluma*, 245–61 (Hebrew); see also D. Ben Gurion, *Diary of War*, entry for 26 July 1948, 663 (Hebrew).

70. D. Ben Gurion, *Diary of War*, entry for 20 September 1948 (Hebrew); also Y. Amnon, *With no Trace*, 204–19.

71. References to the development of chemical weapons can be found in Ben Gurion's *Diary of War*, entries for 1 June, 2 June, 20 June 1948 (Hebrew).

72. According to General Shlomo Shamir, who commanded the 7th brigade in its attempt to take Latrun on the way to Jerusalem, lack of communication due to language difficulties and harsh weather conditions did reduce the efficiency of his men, see Shlomo Shamir to author, Tel Aviv, 17 December 1991.

73. About this see A. Shlaim, *The Politics of Partition*. Abdullah even dispatched his Prime Minister to the British Foreign Minister to explain that his intention was only to take the West Bank. Bevin, according to Sir John Glubb, replied: 'It seems the obvious thing to do. But don't go and invade the areas allotted to the Jews'; see B. Lapping, *End of Empire* (London, 1989) 189.

74. J. B. Glubb, *A Soldier with the Arabs*, 96.

75. Interview with Mohsein Abdel Khalek, Cairo, 19 March 1996, BLA.

76. Interview with Abdel Ghani Kanout, Damascus, 16 October 1996, BLA.

77. Interview with Adel Sabit, 23 February 1997; and with Mourad Ghaleb, 20 March 1996, Cairo, BLA.

78. B. J. Glubb, *A Soldier with the Arabs*, 79.

79. See Order Number 4, which was promulgated by the Provisional Government in *Skira Hodshit* (Tel Aviv, December 1973) (Hebrew).

80. Following the assassination in September 1948 of the UN mediator Count Folke Bernadotte by 'Hazit Ha'am', a group of dissidents close to Lehi, Ben Gurion ordered the arrest of the Lehi leaders, and this was the end of the organization.

81. P. Bernadotte, *To Jerusalem* (Jerusalem, 1952) 63 (Hebrew).

82. D. Ben Gurion, *Diary of War*, entry for 15 June 1948 (Hebrew).

83. G. Rothenberg, *The Anatomy of the Israeli Army*, 60.

84. P. Bernadotte, *To Jerusalem*, 132 and 137 (Hebrew).

85. M. Dayan, *Story of my Life* (London, 1976) 109–16.

86. *New York Times*, 23 October 1979. This censored piece also appears in A. Bregman and J. el-Tahri, *The Fifty Years War*, 40.

87. Interview with George Habash, Damascus, 6 October 1996, BLA.

88. Ben Gurion, in *Transcript of the Meeting of the 16th June 1948*, 21–2, in the author's archive (Hebrew).

89. Y. Rabin, *Pinkas Sherut* (Tel Aviv, 1979) 63 (Hebrew).

90. Y. Rabin, *Pinkas Sherut*, 78 (Hebrew).

91. M. Dayan, *Story of my Life*, 146.

92. The number 5.4 million (of them about 1.5 million children) instead of the commonly known figure of 6 million Jews, is based on the fact that at least 10 per cent of the Jews who were massacred in the Holocaust were Christians, i.e. Jews who had converted to Christianity. For the Nazis, however, a Jew converted to Christianity was still a 'full Jew' (*Volljude*); see B. Lewis, *Semites and anti-Semites* 20. In the Holocaust about one third of world Jewry perished.

93. On the air bombardment of Israeli and Arab cities, see D. Ben Gurion, *Diary of War*, entries for 1 June, 11 June, 16 July, 17 July 1948 (Hebrew).

94. E. Sivan, *The 1948 Generation: Myth, Profile and Memory* (Tel Aviv, 1991) (Hebrew). In comparison with the number of Jews in Israel at the time, this is indeed a high ratio of casualties but compared, for example, with the loss of 60,000 British soldiers on the opening day of the Somme offensive in 1916, this seems an almost insignificant number.

95. The number of those suffering mentally as a result of the war was as high as Britain's during the First World War; see E. Sivan, *The 1948 Generation*, 25 (Hebrew).

96. D. Ben Gurion, *Diary of War*, entries for 5 July, 15 July and 10 November 1948 (Hebrew).

97. G. Rothenberg, *The Anatomy of the Israeli Army*, 67.

98. B. Lewis, *Semites and Anti-Semites*, 23.

CHAPTER TWO

1. On the White Paper of 1939, see Chapter 1.

2. 'Law of Return', in W. Laqueur and B. Rubin (eds) *The Israel-Arab reader*, 109–10. By implication, this law had discriminated against all non-Jews, thus enabling Israelis to establish a closed and exclusive Jewish society. In later years there were also calls, even from non-religious leaders, to encourage all non-Jews to leave the country; see for example what minister Yigal Allon said in the 19 June 1967 cabinet meeting, as cited in R. Pedatzur, *The Triumph of Embarrassment: Israel and the Territories after the Six-Day War* (Tel Aviv, 1996) 51 (Hebrew).

3. Source: D. Ben Gurion (ed.) *The Jews in Their Land* (London, 1974) 318–19; see also U. Bialer, *Between East and West: Israel's Foreign Policy Orientation 1948–1956* (Cambridge, 1990) 198.

4. On the immigration of Jews from Yemen, see S. Yemini, *Memoirs* (Netanya, 1997) (Hebrew).

5. The astonishing story of how Israeli agents had frightened away the Jews of Iraq came to light on 9 November 1972, when an Israeli magazine called *Black Panther* had published the full story. For more details, see D. Hirst, *The Gun and the Olive Branch*, 155–64.

6. B. Lewis, *Semites and Anti-Semites*, 38.

7. For more figures about Jewish immigration to Israel, see M. Sicron, *Immigration to Israel 1948–1953* (Jerusalem, 1957) (Hebrew).

8. At the first census in 1949 Jews listed more than twenty different European and Asiatic languages as their media of speech.

9. The term 'army' is used here to refer to the three branches of the IDF: the air, naval and ground forces.

10. E. Luttwak and D. Horowitz, *The Israeli Army* (London, 1975) 71–7.

11. On just how low standards of fighting were, see Z. Schiff, 'The lessons of the battle of Tel-Muttilla', *Ha'aretz*, 5 June 1951 (Hebrew); U. Milstein, *The History of the Israel Paratroopers* (Tel Aviv, 1985) 106–33 (Hebrew); M. Dayan, 'From Falma to Kadesh', *Ha'aretz*, 17 April 1964 (Hebrew); M. Amit, 'The Sinai campaign: the first experience of the IDF as a regular army', *Ma'arachot*, no. 306–7 (Tel Aviv, Dec. 1986–Jan. 1987) 2 (Hebrew).

12. D. Ben Gurion, *Diary of War*, entry for 26 November 1948 (Hebrew).

13. D. Ben Gurion, *Diary of War*, entry for 27 November 1948 (Hebrew).

14. M. Bar On, *The Gates of Gaza: Israel's Road to Suez and Back 1955–1957* (London, 1994) 23.

15. D. Ben Gurion, speech in the Knesset, 19 August 1952 (Hebrew) (my emphasis).

16. D. Ben Gurion, as cited in G. Rothenberg, *The Anatomy of the Israeli Army*, 71.

17. About this idea see, D. Horowitz, 'The Israel Defence Forces: a civilized military in partially militarized society', in M. Lissak *et al.* (eds) *Army and Security* (Jerusalem, 1981) 274; see also A. Qazzaz, 'Army and society in Israel', *Pacific Sociological Review*, vol. 16, no. 2 (April 1973) 143–65. About the term 'nation-in-arms', see A. Roberts, *Nations in Arms: The Theory and Practice of Territorial Defence* (London, 1976) 37; see also R. Challener, *The French Theory of the Nation in Arms 1866–1939* (New York, 1965) 3–9.

18. On Ben Gurion's meeting with a guest from Switzerland who told him about the Swiss system, see D. Ben Gurion, *Diary of War*, entry for 21 September 1948 (Hebrew).

19. S. Teveth, *The Tanks of Tammuz* (London, 1968) 36.

20. In December 1998 an eleven-judge bench ordered the Knesset to legislate within a year to correct the situation so that Yeshivah boys would serve in the army. The reason for this is that the numbers of exempted Yeshivah students was going up from year to year and this caused resentment within the non-religious population.

21. G. Rothenberg, *The Anatomy of the Israeli Army*, 72.

22. It is estimated that the cost of absorbing a single immigrant in 1949 was about $3,000. Some of the costs were direct, for example, transporting the immigrants from their countries of origin to Israel and providing them with accommodation and other basic needs. There were also indirect costs, mainly paying for the unemployed who constituted 14 per cent of the total Israeli population in 1949; see U. Bialer, *Between East and West*, 199.

23. Figures are from David Ben Gurion's *Diaries*, entry for 13 January 1952, BGA as quoted in U. Bialer, *Between East and West*, 203–4.

24. In fact not only did Arabs steal from Israelis, but Israelis also stole from Arabs. Jordan had 677 head of cattle stolen by Israelis in 1952, whereas Israel lost 539. Of the 677 stolen from Jordan by Israelis, 357 were returned and 320 were not. Of those stolen by Jordanians from Israelis, 362 were returned and 177 were not. Thus in 1952, Jordanians lost 320 head of cattle to Israel while the latter suffered only to the extent of 177 head; see J. B. Glubb, *A Soldier with the Arabs*, 305; see also I. Black and B. Morris, *Israel's Secret Wars: A History of Israel's Intelligence Services* (London, 1991) 118.

25. This tactic was revealed in 1952 after Israel had deported 165 Arabs from the village of Abu Gosh, whose 1948 population of 450 had increased to 800 by virtue of this family reunification tactic.

26. Z. Shalom, *Policy in the Shadow of Controversy: The Routine Security Policy of Israel, 1949–1956* (Tel Aviv, 1996) 12 (Hebrew); see also B. Morris, *Israel's Border Wars 1949–1956: Arab Infiltration, Israeli Retaliation and the Countdown to the Suez war* (Oxford, 1993) 29.

27. About the fedayeen, see E. Ya'ari, *Fatah* (London, 1970); also J. Laffin, *Fedayeen: The Arab–Israeli Dilemma* (London, 1973); also Y. Harkabi, *Fedayeen Actions and Arab Strategy* (Adelphi papers, no. 53, IISS, London, 1969); also Despatch from Shneorson to the Foreign Minister, 15 April 1956, ISA, Fedayeen file, 2440/7; also Cable from Israel to Embassies, 9 April 1956, ISA, foreign ministry files, 2952/2; also M. Burns, *Between Arab and Israeli* (Beirut, 1969) 89. General Burns was the Chief of Staff of the UN truce supervision organization.

28. Figures of violent infiltration can be found in ISA, infiltration files, 2402/12, 2402/13, 2402/14; also M. Dayan, 'Pehulot Ha'tagmoul' ('The reprisals') in Y. Erez, and I. Kphir, *Army and Security*, vol. 1 (Tel Aviv, 1982) 98 (Hebrew).

29. A. Yaniv, *Deterrence without the Bomb*, 58.

30. As cited in Z. Shalom, *Policy in the Shadow of Controversy*, 27 (Hebrew).

31. J. B. Glubb, *A Soldier with the Arabs*, 303.

32. On the doctrine of retaliatory actions, see M. Dayan, 'Retaliatory actions as an instrument for security peace', Lecture of the Chief of Staff, in *Skira Hodshit* (Tel Aviv, August 1955) (Hebrew); also, Y. Gelber, 'The period of retaliatory actions', in *Hetz Shachor: The Gaza Raid and the Israeli Policy of Retaliation during the Fifties* (Tel Aviv, 1994) 13–21 (Hebrew).

33. On this operation, see Ariel Sharon to author, Jerusalem, 7 April 1991; also J. B. Glubb, *A Soldier with the Arabs*, 308–13; also A. Sharon, *Warrior: An Autobiography* (London, 1989) 86–91.

34. On the Gaza raid, see Ariel Sharon to author, Jerusalem, 7 April 1991; Sharon to author, Havat Ha'shikmim, 1 March 1997, BLA; also D. Ben Gurion, *Diaries*, entry for 3 March 1955, BGA; also Letter from Sharett to Ben Gurion, 1 March 1955, correspondence file, BGA; also A. Sharon, *Warrior*, 102–9; also B. Micaelson, 'The Gaza raid: the planning, the execution and the lessons', in *Hetz Shachor*, 17–33 (Hebrew). According to Nasser, this operation caused him to turn to the Russians for arms; see an interview with Nasser in the *New York Times*, 6 October 1955.

35. On 'Operation Kinneret', see Ariel Sharon to author, Jerusalem, 7 April 1991; also A. Sharon, *Warrior*, 124–8.

36. Details of Israel's retaliatory actions between 1953 and 1956 can be found in A. Bregman, 'Civil–military relations in Israel: military influence on war policy', Ph.D. dissertation (Department of War Studies, King's College London, 1993) app. II. On the failure of Israel's policy of retaliatory actions to curb infiltration, see B. Blechman, 'The impact of Israel's reprisals on behaviour of the bordering Arab nations', *The Journal of Conflict Resolution*, vol. 16 (June 1972); see also S. Silverburg, 'The Israeli reaction to terrorism', *New Outlook*, vol. 12, no. 1, 1969.

37. A. Bregman and J. el-Tahri, *The Fifty Years War*, ch. 4.

38. M. Heikal, *Nasser: The Cairo Documents* (London, 1976) 59–60; also a report on the arms deal in *Ha'aretz*, 28 September 1955 (Hebrew). Nasser gave details of the arms deal at the opening of a photographic exhibition on 27 September 1955 in Cairo. On the list were some 300 medium and heavy tanks, T-34/85s and JS-3s, 200 armoured personnel carriers, BTR-152s, 100 SU-100 assault guns, 500 medium field guns and howitzers, 200 57mm anti-tank guns, 134 anti-aircraft guns and 1,000 recoil-less rifles, together with large quantities of scout cars, small

arms, trucks and other military equipment. To provide air power there were fifty twin-engined IL-28 jet bombers and 120 Mig-15 fighters, as well as twenty transport planes. In addition, the Soviets sent two Skory class destroyers, fifteen fast minesweepers, several submarines and scores of torpedo boats. Figures are adapted from G. Rothenberg, *The Anatomy of the Israeli Army*, 96-7; also M. Bar On, *The Gates of Gaza*, 16-17.

39. M. Sharett, *Personal Diary* (Tel Aviv, 1978) entry for 28 September 1955 (Hebrew).
40. *Ma'ariv*, 2 October 1955 (Hebrew).
41. *Davar*, 2 October 1955 (Hebrew).
42. D. Ben Gurion, *Divrai Ha'Knesset* (*Records of the Knesset*) vol. 18, 673 (Hebrew).
43. For this and more, see *Divrai Ha'Knesset*, vol. 19, 64-120 (Hebrew).
44. A. Eban, *My Country* 125-6; see also M. Bar On 'The Czech-Egyptian arms deal', *Ma'arachot*, no. 306-7 (Tel Aviv, Dec. 1986-Jan. 1987) 39 (Hebrew).
45. This and more in M. Bar On, *The Gates of Gaza*, 9.
46. U. Ben-Eliezer, *The Emergence of Israeli Militarism, 1936-1956* (Tel Aviv, 1995) 301-2 (Hebrew).
47. M. Bar On, *The Gates of Gaza*, 10.
48. Defence expenditure as percentage of governmental expenditure remained at a high level throughout the years leading up to the 1967 war. In 1964 it was 32.5 per cent; in 1965, 31.8 per cent; and in the year before the 1967 war, 31.2 percent. See M. Barnett, *Confronting the Costs of War: Military Power, State, and Society in Egypt and Israel* (Princeton, 1992) 154.
49. It was named Kadesh after the desert post where the Israelites had rested on their way to the Promised Land. The account of the operation in this chapter is relatively short because there is a voluminous literature covering every detail, by military and other historians, as well as by the commanders involved; for more about the political background from an Israeli point of view, see Y. Evron, *A New Look at the 1956 Suez War* (Tel Aviv, 1986) (Hebrew); also M. Dayan, 'Sinai: ten years after', *Ma ariv*, 11 November 1966 (Hebrew); also M. Dayan, *Diary of the Sinai Campaign* (London, 1965).
50. G. Rafael, *Destination Peace: Three Decades of Israeli Foreign Policy* (London, 1981) 54.
51. The Canal company, with its British and French shareholders, did not actually own the Canal, but had acquired a concession to operate it for ninety-nine years after its opening, that is until November 1968.
52. In a speech at the Guildhall on 9 November 1955, Prime Minister Anthony Eden said that in order to prevent future wars Israel should give up land, especially in the Negev. See on this Y. Ne'eman, 'Contacts with the French and British during the Sinai campaign', *Ma'arachot*, no. 306-7 (Tel Aviv, Dec. 1986-Jan. 1987) 31 (Hebrew); see also Ben Gurion's response to Eden's proposal in *Divrai Ha'Knesset* (*Records of the Knesset*) 15 November 1955 (Hebrew).
53. More on this in M. Sharett, *Personal Diary*, 266, 947 (Hebrew).
54. K. Kyle, *Suez* (London, 1992) app. A.
55. *ibid.*; see also H. Wilson, *The Chariot of Israel: Britain, America and the State of Israel* (London, 1981) 280.
56. M. Dayan, *Diary of the Sinai Campaign* 60-1; for more on the planning of the campaign with the French and British, see Shimon Peres to author, Jerusalem, 11 March 1991; see also Y. Ne'eman, 'Contacts with the French and British in the Sinai campaign', *Ma'arachot*, no. 306-7 (Tel Aviv, Dec. 1986-Jan. 1987) (Hebrew). Colonel Ne'eman, then Deputy Director of Military Intelligence, was involved in these talks.

57. A. Eban, *My Country*, 141; for more about Israel's war aims see D. Ben Gurion, 'The political and military situation', a speech in the Knesset, *Divrai Ha'Knesset*, 7 November 1956, 197 (Hebrew); also a speech he delivered to the Knesset on 22 April 1956, 1685 (Hebrew); also M. Amit, 'The Sinai campaign: the first test of IDF as a regular army', *Ma'arachot*, no. 306–7 (Tel Aviv, Dec. 1986–Jan. 1987) 4 (Hebrew).

58. M. Dayan, 'Israel army formations taking part in operation Kadesh', in *Diary of the Sinai Campaign*, app. 4.

59. B. Z. Tehan, *The Sinai Campaign* (n.d, n.p.) (Hebrew). This is an internal IDF publication and a most reliable source.

60. Less successful, though, was the Anglo-French operation. They sent their ultimatum on 30 October to both Egypt and Israel and, with the ultimatum expiring on the morning of the 31st, their first bombs were dropped that evening. On 5 and 6 November, British and French troops had landed from the sea to occupy positions along the Suez Canal, but by now time had run out politically, and the campaign was called off before Britain and France could reach their objectives.

61. Although the fighting was mainly against the Egyptians in the Sinai, Israeli forces elsewhere took advantage of the fog of battle to finish the uncompleted job of the 1948 war. As the then head of Northern Command Yitzhak Rabin testified: 'exploiting the war with the Egyptians. ... I have solved one problem in the north [of Israel] ... we have transferred [meaning expelled] about 2,000 Arabs, who were a major security problem ... to the eastern side of the Jordan'. Y. Rabin, *Pinkas Sherut*, 97 (Hebrew).

62. A. Yaniv, *Deterrence without the Bomb*, 75.

63. Concocted by the Russian Czars' disinformation service, the *Protocols of the Elders of Zion* has served as the basis for worldwide anti-semitic propaganda. It was successively used by the czarist police, the Whites in the Russian civil war, the German and other Nazis, and certain Arab governments and organizations in their anti-Jewish propaganda; see B. Lewis, *Semites and Anti-Semites*, 23.

64. A. Eban, *My Country*, 162.

65. A. Eban, *My Country*, 164.

66. G. Rothenberg, *The Anatomy of the Israeli Army*, 116.

CHAPTER THREE

1. Memorandum of conversation, 31 January 1967, LBJ Library, E.O.12356, sec. 3.4, NEJ 93–120. Moshe Dayan, who would become the hero of the 1967 war, had said after the war: 'Many wars had started unexpectedly, but it is doubtful if there has been ever in the history of Israel, such an unexpected war as the [June 1967 war]'. M. Dayan, 'Midron el Milchama', *A New Map, New Relationships* (Tel Aviv, 1968) (Hebrew). This he said, of course, before the surprising Yom Kippur War of October 1973.

2. The civil war in Yemen broke out on 26 September 1962. Egypt intervened in the war, seeing it as an opportunity to teach King Saud of Saudi Arabia, who had led a campaign against Egypt, a lesson. Egypt supported the Republicans, and Saudi Arabia the Royalists. Egypt's involvement in Yemen steadily increased from a brigade to two divisions – 70,000 troops.

3. This happened in four major border clashes: 17 March 1965, 13 May 1965, 12 August 1965 and 14 July 1966. For more see Y. Tal, *National Security: The Few against the Many* (Tel Aviv, 1996) 136–8 (Hebrew).

4. E. Haber, *Today War Will Break Out: The Reminiscences of Brig. Gen. Yisrael Lior, Aide-de-Camp to Prime Ministers Levi Eshkol and Golda Meir* (Tel Aviv, 1987) 146 (Hebrew).
5. Nasser's speech at UAR Advanced Air Headquarters, 25 May 1967, in W. Laqueur and B. Rubin (eds) *The Israel-Arab Reader*, 144–9.
6. About Eshkol's statements, see E. Haber, *Today War Will Break Out*, 147 (Hebrew).
7. See Chapter 1.
8. Interview given by Moshe Dayan in 1976 to Rami Tal and published in *Yediot Aharonot*, 27 April 1997 (Hebrew).
9. Interview with Syrian general Abdel Razzak Al-Dardari (Damascus, n.d.) in the author's archive.
10. Y. Sayigh, and A. Shlaim (eds) *The Cold War and the Middle East* (Oxford, 1997) 291, 293.
11. For strong evidence in support of this approach, see A. Bregman and J. el-Tahri, *The Fifty Years War*, 64–6.
12. A. el-Sadat, *In Search of Identity: An Autobiography* (New York, 1977) 172.
13. The Jordanians were cross with Nasser for failing to rescue them when the Israelis attacked in April that year at Samua. About Arab pressure on Nasser to stand up to Israeli aggression, see Nasser's speech to Arab trade unionists, 26 May 1967, in W. Laqueur and B. Rubin, *The Israel-Arab Reader*, 149–52; also interview with Egyptian Minister of War Shams el-Din Badran, London, 5 June 1997, BLA.
14. Interview with Egyptian general Ahmed Fakher, Cairo, 27 February 1997, BLA.
15. Interview with Mohammed Fawzi, Cairo, 28 February 1997, BLA.
16. Interview with Syrian general Abdel Razzak Al-Dardari.
17. Eshkol made the same offer on the night of 27 May, when the Soviet Ambassador came to visit him at the Dan Hotel at 2 a.m. The Ambassador had complained that Israel was mobilizing its forces and Eshkol proposed to change his pyjamas and to accompany the Ambassador to the border with Syria to see that Israel had not mobilized forces. About 'the night of the pyjamas', see Miriam Eshkol to author, Jerusalem, 30 January 1997.
18. A. Eban, *My Country*, 198.
19. Interview with Evgeny Pyrlin, Moscow, March 1997, BLA; also A. Bregman and J. el-Tahri, *The Fifty Years War*, 65.
20. 'Soviet official's comments on Soviet policy on the Middle East war – CIA report of conversation with Soviet official re June War', LBJ Library, 82–156, doc. 8420.
21. Nasser to Eric Rouleau, *The Times*, 19 February 1970.
22. Israel's representative to the UN, Gideon Rafael, met with the Secretary General, U Thant, and read him an extract from a United Nations document: 'if the United Nations buffer should be removed, serious fighting would, quite likely, soon be resumed'. U Thant, somewhat bewildered, asked Rafael who had written this report, to which Rafael replied, 'It was submitted by yourself, Mr Secretary General, on 7 September 1966 to the General Assembly'; see G. Rafael, *Destination Peace*, 139.
23. On Nasser's demand that UNEF leave, see W. Laqueur, *The Road to War: The Origin and Aftermath of the Arab–Israeli Conflict 1967–8* (London, 1993) 101–2.
24. Nasser's speech at UAR Advanced Air Headquarters, 25 May 1967; also interview with Nasser, *World in Action*, 29 May 1967.
25. See Chapter 2.
26. A. Yaniv, *Deterrence without the Bomb*, 81.
27. Quoted in S. Segev, *Sadin Adom: The Six Day War* (Tel Aviv, 1967) 51 (Hebrew); also G. Rafael, *Destination Peace*, 65.
28. A. el-Sadat, *In Search of Identity*, 172.

29. A. J. P. Taylor, *English History* (London, 1965) 580.

30. A. el-Sadat, *In Search of Identity*, 173.

31. See Chapter 1

32. Y. Allon, *A Curtain of Sand* (Tel Aviv, 1959) 376 (Hebrew); also N. Lorch, 'Kavei Dimyon ve Shoni be'Milchamot Israel Arav', *Ma ariv*, 26 May 1974 (Hebrew).

33. That the Straits of Tiran were not blocked we know from an interview with Edin Bahey Noufal, Cairo, 25 February 1997, BLA. Noufal was Deputy Chief of Operations during the 1967 war and Chief of Operations in the federal army command during the 1973 war.

34. R. Gilo (ed.) *Bamachane – The IDF Journal: 30 Years to the Six Day War* (Tel Aviv, 30 May 1997) 8 (Hebrew).

35. J. Hunt, *Hussein of Jordan* (London, 1989) 141–2.

36. About the signing of the pact with Egypt, see an interview with King Hussein, Amman, 2 March 1997; also an interview with Jordan's Prime Minister Zaid al Rifai, Amman, 6 March 1997, BLA.

37. Source: Y. Tal, *National Security*, 142 (Hebrew); another source indicates that Israel had 275,000 men, 1,093 tanks and 203 fighter-bombers, while the Arabs had 456,000 men, 2,750 tanks, and 602 jets and bombers, see R. Gilo (ed.) *Ba'machane – The IDF Journal: 30 Years to the Six Day War*, 20 (Hebrew).

38. On IDF's doctrine of warfare, see A. Levita, *Offense and Defence in Israeli Military Doctrine* (London, 1990).

39. Y. Tal, *National Security*, 144 (Hebrew).

40. R. Gilo (ed.) *Bamachane – The IDF Journal: 30 Years to the Six Day War*, 11 (Hebrew).

41. Y. Rabin, *Pinkas Sherut*, 160, 162 (Hebrew); also Moshe Dayan in a summary of the 1967 war, 28 July 1967, YTA, 15 (Galili) 48/1/3, 3 (Hebrew).

42. Nasser's speech to Arab trade unionists, 26 May 1967, in W. Laqueur and B. Rubin (eds) *The Israel-Arab Reader*, 149–52.

43. E. Downton, 'Report from Cairo', *Sunday Telegraph*, 21 May 1967.

44. Interview with Uzi Narkiss, Jerusalem, 21 January 1997, BLA.

45. D. Hall-Cathala, *The Peace Movement in Israel, 1967–87* (London, 1990) 4.

46. Former general Matityahu Peled to author, Tel Aviv, 7 April 1991.

47. A. Eban, *My Country*, 214.

48. Miriam Eshkol to author.

49. About how and why, see Miriam Eshkol to author.

50. *Ha'aretz*, 29 May 1967 (Hebrew); also Miriam Eshkol to author.

51. Moshe Dayan in a summary of the 1967 war (28 July 1967) YTA, 15 (Galili) 48/1/3, 3 (Hebrew).

52. M. Dayan, *Story of my Life*, 340.

53. M. Dayan, *Story of my Life*, 331; see also interview with Yeshayahu Gavish, Ramat Ha'sharon, 20 January 1997, BLA.

54. M. Dayan, *Story of my Life*, 341.

55. G. Rafael, *Destination Peace*, 64.

56. Aharon Yariv to author, Tel Aviv, 27 March 1991; also letter from Aharon Yariv to author, 2 June 1992, Tel Aviv (Hebrew).

57. 'The offensive plan of the southern command' (IDF internal publication) (Hebrew); The Operations Diary of the Southern Command as cited in the *Four Days War* (internal publication, The Southern Command Press) 2 June 1967 (Hebrew).

58. Y. Rabin, *Pinkas Sherut*, 182 (Hebrew).

59. Interview with Minister of War Shams el-Din Badran, London, 5 June 1997, BLA.

60. Interview with Pavel Akopov Sememovich, Moscow, March 1997, BLA. Akopov was present at the meeting between Kosygin and Badran. He was a Soviet diplomat and worked for the Middle East desk of the Politburo.

61. Interview with President Nasser, 29 May 1967, *World in Action*, tape number 1148; see also interview with Minister of War Shams el-Din Badran.

62. Interview with Egyptian Minister of War Shams el-Din Badran.

63. For more about Israeli diplomatic attempts to resolve the conflict, particularly the Eban's mission, see A. Bregman and J. el-Tahri, *The Fifty Years War*, 70–5.

64. From Amit's report to the cabinet, Meir Amit's archive.

65. *ibid.*

66. Interview with Meir Amit, Ramat Gan, 20 January 1997, BLA; also interview with Robert McNamara, 21 April 1997, Washington, BLA.

67. As cited in J. Lunt, *Hussein of Jordan*, 143–4.

68. R. Gilo (ed.), *Ba machane – The IDF Journal: 30 Years to the Six Day War*, 26 (Hebrew).

69. In fact, when Dayan ordered the advancing forces to pull back they were not yet at the water's edge. A field commander who had arrived at a place called 'Rumani' mistakenly thought, and so reported, that he had reached the Suez Canal; see Yitzhak Rabin to author, Tel Aviv, 21 March 1991. Israeli forces reached the Suez Canal on 9 June 1967 at 1 a.m.

70. Interview with Ezer Weizman, Jerusalem, 3 March 1997, BLA.

71. Interview with King Hussein of Jordan, Amman, 2 March 1997, BLA.

72. *ibid.*

73. J. Lunt, *Hussein of Jordan*, 144.

74. The conversation between Nasser and the King can be found in A. Bregman and J. el-Tahri, *The Fifty Years War*, 90; see also an interview with King Hussein of Jordan; also an off-the-record interview with the King, Amman, 28 January 1997, in the author's archive; also an interview with Zaid al-Rifai, Amman, 6 March 1997, BLA.

75. Interview with King Hussein of Jordan.

76. R. Tal, 'Moshe Dayan: soul searching', *Yediot Aharonot*, 27 April 1997 (Hebrew).

77. Interview with General Reshetinikov Vassily Vassilievich, Commander of Strategic Aviation Corps, Moscow, 27 September 1996 (in the author's archive) and as cited in A. Bregman and J. el-Tahri, *The Fifty Years War*, 95; also interview with Evgeny Pyrlin, Moscow, March 1997, BLA.

78. Interview with Chief of IAF Mordecahi Hod, Tel Aviv, 21 January 1997, BLA.

79. Interview with Syrian General Abdel Razzak Al-Dardari.

80. NEJ 95–157 hot-line message from Chairman Kosygin to President Johnson, 10 June 1967 (8.45 a.m.) LBJ Library.

81. A. Eban, *My Country*, 279.

82. A. M. Farid, *Nasser: The Final Years* (Reading, 1994) 6–7. For eleven years, until 1970, Abdel Magid Farid had served as Secretary-General of the Egyptian presidency with the rank of minister, and attended all of Nasser's meetings on domestic and international affairs.

83. *ibid.*, 14.

84. *ibid.*, 23.

85. *ibid.*, 10, 14.

86. *ibid.*, 124.

87. 'Middle East artillery battle provokes bitter debate', *The Christian Science Monitor*, 10 September 1968; see also U. Milstein, 'Attrition 1961–84', *Monitin*, no. 71 (Tel Aviv, August 1984) 26 (Hebrew).

88. A. Aden, *On the Bank of the Suez: An Israeli General's Personal Account of the Yom Kippur War* (London, 1980) 43.

89. M. Heikal, *The Road to Ramadan* (London, 1975) 28–9.
90. *Al-Aharam*, 21 January 1969.
91. A. M. Farid, *Nasser: The Final Years*, 135.
92. *ibid.*, 135–6.
93. Haim Bar Lev to author, Jerusalem, 19 March 1991.
94. D. Thomson, *Europe since Napoleon* (London, 1966) 736.
95. Haim Bar Lev to author.
96. For more about this critical debate, see Haim Bar Lev to author; former general Yeshayahu Gavish to author, Ramat Ha'sharon, 5 January 1992; former general Avraham Tamir to author, Tel Aviv, 28 March 1991; also H. Bar Lev, speech in the Knesset, *Divrai Ha'Knesset*, 11 December 1985; also U. Milstein, *The Lesson of a Collapse: From Sadat to Arafat* (Kiron, 1993) 105 (Hebrew).
97. S. El-Shazli, *The Crossing of Suez: The October War (1973)* (London, 1980) 16.
98. *ibid.*
99. On Operation Boxer, see Ezer Weizman to author, Caesaria, 17 February 1992.
100. Mordechai Hod to author, Lod, 8 April 1991.
101. 'Dayan outlines Israel's military strategy', *Financial Times*, 29 January 1970; also Moshe Dayan in *Davar*, 29 January 1970 (Hebrew); also Golda Meir speaking in Labour's central committee, 12 October 1970, LPA, 23/70, 6 (Hebrew); also Meir in *Ha'aretz*, 2 March 1970; and her announcement in the Knesset on 17 February 1970 (Hebrew).
102. Mordechai Hod to author and Ezer Weizman to author. The contract to obtain forty-eight Skyhawks was signed in February 1966 and that for the Phantoms a little later. Visits by both Weizman and Hod to the United States led to the arrival of the aeroplanes in Israel around the time that the idea of using air power deep into Egypt really took off; see A. Shlaim and R. Tanter, 'Decision process, choice and consequences: Israel's deep-penetration bombing in Egypt, 1970', *World Politics*, vol. 30, no. 4 (1978) 489, 491.
103. On the IAF's first strike on 7 January 1970, see Z. Schiff, *Phantom over the Nile: The Story of the Israeli Air Corps* (Haifa, 1970) 193 (Hebrew).
104. S. El-Shazli, *The Crossing of Suez*, 17.
105. 'The announcement of the Prime Minister regarding the political situation', *Divrai Ha'Knesset*, 17 February 1970 (Hebrew).
106. See reports in *The Times*; the *International Herald Tribune*; the *Guardian* and the *Financial Times*, all from 9 April 1970; also Mordechai Hod to author.
107. The success of the Egyptians was much due to direct Soviet intervention in the war; see for example the testimony of Popov, Konstantin Ilych, who shot down five Israeli Phantoms in August 1970 (interview, Balashikha, 28 September 1996, in the author's archive); also classified intelligence reports regarding Soviet intervention in the war, YTA, Section 15 (Galili) 54/2–6; on how Israel shot down five Migs manned by Soviet pilots, see Mordechai Hod to author; see also Y. Amir, 'This is how five Migs flown by Russian pilots were shot down', *The IAF Journal*, no. 91, (July 1973) 6–16 (Hebrew).
108. One is Y. Bar-Siman Tov, *The Israeli–Egyptian War of Attrition 1969–1970* (New York, 1980); also A. Khalidi, 'A perspective on the strategy of attrition: the Egyptian–Israeli war of attrition, 1969–1970' (Ph.D. dissertation, King's College London, 1982); also D. Schueftan, *Attrition: Egypt's Postwar Political Strategy 1967–1970* (Tel Aviv, 1989) (Hebrew).
109. D. Schueftan, *Attrition*, 440 (Hebrew); around 10,000 Egyptians and civilians were killed, most of the cities along the Suez Canal were destroyed, and their inhabitants became refugees in their own country.
110. M. N. Bernett, *Confronting the Costs of War*, 154.

CHAPTER FOUR

1. Interview with former foreign ministry official Gideon Rafael, Jerusalem, 19 January 1997, BLA.
2. Interview with Donald Bergus, Washington, 29 October 1996, in the author's archive.
3. A. el-Sadat, *In Search of Identity*, 1.
4. Sadat moved against the Ali Sabri group on 14 May 1971, arresting them and putting many of them on trial; see the very interesting interview with Sadat's widow Jihan el-Sadat, Cairo, 28 February 1997, BLA.
5. As cited in C. Herzog, *The War of Atonement: The Inside Story of the Yom Kippur War, 1973* (London, 1998) 18.
6. A. el-Sadat, *In Search of Identity*, 219.
7. *ibid.*
8. Z. Schiff, 'Was there a warning?', *Ha'aretz*, 12 June 1998 (Hebrew).
9. See Chapter 3
10. M. Dayan, *Story of my Life*, 469; also V. Shem-Tov, *One of Them* (Kibbutz Dalia, 1997) 56 (Hebrew); also A. Braun, *Moshe Dayan and the Yom Kippur War* (Tel Aviv, 1992) 11–12 (Hebrew).
11. Interview with Gideon Rafael.
12. As cited in A. Braun, *Moshe Dayan and the Yom Kippur War*, 16 (Hebrew).
13. Interview with Joseph Sisco, Washington, 19 March 1997, BLA; also A. Bregman and J. el-Tahri, *The Fifty Years War*, 108–9.
14. Interview with Joseph Sisco; also interview with Alfred 'Roy' Atherton, who had accompanied Sisco on this visit, Washington, 19 October 1996, in the author's archive.
15. For Sadat's motives in expelling the Soviets, see his address to the executive committee of ASU, 18 July 1972, in I. Raphael, *The Public Diary of President Sadat* (Leiden, 1978) 221–2.
16. The *Sunday Times* Insight Team, *The Yom Kippur War* (London, 1974) 58.
17. Interview with General Saad el-Din Shazli, Cairo, 24 February 1997; see also A. Bregman and J. el-Tahri, *The Fifty Years War*, 113.
18. C. Herzog, *The War of Atonement*, 25.
19. Sadat's address to the Conference of the Non-Aligned Countries in Algiers, 6 September 1973, in I. Raphael, *The Public Diary of President Sadat*, 109; also I. Fahmy, *Negotiating for Peace in the Middle East* (London, 1983) 5. Ismail Fahmy was Egypt's Deputy Prime Minister and Foreign Minister until 17 November 1977.
20. Interview with General Saad el-Din Shazli and with Field Marshal Abdul Ghani el-Gamassy, Cairo, 24 February 1997, BLA.
21. On this visit to Moscow, see M. Heikal, *The Road to Ramadan*, 83–90; also E. Zeira, *The October '73 War: Myth Versus Reality* (Tel Aviv, 1993) 87 (Hebrew).
22. A. el-Sadat, *In Search of Identity*, 318 (my emphasis).
23. Letter A. el-Sadat to Brezhnev, as cited in A. el-Sadat, *In Search of Identity*, 320; and interview with Pavel Akopov, Moscow, March 1997, BLA.
24. Scud missiles were finally delivered to Egypt around August 1973, but became operational only at the beginning of 1974.
25. Interview with Field Marshal Abdel Ghani el-Gamassy.
26. S. el-Shazli, *The Crossing of Suez*, 122.
27. Interview with Field Marshal Abdel Ghani el-Gamassy.
28. S. el-Shazli, *The Crossing of Suez*, 123; see also M. Heikal, *The Road to Ramadan*, 181.
29. Interview with Saad el-Din Shazli.
30. A. el-Sadat, *In Search of Identity*, 241.

31. *ibid*.

32. Much of the following information has never been published before and is still one of the most guarded secrets in Israel. It is based on lengthy interviews with people who were close to the events and are very reliable, but whose names, for obvious reasons, cannot be revealed.

33. The outbreak of war also surprised the Americans, and the Israelis were not alone in error. The CIA bulletin of 6 October, obviously prepared before the start of the war, stated:

> Israel, Egypt and Syria are becoming increasingly concerned about the military activities of each other, although neither side appears bent on initiating hostilities. For Egypt a military initiative makes little sense at this critical juncture. ... For the Syrian president, a military adventure now would be suicidal.

As cited in G. Rafael, *Destination Peace*, 290.

34. I. Black and B. Morris, *Israel's Secret Wars*, 286.

35. A. el-Sadat, *In Search of Identity*, 318.

36. Director of Military Intelligence Eli Zeira to Uri Milstein, 23 May 1974, 8 in YTA, 25M/60/2 (Hebrew).

37. A. Barzilai, 'Zeira: a double agent had strengthened my adherence to a wrong conception in Yom Kippur', *Ha'aretz*, 28 October 1998 (Hebrew).

38. Y. Ben Porat, 'The Yom Kippur War: a mistake in May leads to a surprise in October', *IDF Journal*, vol. 3, no. 3, (Summer 1986) 53.

39. A. Braun, *Moshe Dayan and the Yom Kippur War*, 25–34 (Hebrew).

40. H. Bartov, *Daddo: 48 years and more 20 days*, vol. I (Tel Aviv, 1978) 273–4 (Hebrew). Daddo – David Elazar – was Israel's Chief of Staff during the 1973 war.

41. A. el-Sadat, *In Search of Identity*, 241.

42. Interview with Field Marshal Abdel Ghani el-Gamassy.

43. Interview with Egyptian general Fuad Awidi, *Ma ariv*, 24 September 1993 (Hebrew).

44. Interview with Syrian general Abdel Razzak Al-Dardary, who was then chief of operations; see also Interview with Egyptian general Bahieddin Noufal. Noufal was the Chief of Staff of the joint Egyptian–Syrian federal operation; also M. Heikal, *The Road to Ramadan*, 11–18.

45. Interview with Egyptian general Saad el-Din Shazli; also M. Heikal, *The Road to Ramadan*, 12.

46. On this agent telling the Israelis that Sadat had decided to postpone the war, see A. Braun, *Moshe Dayan in the Yom Kippur War*, 68 (Hebrew).

47. Interview with Syrian former minister of information George Saddeqni, Damascus, 16 October 1996, in the author's archive.

48. *ibid*.

49. Interview with former Jordanian prime minister Zeid Rifai.

50. This document was first published in A. Bregman and J. el-Tahri, *The Fifty Years War*, 118–19. By publishing this rare document we have managed to confirm rumours of the King's visit to Israel. For more see, M. Zak, 'The warning', *Ma ariv*, 24 September 1993, 29 (Hebrew); Z. Schiff, 'What did Golda conceal?', *Ha'aretz*, 27 September 1989 (Hebrew); Z. Schiff, 'A foreign leader warned: the intelligence and Golda ignored', *Ha'aretz*, 15 September 1993 (Hebrew).

51. The above quotations are based on unpublished transcripts, but the reader can find extracts of this crucial discussion in A. Braun, *Moshe Dayan and the Yom Kippur War*, 39–40 (Hebrew).

52. M. Heikal, *The Road to Ramadan*, 32; A. Bregman and J. el-Tahri, *The Fifty Years War*, 116.
53. Interview with former Syrian minister of information George Saddeqni.
54. Interview with Egyptian general Bahieddin Noufal; also M. Heikal, *The Road to Ramadan*, 31.
55. Interview with Syrian Minister of Defence Mustapha Tlas, Damascus, 3 July 1997, BLA; Interview with General Saad el-Shazli, Cairo, 28 September 1996, in the author's archive; also interview with Field-Marshal Abdel Ghani el-Gamassy; also interview with general Bahieddin Noufal.
56. A. el-Sadat, *In Search of Identity*, 246.
57. A. Braun, *Moshe Dayan and the Yom Kippur War*, 57 (Hebrew); Brig. Gen. Y. Ben-Porat, *Neila: Locked On*, (Tel Aviv, 1991) 15 (Hebrew).
58. A. el-Sadat, *In Search of Identity*, 247.
59. A. Braun, *Moshe Dayan and the Yom Kippur War*, 62–4 (Hebrew).
60. E. Zeira, *The Yom Kippur War*, 156–7 (Hebrew); M. Dayan, *Story of my Life*, 477; 'The Commission inquiry: the Yom Kippur War', *The Agranat Report* (Jerusalem, 1974) 50 (Hebrew).
61. Chief of Staff David Elazar, *Ma ariv*, 29 October 1973 (Hebrew).
62. The war was to begin on 6 October, which was also the tenth day of Ramadan, the day in the year 624 in which the prophet Mohammad began to prepare for the battle of Badr, which led six years later to his victory over the Meccans and his triumphant entry into Mecca.
63. Interview with Egyptian general Saad el-Din Shazli.
64. A. Hashavia, *The Yom Kippur War* (Tel Aviv, 1974) 15 (Hebrew); E. Zeira, *The Yom Kippur War*, 68 (Hebrew).
65. S. el-Shazli, *The Crossing of Suez*, 23.
66. Interview with Egyptian general Saad el-Din Shazli and Interview with Egyptian general Bahieddin Noufal.
67. Interview with Syrian Minister of Defence Mustapha Tlas.
68. H. Bartov, *Daddo*, 258–60 (Hebrew). For more about the Israeli defence plan, see A. Adan, *On the Bank of the Suez: An Israeli General's Personal Account of the Yom Kippur War* (London, 1980) 57. The IDF also had four sets of plans for crossing into the enemy's land. These were called 'Operation Zefania', 'Operation Ben Hail', 'Operation Hatul Midbar' and 'Operation Abirei Lev'; see U. Milstein, *The Lesson of a Collapse: from Sadat to Arafat*, 121–2 (Hebrew).
69. Haim Bar Lev to author; also an interview with Ariel Sharon's successor Shmuel Gonen in *Yediot Aharonot*, 21 September 1977 (Hebrew).
70. C. Herzog, *The War of Atonement*, 62–3.
71. E. Zeira, *The Yom Kippur War*, 40 (Hebrew).
72. Y. Tal, *National Security*, 166–7 (Hebrew).
73. S. Nakdimon, *Low Probability* (Tel Aviv, 1982) 29 (Hebrew).
74. H. Bartov, *Daddo*, vol. 1, 282–5 (Hebrew).
75. Yitzhak Hofi to author, Ramat Gan, 21 October 1996.
76. Dayan's tour of the Golan Heights came a day after King Hussein's visit to Israel when he had warned that Egypt and Syria intended to launch an attack on Israel. It might be that Dayan's trip to the north was partially a result of Hussein's warning. M. Dayan, *Story of my Life*, 473; A. Braun, *Moshe Dayan and the Yom Kippur War*, 41 (Hebrew); *The Agranat Report*, 21–2 (Hebrew).
77. Y. Tal, *National Security*, 167 (Hebrew); M. Dayan, *Story of my Life*, 470.
78. Interview with former Syrian Minister of Information George Saddeqni.
79. See interview with Syrian Minister of Defence Mustapha Tlas. Jordan did not join the war. General Amer Khammash, number three in the Jordanian army, met

with Syria's President Assad on Monday 8 October and was requested that Jordan join the war, which Khammash declined. At first President Sadat of Egypt also asked the Jordanians to join the war. Khammash travelled to Cairo and met with Sadat, who eventually said: 'I don't recommend Jordan to do anything because this would be sheer suicide'; see interview with General Amer Khammash, Amman, 4 October 1996, in the author's archive.

80. Chief of Staff David Elazar to Uri Milstein, 4 June 1974, YTA, N125/60/1, 9–11; also Moshe Dayan, *Story of my Life*, 467; also David Elazar, interview, *Ma ariv*, 29 October 1973 (Hebrew); also A. Braun, *Moshe Dayan and the Yom Kippur War*, 70–1, 72–3; also *The Agranat Report*, 21 (Hebrew).

81. G. Meir, *My Life*, 358; David Elazar to Uri Milstein; also *The Agranat Report*, 23–4 (Hebrew); also letter from Elazar to the government as published in *Ma'ariv*, 20 April 1976 (Hebrew).

82. A. Braun, *Moshe Dayan and the Yom Kippur War*, 86 (Hebrew); G. Meir, *My Life*, 359; V. Shem-Tov, *One of Them*, 51 (Hebrew).

83. S. el-Shazli, *The Crossing of Suez*, 150.

84. Interview with Field Marshal Abdel Ghani el-Gamassy.

85. S. el-Shazli, *The Crossing of Suez*, 157.

86. Chief of Staff David Elazar to Uri Milstein; also A. Braun, *Moshe Dayan and the Yom Kippur War*, 83 (Hebrew); also *The Agranat Report*, 43 (Hebrew); also Haim Bar Lev to author; also interview with Shmuel Gonen, *Yediot Aharonot*, 21 September 1977 (Hebrew).

87. E. Zeira, *The October War*, 66 (Hebrew).

88. Yisrael Tal to Uri Milstein, 8 January 1984, YTA, 25/60/2 (Hebrew).

89. Yisrael Tal to Uri Milstein; also M. Heikal, *The Road to Ramadan*, 215.

90. M. Dayan, *Story of my Life*, 488; G. Meir, *My Life*, 361.

91. Although the war on the Golan Heights had more or less ended, still the Hermon stronghold was in Syrian hands. On 22 October, the Israelis completely routed and expelled the last Syrians from the Heights.

92. M. Dayan, *Story of my Life*, 494.

93. During the Second World War, in April and June 1941, for example, the German general Rommel had produced a British retreat – in the first case a collapse – by a similar strategic thrust that was made in lesser strength; see B. H. Liddell Hart, *History of the Second World War* (London, 1970) 201.

94. M. Dayan, *Story of my Life*, 503; Yisrael Tal to Uri Milstein, 8 January 1984, YTA, 25/60/2 (Hebrew); *The Agranat Report*, 80–2 (Hebrew).

95. S. el-Shazli, *The Crossing of Suez*, 162; M. Heikel, *The Road to Ramadan*, 212; E. Tavor, 'The longest day', *Ha'olam Ha'ze*, 11 December 1974 (Hebrew).

96. On Syrian pressure on Egypt to move deeper into the Sinai, see interviews with Egypt's Field Marshal Abdel Ghani el-Gamassy and Syria's Minister of Defence Mustapha Tlas.

97. Interview with General Saad el-Din Shazli; also S. el-Shazli, *The Crossing of Suez*, 37–40.

98. M. Heikal, *The Road to Ramadan*, 227.

99. Yisrael Tal to author.

100. A. Sharon, *Warrior*, 311; see also Ariel Sharon to author.

101. M. Dayan, *Story of my Life*, 590.

CHAPTER FIVE

1. In the following passage I only identify local players on the Lebanese scene. But the superpowers were also involved. American involvement is fairly well known,

notably because of the attack by a suicide bomber who drove a semi-trailer loaded with explosives into the Marine barracks in Beirut on 23 October 1983, killing 241 marines and wounding 100. Less is known, however, about Soviet involvement in Lebanon, which was mainly concerned with assisting the Syrians to operate its missile system in the Beka'a. On American and Soviet involvement, see M. Binyon, 'Sadder but wiser Reagan leaves Lebanon to stew', *The Times*, 30 May 1985; R. Owen, 'Moscow is kept on the sidelines', *The Times*, 30 May 1985.

2. Interview with King Hussein of Jordan.
3. On this, see P. Snow and D. Phillips, *Leila's Hijack War: From the Day of the Mass Hijack to the Day of Nasser's Funeral* (London, 1970).
4. The events in Jordan in 1970–1 became known as 'Black September'. For more, see J. Lunt, *Hussein of Jordan* 193–223.
5. The 1932 population census was the last officially taken in Lebanon. Subsequent governments have refused to repeat the exercise. In the 1932 census, the Maronites formed some 29 per cent of the population, the Sunnis 22.5 per cent and the Shiites 20 per cent. The country's religion is complex: Moslem 57 per cent; Sunni 20 per cent; Shiite 31 per cent; Druze 6 per cent; Christians 43 per cent; Maronite 25 per cent; remainder Greek/Syrian/Armenian/Catholic and Protestant. Total Christians 53.7 per cent, total Muslims 45.3 per cent; see A. Bregman and J. el-Tahri, *The Fifty Years War*, 287; also G. Ben-Dor, 'Lebanon: the disintegration of a state', in *Lebanon: War and Reconstruction* (Haifa, 1982) 36 (Hebrew).
6. The Lebanese Front was officially formed in September 1976, and the Lebanese National Movement in April 1975. Nevertheless, and even before formally united in its opposing blocks, the different groups within each block had worked together.
7. On how this incident affected relations in Lebanon, see Interview with the Maronite leader Josef Abu Khalil, Beirut, 19 February 1997, BLA; also Interview with Bashir Gemayel's adviser Karim Pakradouni, Beirut, 21 February 1997, BLA.
8. Y. Rabin, *Pinkas Sherut*, 503 (Hebrew); M. Tlas, *The Israeli Invasion of Lebanon* (Tel Aviv, 1988) 24 (Hebrew). This important book is the official Syrian version of the 1982 war in Lebanon. It was prepared by a group of Syrian officers under the supervision of Minister of Defence Dr Mustapha Tlas. It was translated into Hebrew and comments were added by the Israelis.
9. Based on an interview with a senior agent of Mossad who wished to stay anonymous; see also A. Bregman and J. el-Tahri, *The Fifty Years War*, 158; also an interview with the Christian leader Josef Abu Khalil, who confirms the story.
10. Shimon Peres to author, Tel Aviv, 9 July 1997, BLA; Interview with Joseph Abu Khalil.
11. David Kimche, interview in *Hadashot*, 17 February 1989 (Hebrew); R. Bergman, 'Hadacha Be'Zameret Ha'Mossad', *Ha'aretz*, 3 January 1997 (Hebrew).
12. I. Black and B. Morris, *Israel's Secret Wars*, 581.
13. On the terrorist attack, see A. Naor, *Begin in Power: A Personal Testimony* (Tel Aviv, 1993) 244–5 (Hebrew).
14. IDF spokesman, 'The Litani operation', 26 March 1978, 2 (Hebrew); see also M. Tlas, *The Israeli Invasion of Lebanon*, 49–60 (Hebrew).
15. A. Naor, *Begin in Power*, 253 (Hebrew).
16. *ibid.*
17. I. Black and B. Morris, *Israel's Secret Wars*, 370. Begin refused to call the Habib agreement a 'ceasefire' because it implied that Israel was apparently negotiating with the PLO. He called it 'an agreement to stop terrorist acts from Lebanon to Israel'.

18. On why so many objected to having Sharon as Defence Minister, see D. Margalit, *I Have Seen Them All* (Tel Aviv, 1997) 90 (Hebrew); A. Naor, *Begin in Power*, 262 (Hebrew); also A. Bregman and J. el-Tahri, *The Fifty Years War*, 161.

19. A. Sharon, 'Facts as they are about the war in Lebanon', lecture at the Centre for Strategic Studies (Tel Aviv, 11 August 1987) 4 (Hebrew).

20. M. Zipori, *In a Straight Line* (Tel Aviv, 1997) 268–9 (Hebrew). Mordechai Zipori was a minister in Begin's cabinet and one of Sharon's critics; also I. Black and B. Morris, *Israel's Secret Wars*, 368; A. Naor, *Begin in Power*, 255 (Hebrew); IDF Spokesman, *Ha'aretz*, 28 April 1981 (Hebrew).

21. David Kimche to author, Ramat Ha'sharon, 3 October 1996, in the author's archive.

22. M. Tlas, *The Israeli Invasion of Lebanon*, 25 (Hebrew); Y. Kordova, 'From the missile crisis to war', *Ma'arachot*, no. 285 (December 1982) 25–6 (Hebrew).

23. A. Naor, *Begin in Power*, 256 (Hebrew); the operation against the Iraqi nuclear reactor was carried out by the IAF on 7 June 1981, see S. Nakdimon, *Tammuz in Flames* (Tel Aviv, 1993) (Hebrew).

24. A. Sharon, 'Facts as they are about the war in Lebanon', 10 (Hebrew).

25. Z. Schiff, *Ha'aretz*, 23 May 1982 (Hebrew).

26. Y. Marcus, 'The war is inevitable', *Ha'aretz*, 23 May 1982 (Hebrew).

27. A. Sharon, 'Facts as they are about the war in Lebanon', 10 (Hebrew).

28. It was, in fact, presented to them as a precaution in case Damascus were to react aggressively to Israel's decision, made on 14 October 1981, to annex the Golan Heights; see M. Raviv, *Israel at Fifty: Five Decades of Struggle for Peace – A Diplomat's Narrative* (London, 1998) 207.

29. A. Bregman and J. el-Tahri, *The Fifty Years War*, 165.

30. Interview with Morris Draper, Washington, 13 October 1996, in the author's archive.

31. Interview with Alexander Haig, Washington, 18 March 1997, BLA; Ariel Sharon to author, Havat Ha'shikmim, 1 March 1997, BLA; A. Sharon, *Warrior*, 450; A. Sharon, Speech in the Knesset, *Divrai Ha'Knesset*, 29 June 1982, 2935 (Hebrew).

32. According to Ambassador Morris Draper, 'Haig was too open-ended' with the Israelis; see interview with Draper, Washington, 13 October 1996, in the author's archive.

33. G. Ball and D. Ball, *The Passionate Attachment: America's Involvement with Israel, 1947 to present* (New York, 1992) 123.

34. *ibid.*

35. A. Yaniv, *Deterrence without the Bomb*, 108.

36. I. Black and B. Morris, *Israel's Secret Wars*, 374.

37. As cited in H. Sachar, *A History of Israel*, vol. II (Oxford, 1987) 175.

38. Z. Schiff and E. Ya'ari, *Israel's Lebanon War* (London, 1984) 98; About Abu Nidal, see P. Seale, *Abu Nidal: A Gun for Hire* (London, 1993).

39. M. Begin, speech in the Knesset, *Divrai Ha'Knesset*, 12 August 1982 (Hebrew); A. Sharon, speech in the Knesset, *Divrai Ha'Knesset*, 29 June 1982, 2936 (Hebrew); Chief of Staff Rafael Eitan, interview, *Ma ariv*, 2 July 1982 (Hebrew). Two other paragraphs in this decision were: '(e) the following committee will decide the timing [of the operation]: the Prime Minister, his deputy and defence, health, foreign and interior ministers; (f) [the cabinet decides] to approve the [war] plan which was presented by the Defence Minister and the Chief of Staff', see A. Sharon, 'Facts as they are about the war in Lebanon', 29 (Hebrew).

40. The question whether or not the depth of the invasion was defined later caused a heated debate in Israel; see M. Zipori, *In a Straight Line*, 272 (Hebrew); also A. Sharon, *Warrior*, 456; also M. Zipori, 'The depth was well confined', *Ha'aretz*, 18

September 1992 (Hebrew); also M. Begin, *Divrai Ha'Knesset*, 8 June 1982 (Hebrew). On the fifth day of the war (10 June) Sharon explained that: 'in order to maintain a security strip of 40 kilometres it was essential to destroy the infrastructure of terror and hit the terrorists as severe a blow as possible even at a range beyond 40 kilometres', see interview with Sharon on Israeli Television, 21.34 GMT, 10 June 1982. In July 1982 when Israeli forces were more than 80 kilometres north of the Israeli border, Sharon said that whereas the initial goal was to 'push them 45 kilometres', still Israel had never said it would 'give any guarantee to the terrorists beyond this line'; see A. Sharon, 'Israel's war: we tried so hard to spare civilians', *The Times*, 14 July 1982; see also *Ma ariv*, 18 June 1982 (Hebrew); also A. Sharon, 'A defence of peace for Galilee', *International Herald Tribune*, 30 August 1982.

41. Ariel Sharon to author; also Sharon in the cabinet meeting of 5 June 1982; also M. Zipori, *In a Straight Line*, 275 (Hebrew); also R. Eitan, *A Story of a Soldier* (Tel Aviv, 1985) 210 (Hebrew).
42. Y. Shamir, *Summing Up* (New York, 1994) 132.
43. Chief of Staff Rafael Eitan to author, Jerusalem, 20 March 1991.
44. A. Sharon, 'Facts as they are about the war in Lebanon', 14 (Hebrew).
45. A. Sharon, 'Facts as they are about the war in Lebanon', 14, 20 (Hebrew); Chief of Staff Rafael Eitan to author.
46. Former Director of Military Intelligence Yehoshua Saguey to author, Bat Yam, 7 March 1991.
47. Ariel Sharon to author; also interview with Karim Pakradouni.
48. Ariel Sharon in *Yediot Aharonot*, 28 June 1982, 5 (Hebrew); also A. Sharon, 'Facts as they are about the war in Lebanon', 19 (Hebrew).
49. Interview with Karim Pakradouni.
50. The above quotations are based on the interview with Karim Pakradouni.
51. See Map 6.
52. Ariel Sharon at a meeting with commanders at the Northern Command on 15 December 1981, as cited in his lecture, 'Facts as they are about the war in Lebanon', 13 (Hebrew).
53. A. Cordesman and A. Wagnar, *The Lesson of Modern War: The Arab–Israeli Conflict*, vol. I (London, 1990) 118; also Table 3, 'Syrian order of battle in Lebanon', in R. Gabriel, *Operation Peace for Galilee* (New York, 1984) 233.
54. R. Avi Ran, *The War of Lebanon: Arab Documents*, vol. II (Tel Aviv, 1997) 109 (Hebrew).
55. R. Avi Ran, *The War of Lebanon: Arab Documents*, 13.
56. It is hard to be accurate with regard to the number of Palestinian combatants because among the Palestinian refugees there were many who were carrying guns and on some occasions did join the fighting.
57. B. Mem, 'The peace for Galilee war: the main military stages', *Ma'arachot*, no. 284 (September 1982) 27 (Hebrew).
58. Former Chief of Operations 96th division, Brigadier (Res.) Shimon Nave to author, 15 May 1993, London; M. Eldar, 'The landing at the Aouali, *Ma'arachot*, 299 (July/August 1985) 26–34 (Hebrew); also Y. Yair, *With me from Lebanon: The Paratroops Brigade in the Peace for Galilee Campaign* (Tel Aviv, 1990) 22–6 (Hebrew); On the Palestinian view of this landing, see R. Avi Ran, *The War of Lebanon: Arab Documents*, document 17, 35–6.
59. Avigdor Ben Gal to author, Tel Aviv, 16 January 1992.
60. Avigdor Ben Gal to author; also Director of Military Intelligence Yehoshua Saguey to author.

61. An interview with OC Northern Command Amir Drori, *Ma ariv*, 1 July 1994 (Hebrew) (my emphasis).

62. Y. Erez, 'The military actions: a snowball', *Ma ariv*, 3 June 1983 (Hebrew).

63. A. Naor, *Cabinet at War: The Functioning of the Israeli Cabinet during the Lebanon War* (1982) (Jerusalem, 1986) 36 (Hebrew).

64. Chief of Staff Eitan in a radio interview as cited in the *Guardian*, 8 June 1982; also report in *Israel Home Service 2000*, 6 June; also R. Eitan, *A Story of a Soldier*, 242 (Hebrew).

65. Minutes of a cabinet meeting, 6 June 1982, as quoted by Sharon in his speech in the Knesset, *Divrai Ha'Knesset*, 29 June 1982, 2936 (Hebrew).

66. Ariel Sharon to author, 7 April 1991, Jerusalem.

67. A. Sharon, Speech in the Knesset, *Divrai Ha'Knesset*, 29 June 1982, 2937 (Hebrew).

68. M. Tlas, *The Israeli Invasion of Lebanon*, 144 (Hebrew).

69. A first hand account of the armoured battle at Jezzin based on interviews with soldiers who took part in the battle; see Anonymous, 'An armoured force in a mountainous and urban area: the Brigade Benai Or in Jezzin, 8 June 1982', *Ma'arachot*, no. 296 (December 1984) 41–4 (Hebrew).

70. M. Tlas, *The Israeli Invasion of Lebanon*, 153–4 (Hebrew).

71. Z. Schiff and E. Ya'ari, *Israel's Lebanon War*, 163.

72. He passed a note to Amos Amir, Deputy Commander of the IAF, who was present at the meeting. 'Amos', it went, 'I ride horses [and I know, that] when you jump over obstacles the highest obstacle is the most difficult. [Minister] Burg has been the highest obstacle and we have overcome it … Arik', see Amos Amir to author, Tel Aviv, 27 February 1997, BLA; also Dr Yosef Burg to author, Jerusalem, 18 March 1991. On the cabinet decision to approve the operation see A. Sharon, Speech in the Knesset, *Divrai Ha'Knesset*, 29 June 1982, 2937 (Hebrew).

73. Deputy Chief of IAF Amos Amir to author; also *Davar*, 13 June 1982, 11 (Hebrew); also M. Tlas, *The Israeli Invasion of Lebanon*, 188–90 (Hebrew).

74. E. Geva, in *Ma ariv*, 26 September 1982 (Hebrew). For more on the Geva affair, see interview with Geva in *Yediot Aharonot*, 26 July 1982 and 30 July 1982 (Hebrew); also R. Eitan, *A Story of a Soldier*, 222–3 (Hebrew).

75. Interview with Lebanese Chief of Intelligence Jonny Abdo, Beirut, 1 April 1997, BLA.

76. Interview with former prime minister Shafiq al-Wazzan, Beirut, 19 February 1997, BLA.

77. R. Avi-Ran, *The War of Lebanon: Arab Documents*, 193; also R. Eitan, *A Story of a Soldier*, 295–7 (Hebrew).

78. Ariel Sharon to author.

79. The force was probably led by the commander of the brigade, Brigadier General Yoram Yair, and upon instructions left the camps soon after it entered in order not to be blamed for taking part in the killing. The Israeli insistence that no Israeli forces were in the camps is untrue. This is based on an interview with an Israeli journalist who wishes to stay anonymous.

80. For the text of this letter, see I. and D. Menuhin (eds) *The Limits of Obedience* (Tel Aviv, 1985) 175 (Hebrew).

81. A. Dequel 'Yesh Gvul', *Ha'aretz*, 3 May 1983 (Hebrew).

82. *New York Times*, 2 May 1983.

83. K. Hana, 'The resisters', *Hotam*, 11 March 1983, 6–7 (Hebrew); R. Lin 'The moral judgement of the Lebanon war refusers' *Iyunim Be'hinuch*, no. 42 (Haifa University, November 1985) 19–20 (Hebrew).

84. M. Zipori, *In a Straight Line*, 305 (Hebrew).

85. H. Sachar, *A History of Israel*, 197.

CHAPTER SIX

1. *Intifada* is literally the shivering that grips a person suffering from fever. It is often used to refer to brief upheavals. When the disturbances began Yasser Arafat, leader of the PLO, referred to it as 'intifada' which shows that he had expected a short upheaval. His deputy, Halil el Wazir (Abu Jihad), attempted to coin the name *haba* meaning 'storm' or 'tempest' but by then the name *Intifada* had already stuck.
2. Interview with Mohamad Labadi, Gaza, 6 July 1997, BLA. Labadi was a prominent leader of the *Intifada*.
3. As cited in M. Palumbo, *Imperial Israel: The History of the Occupation of the West Bank and Gaza* (London, 1992) 331. Arafat's statement seems intended to incite the Palestinians rather than to reflect reality.
4. Eitan Haber to author, Ramat Gan, 20 January 1997, BLA. Haber was Defence Minister Rabin's assistant; also former general Amram Mitzna to author, Haifa, 27 January 1997, BLA. General Mitzna was the overall commander of Judea and Samaria (the West Bank) at the time of the *Intifada*.
5. Z. Schiff and E. Ya'ari, *Intifada: The Palestinian Uprising: Israel's Third Front* (New York, 1989) 118; also G. Frankel, *Beyond the Promised Land: Jews and Arabs on the Hard Road to a New Israel* (New York, 1996) 24.
6. The statements of both Rabin and Shamir also contradicted IDF's own figures of the time, which showed that about 80 per cent of violent incidents in the territories were initiated locally. According to Arab sources: 'There is no room to doubt that the protests are not stirred from outside ... they are a direct result of the occupation'. As cited in G. Frankel, *Beyond the Promised Land*, 39; also M. Palumbo, *Imperial Israel*, 225.
7. D. Hiro, *Sharing the Promised Land: An Interwoven Tale of Israelis and Palestinians* (London, 1996) 385.
8. Z. Schiff and E. Ya'ari, *Intifada*, 30.
9. As cited in D. Peretz, *Intifada: The Palestinian Uprising* (Boulder CO, 1992) 35.
10. Z. Schiff and E. Ya'ari, *Intifada*, 79.
11. According to figures published by Israel's Central Bureau of Statistics (1986), on the eve of the *Intifada* there were in the Gaza Strip – which is twenty-five miles long and between 3.5 and 8 miles wide – 634,000 Palestinians. This meant that the population had grown by over 75 per cent during the two decades since Israel had occupied it in 1967. In the five years between 1981 and 1986, the Palestinian population of the Strip grew from 507,000 to 634,000 and annual growth rate since then had been 4.3 per cent.
12. D. Peretz, *Intifada*, 32.
13. This became known in Israel as 'The night of the hang-gliders'; see the *New York Times*, 31 July 1987; also I. Black and B. Morris, *Israel's Secret Wars*, 462.
14. As cited in D. Peretz, *Intifada*, 37.
15. Ehud Barak to author, Ramat Yishai, BLA.
16. Chief of Staff Dan Shomron, *Yediot Aharonot*, 15 January 1998 (Hebrew); also Ehud Barak to author.
17. On how the first leaflet came about, see Interview with Mohamad Labadi.
18. Z. Lockmann (ed.) *Intifada* (Boston, 1989) Communiqué no. 1, 328–9.
19. Where he settled in the Moslem quarter of Jerusalem in a move which outraged the Arabs and was aimed to show that Jerusalem belongs to the Jewish people.
20. Source: B'Tselem, The Israeli Information for Human Rights in the Occupied Territories.

21. These figures are cited in Z. Schiff and E. Ya'ari, *Intifada*, 113.
22. D. Peretz, *Intifada*, 43.
23. W. Laqueur and B. Rubin (eds) 'Hamas: Charter, August 1988', in *The Israel-Arab Reader*, 529–37.
24. These figures are cited in Z. Schiff and E. Ya'ari, *Intifada*, 225.
25. Source: B'Tselem, The Israeli Information for Human Rights in the Occupied Territories. These details are based on Palestinian sources.
26. Designed to wound rather than kill, these rubber bullets fired at close range are as lethal as live ammunition, especially if they strike the head or a vital organ. At least fifty-seven Palestinians were killed between December 1989 and 1998 by rubber bullets. Of these fatalities, twenty-eight were children under the age of seventeen, and thirteen were less than thirteen years old; see A. Hass, 'Rubber bullets fatal', *Ha'aretz*, 6 December 1998 (Hebrew).
27. General Amram Mitzna to author.
28. Z. Schiff and E. Ya'ari, *Intifada*, 150.
29. *ibid.*, 152.
30. These figures are cited in *ibid.*, 261.
31. Israel also paid heavily for this war of attrition. As a consequence of the *Intifada*, its commercial turnover fell 25 per cent below the original forecast for 1988, which translated into a loss of almost $1 billion. In the building and textile trades, the decline reached as much as 10–15 per cent; tourism dropped by 14 per cent and total exports from Israel to the territories diminished by no less than 34 per cent.
32. D. Hiro, *Sharing the Promised Land*, 390. Red in the flag signified the blood of the martyrs, green the fertility of the Palestinian plains, white, peace, and black the oppression of occupation to be removed when Palestine was liberated.
33. Source: B'Tselem, The Israeli Information for Human Rights in the Occupied Territories. It is hard to establish the exact number of casualties. Israeli authorities tend to reduce the numbers, while the Palestinians keep them high. A study by Dr Samir Salamen Khalili, a paediatrician, indicated that during the first year of the *Intifada* 540 Palestinians were killed, of them 339 on the West Bank and 201 in the Gaza Strip. Of these, 76 per cent were killed from bullet wounds, 16 per cent of gas, 4.5 per cent were trampled to death and 3.5 per cent died from beatings. About 25 per cent of the dead were under sixteen and half between seventeen and twenty-five; see M. Palumbo, *Imperial Israel*, 267. Figures produced by the PLO information centre suggest an even higher number of casualties. According to these figures, by the end of the first year, more than 434 Palestinians were killed, 46,000 were seriously injured, at least thirty-two were deported, and another fifty-six received deportation orders. About 5,000 were placed under administrative detention; 584 homes were demolished or sealed, and over 5,000 people were displaced. Source: *Palestine Today*, 31 December 1988.
34. But even after the signing of the agreement disturbances had continued. In Hebron in February 1994, a Jewish settler, Baruch Goldstein, opened fire on Palestinian worshippers, killing many of them; subsequent suicide bomb attacks by Hamas on passenger buses killed dozens of Israelis. Between 14 September 1993 (the day after the signing of the Oslo Accord) and 31 October 1998, 263 Palestinian civilians were killed by Israeli security forces in the occupied territories and another eleven in Israel itself. Additionally, fifty-eight Palestinian civilians were killed in the territories by Israeli civilians and six others in Israel. Eighteen members of the Palestinian security forces were killed by Israeli security forces. Forty-three Israeli citizens were killed by Palestinian civilians in the territories and 122 more in Israel. One Israeli civilian was killed by Palestinian security forces; twenty-eight members of the Israeli security forces were killed by Palestinian

civilians in the territories, and forty-one more in Israel itself. Sixteen members of the Israeli security forces were killed by Palestinian security forces. In the same period, 676 Palestinian houses were demolished. Source: B'Tselem, The Israeli Information for Human Rights in the Occupied Territories.

35. Source: B'Tselem, The Israeli Information for Human Rights in the Occupied Territories.

36. Z. Schiff and E. Ya'ari, *Intifada*, 40–1.

37. As cited in G. Frankel, *Beyond the Promised Land*, 22.

38. On the Arabs of Israel and their response to the *Intifada*, see U. Benziman and A. Mansour, *Subtenants* (Jerusalem, 1992) (Hebrew).

39. They were warned by Israeli leaders that they would be deported; see for example the statement of minister Yuval Ne'eman, *Ha'aretz*, 9 December 1990 (Hebrew).

40. A 1988 survey, conducted before the general election, which had investigated the impact of the *Intifada* on the political views of Israelis, showed that 48 per cent reported no change in their views because of the uprising, 31 per cent reported a move to the right and 17 per cent a move to the left; see A. Arian, *Security Threatened: Surveying Israel's Opinion on Peace and War (Cambridge, 1995)* 80.

41. B. Josephs, 'Pubios say refusal campaign is growing', *Jerusalem Post*, 23 October 1987, 2.

42. L. Galili, '16 Sheministim nosafim katvu le Rabin', *Ha'aretz*, 30 December 1987, 5 (Hebrew).

43. A. Court, '160 reservists say they won't serve in occupied territories', *Jerusalem Post*, 1 January 1988.

44. L. Galili, '260 miluimnikim hodiu', *Ha'aretz*, 15 Feb 1988 (Hebrew).

CHAPTER SEVEN

1. S. Hareven, 'The first forty years', *The Jerusalem Quarterly*, no. 48, (Jerusalem, autumn 1988) 8.

2. A. Eban, *My Country*, 287 (my emphasis).

3. A. Arian, *Security Threatened*, 27.

4. Recorded and edited by a group of young Kibbutz members: *The Seventh Day: Soldiers Talk about the Six Day War* (London, 1971) 217–18.

5. A. Arian, *Security Threatened*, 27.

6. A. O'Sullivan, 'Money, not Zionism, attracts today's Israeli army officers', *Jerusalem Post*, 6 September 1996.

7. A. Arian, *Security Threatened*, 79, also 27, 64.

Select bibliography

For reasons of space, this list is very selective and concentrates on works in English and on books, as these are more accessible. Details of other relevant material can be found in the bibliographies of the works cited and in the notes of this book.

Abbas, M., *Through Secret Channels* (Reading, 1995).

Adan, A., *On the Bank of the Suez: An Israeli General's Personal Account of the Yom Kippur War* (London, 1980).

Allon, Y., *Shield of David: The Story of Israel's Armed Forces* (London, 1970).

Arens, M., *Broken Covenant* (New York, 1995).

Ashrawi, H., *This Side of Peace* (New York, 1995).

Baker, J., *The Politics of Diplomacy: Revolution, War and Peace 1989–1992* (New York, 1995).

Bar On, M., *The Gates of Gaza: Israel's Road to Suez and Back, 1955–1957* (London, 1994).

Bar-Siman Tov, Y., *The Israeli–Egyptian War of Attrition, 1969–1970* (New York, 1980).

Bialer, U., *Between East and West: Israel's Foreign Policy Orientation 1948–1956* (Cambridge, 1990).

Black, I. and Morris, B., *Israel's Secret Wars: A History of Israel's Intelligence Services* (London, 1996).

Bregman, A., 'Civil–Military Relations in Israel: Military Influence on War Policy', Ph.D. dissertation submitted in 1993 to the Department of War Studies, King's College London.

Bregman, A. and el-Tahri, J., *The Fifty Years War: Israel and the Arabs* (London, 1998, New York, 1999).

Burns, E. L. M., *Between Arab and Israeli* (London, 1962).

Collins, L. and Lapierre, D., *O Jerusalem!* (Bnei Brak, 1993).

Dayan, M., *Diary of the Sinai Campaign* (London, 1965).

—— *Story of my Life* (London, 1976).

Eban, A., *An Autobiography* (London, 1977).

—— *My Country: The Story of Modern Israel* (London, 1973).

el-Shazli, S., *The Crossing of Suez: The October War (1973)* (London, 1980).

Eytan, W., *The First Ten Years: A Diplomatic History of Israel* (New York, 1958).

Fahmy, I., *Negotiating for Peace in the Middle East* (London, 1983).

Farid, A. M., *Nasser: The Final Years* (Reading, 1994).

Fisk, R., *Pity the Nation* (London, 1990).

Flapan, S., *The Birth of Israel: Myths and Realities* (New York, 1987).

Frankel, G., *Beyond the Promised Land: Jews and Arabs on the Hard Road to a New Israel* (New York, 1996).

Gal, R., *A Portrait of the Israeli Soldier* (New York, 1986).

Harkabi, Y., *Fedayeen Actions and Arab Strategy* (London, 1969).

Heikal, M., *The Road to Ramadan: The Inside Story of how the Arabs Prepared for and almost Won the October War of 1973* (London, 1975).

—— *Secret Channels* (London, 1996).

Herzog, H., *The War of Atonement: The Inside Story of the Yom Kippur War, 1973* (London, 1998).

Hiro, D., *Sharing the Promised Land: An Interwoven Tale of Israelis and Palestinians* (London, 1996).

Kimche, J., *Both Sides of the Hill* (London, 1960).

Koestler, A., *Promise and Fulfilment: Palestine 1917–1949* (London, 1983).

Laqueur, W. and Rubin, B., *The Israel–Arab Reader: A Documentary History of the Middle East Conflict* (London, 1995).

Levita, A., *Offense and Defence in Israeli Military Doctrine* (London, 1990).

Lewis, B., *Semites and Anti-Semites* (London, 1986).

Meir, G., *My Life* (London, 1975).

Morris, B., *1948 and After: Israel and the Palestinians* (Oxford, 1990).

—— *The Birth of the Palestinian Refugee Problem, 1947–1949* (Cambridge, 1988).

Ovendale, R., *The Origins of the Arab-Israeli Wars* (London, 1984).

Pappe, I., *The Making of the Arab-Israeli Conflict 1947–1951* (London, 1994).

Pasha, G., *A Soldier with the Arabs* (London, 1958).

Peres, S., *David's Sling* (London, 1970).

—— *Battling for Peace: Memoirs* (London, 1995).

Rabin, Y., *The Rabin Memoirs* (London, 1979).

Rabinovich, I., *The Road not Taken: Early Arab–Israeli Negotiations* (Oxford, 1991).

—— *The War for Lebanon, 1970–1983* (New York, 1984).

Rafael, G., *Destination Peace: Three Decades of Israeli Foreign Policy – a Personal Memoir* (London, 1981).

Randal, J., *The Tragedy of Lebanon* (London, 1990).

Riad, M., *The Struggle for Peace in the Middle East* (London, 1981).

Rothenberg, G., *The Anatomy of the Israeli Army* (London, 1979).

Sachar, H., *A History of Israel* (Oxford, 1987).

Sadat, A. el-, *In Search of Identity: An Autobiography* (New York, 1977).

Said, E., *The Question of Palestine* (New York, 1980).

Savir, U., *The Process* (New York, 1998).

Schiff, Z. and Ya'ari, E., *Israel's Lebanon War* (London, 1984).

—— *Intifada: The Palestinian Uprising – Israel's Third Front* (New York, 1989).

Seale, P., *The Struggle for Syria* (Oxford, 1965).

Shamir, Y., *Summing Up: An Autobiography* (Boston, 1994).

Sharon, A., *Warrior: The Autobiography of Ariel Sharon* (London, 1989).

Shlaim, A., *The Politics of Partition: King Abdullah, the Zionists and Palestine 1921–1951* (Oxford, 1988).

Sykes, C., *Cross Roads to Israel: Palestine from Balfour to Bevin* (London, 1965).

Weizman, E., *On Eagles' Wings* (London, 1976).

Ya'ari, E. and Haber, E., *The Year of the Dove* (New York, 1979).

Yaniv, A., *Deterrence without the Bomb: The Politics of Israeli Strategy* (Massachusetts, 1987).

Index